KIRBY'S WAY

KIRBY'S WAY

HOW KIRBY AND CAROLINE RISK BUILT THEIR COMPANY ON KITCHEN-TABLE VALUES

BY ANGIE KLINK

PURDUE UNIVERSITY PRESS WEST LAFAYETTE, INDIANA

Library of Congress Cataloging-in-Publication Data
Klink, Angie, 1959-
   Kirby's way : how Kirby and Caroline Risk built their company on kitchen-table values / by Angie Klink.
      p. cm.
   ISBN 978-1-55753-614-3 (pbk. : alk. paper) ~ ISBN 978-1-61249-221-6 (epdf) ~ ISBN 978-1-61249-220-9 (epub) 1. Risk, Kirby, 1901-1989. 2. Risk, Caroline, 1912- 3. Kirby Risk Corporation~History. 4. Electric industries~Indiana~History. 5. Businesspeople~Indiana~Biography. I. Title.
   HD9697.A3U5453 2012
   338.7'62130922772~dc23
   [B]
                                        2012016836

Also by Angie Klink
Divided Paths, Common Ground: The Story of Mary Matthews and Lella Gaddis, Pioneering Purdue Women Who Introduced Science into the Home

In memory of my father, Jack Lipp,
Purdue electrical engineer,
quiet man of integrity,
cheerleader to a grateful daughter.

—for all the Sunday drives
to see high-voltage transformers.

CONTENTS

A Christmas Carol, Charles Dickens, 1843

"But you were always a good man of business, Jacob," faltered Scrooge, who now began to apply this to himself.

"Business!" cried the Ghost, wringing its hands again. "Mankind was my business. The common welfare was my business; charity, mercy, forbearance, and benevolence, were, all, my business. The dealings of my trade were but a drop of water in the comprehensive ocean of my business!"

FOREWORD

Kirby Risk always seemed to me to have the perfect name. My best memory of Mr. Risk (he'll always be "Mr." to me) goes back to my high school years at Lafayette Jefferson High School. His son, Jim (James Kirby Risk III), was a starter on our basketball team and I was one of the managers. More than once after a basketball game, Mr. Risk told us kids to pile in his stretch Packard so he could take us to Miller's Fish House in Colfax, Indiana. Once inside Miller's, he'd order fried everything—fried catfish with French fries, and onion rings. And just about the time everyone was finished eating, he'd order another round. Kirby Risk loved food, and he especially enjoyed seeing others enjoy themselves in his company. That's just one of the many reasons he was such a success in Lafayette, as Angie Klink tells us in this interesting account of his life, *Kirby's Way*.

Kirby Risk knew an amazing number of people in Lafayette. As a result, as Angie notes, the Risk children "grew up with a constant swirl of fans." Caroline, his wife and the mother of Carol, Sherry, Jim, and Julie, said it best, "There's nobody else in the world like him."

Kirby's Way has many stories that illustrate what made this man and his family unique. He was a constant supporter of Lafayette Jefferson High School and Purdue University sports (everyone loved to get tickets to the Risk Football Saturdays). He lived and breathed Lafayette, traded with its businesses, and boosted its young people through his financial and moral support of Junior Achievement.

One of my favorite stories in the book revolves around Mr. Risk's interaction with a character that most twentieth-century Lafayette natives remember well. Known as the "cone lady," Elinor Stingly worked for over fifty years at the Frozen Custard stand across from Columbian Park. She died in 2009 at age 101, but until the last five years of her life you could see her taking orders at the cone window every summer day. Elinor was so popular and worked to such a ripe old age that "the Custard" would hang a sign in the window on days she wasn't there that read "I'm not dead; I'm just at the doctor."

Elinor and Mr. Risk didn't always see eye-to-eye on the subject of cones, however. Lafayette native Anne Price tells of the time Mr. Risk got so mad at the Frozen Custard that he refused to go up to the window to place his order and would instead send his kids. "He would be out in the car," Anne recalls, "but wouldn't go up. Something upset him; he wouldn't go up because it was just the principal of things."

What upset Mr. Risk was Elinor Stingly's refusal to mix flavors when she sold cones. In short, she simply wouldn't allow a scoop of chocolate to be mixed with vanilla. Those were the rules, like it or not. Elinor's rules of ice cream management just didn't fly with the Risk code of business where the customer is always right.

Mr. Risk passed on the Risk code of business to his son, Jim, who has been my close friend for fifty-seven years. Back in our Lafayette Jefferson High School days, Jim was picked by our classmates as most likely to succeed. We gave him a tough assignment, because it's not always easy for a son to follow his father in a successful business. Mr. Risk clearly taught Jim well, for under Jim's leadership, Kirby Risk Electric grew even bigger and better. It is important to give some of the credit for this to his wife, Mary Jo, who wisely rejected my advances in the first grade when we were both six. I'm pretty sure she got the better deal when she married Jim many years ago.

There is a lot to read in *Kirby's Way*, stories that will be enjoyable to his family and friends and even for those who never met him. Mr. Risk never took a drink of alcohol in his life; he worked hard and played hard. In my experience, Jim seems to live life much like his father—always a positive person; he's loyal to his friends, his community, and his customers. Enjoy the many stories in the pages that follow.

-Brian Lamb
Founder and Executive Chairman of C-SPAN

PREFACE

KR University is an online educational opportunity for employees of Kirby Risk Corporation. Kirby Risk—the man—would have liked such a teaching advantage to help his people. Yet a more powerful KR University lies within the pages of this book.

To be a graduate of the school of Kirby Risk would mean one had earned a doctorate in kindness. Kirby, himself, held a PhD in caring, a master's in benevolence, and a bachelor's degree in noticing people. He used his "degrees" wisely, building his life and company with what he learned from his textbook, the Bible. "Kirb," as he sometimes was called, was quietly quirky, bullheaded, and fun. He had a signature style, from his bow tie and invariable tardiness, to his frank remarks and night owl hours. He showed love to people by serving them food, particularly gallons and gallons of ice cream that burst the hinges of his basement freezer.

Petite Caroline was Kirby's impeccable partner. Their wedding at the 1933 Chicago World's Fair is the fabric of fairytales. Together they built a life and company that, today in our disjointed world, we long to emulate. Kirby conducted business on a handshake. He was friends with the men who headed companies in his community and with others he came to know across the United States. Kirby and Caroline knew how to knit deep and lasting friendships wherever they landed. Caroline was Kirby's loving co-player. She was the eloquent letter writer, the gracious dinner hostess, and the rock-solid manager of their four children, while handling the company payroll and much more from her office in the enclosed front porch of their home.

I extend a heartfelt thank-you to Jim Risk for asking me to write down some of his mother's memories of her life with Kirby. I thank dear Caroline, who turns 100 in 2012, for allowing me to read her journals and personal notes. She wrote lists, a condensed history of the company, and paragraphs recording snippets of the remarkable moments she spent with her husband, as if she knew one day their story would be told. In 2009, I began writing what was at first to be a simple record for the Risk family. The modest account blossomed to become this book—a broad brushstroke of lives so well lived.

Kirby noticed people. He made them feel important, and they loved him. In turn, people wanted to help Kirby. The relationships he built shaped the success of his life and his company. Jack Scott, former publisher of the Lafayette *Journal and Courier* and retired chairman of the Gannett Foundation, said, "Kirby's got more compassion per corpuscle than any person I've ever known."

Kirby was fearless in his conviction to help others and do right by them. He was forthright in deed and word. His presence alone could get things done. Kirby garnered respect.

Can people today live like Kirby and Caroline did, giving genuinely to those with whom they work, worship, and play, building relationships along the way? Or is the world too big, its people too mobile, too distrusting, and too self-centered? My hope is that after reading *Kirby's Way*, more of us, when going about our days, may experience the occasional "lightbulb Kirby Risk moment."

More than likely, if J. Kirby Risk Jr. were still with us, he would not want this book to be published. In his day, he ducked out of a few banquet rooms when he heard he would be thanked publicly for his good work. Yet if he thought about the book's potential, he might see his and Caroline's narrative as a parable, like those stories Jesus told to convey spiritual truths. A parable compels readers to discover certainties for themselves. Perhaps Kirby would like to pass on his stories of giving and fun if he thought people would be inspired to help others and have a good time doing so.

Roger Swindle, a longtime employee of Kirby Risk Corporation, sums up Kirby's personality with this story:

There was a businessman who came to town, and he was looking for people to model his business after. He heard about Kirby. Somebody said to him, "Who is Kirby Risk?" The businessman said, "Well, Kirby is the guy that if he took a bucket of purple paint and went out here on Main Street and started to paint that center line, nobody would even ask him why."

–Angie Klink

Author's Note: Unless otherwise noted, all images are courtesy of the Risk family.

CHAPTER 1

FROM THE BANKS OF THE WABASH

Beginning in the 1890s, Highland Park, formerly Ross and Reynolds farm pasture, was *the* place to live in Lafayette, Indiana, a city in the northwest lobe of the state, a quiet "rose" between two bustling city "thorns," Indianapolis and Chicago. Highland Park became a close-knit neighborhood brimming with leading business owners, lawyers, judges, doctors, famous politicians, and summertime actors. An advertisement printed in *Greater Lafayette: A Pictorial History* touted Highland as "elegant avenues, perfect drainage and a healthy place with a 15-minute walk from the courthouse."

On September 1, 1899, James Kirby Edward Risk and his wife Dora Dean Jolley Risk paid $4,345 for their lot and newly built home surrounded by tulip trees (Indiana's state tree), maples, and oaks. There were no sidewalks or paved streets. Homes had gaslights. Every house was different, yet most had front porches for visiting. A little triangular-shaped park sat in the middle of the development beckoning children to play ball. Today, the grassy triangle is still there, and it has become a place where children and neighbors gather.

In 1901, Kirby was born in the second-floor front bedroom at 719 Owen Street in Lafayette, Indiana's Highland Park Neighborhood. Kirby is on the left in knickers, playing croquet with his family. His father, James Kirby Risk Sr., stands on the front porch. Kirby's teddy bear and tricycle wait at the front steps.

This is where James Kirby Risk Jr. was born, grew up, and never left.

On September 22, 1901, Kirby was born in the front bedroom of his parents' two-story Victorian at 719 Owen Street. He arrived ten years after his parents' wedding. A daughter born previously died at birth. The five-cent interurban ran outside the Risk's front door. The clanging streetcar took passengers down the hill and into the valley where the downtown merchants and canal traders sold their wares along the meandering Wabash River. One day Kirby would start a business there.

Kirby's cousin Dora Fiddler was raised by the Risks. She was the daughter of Kirby's Aunt Jane Haggard of Detroit (or Aunt Jen, she was called by some), his mother's sister. Dora, nicknamed Dodie, was twelve years older than Kirby, and presumably was named after his mother. Dora was like a big sister—or maybe even a second mother—to young Kirby.

KIRBY'S FATHER

At an early age, Kirby's father began to support his mother and seven younger siblings. In 1880, at the age of fifteen, James Kirby Sr. left his family's farm in Ripley County, Indiana, to find work. Eighteen years later, he would be a stalwart Democrat, elected to the office of city clerk in Lafayette. A biographical account from that time described Kirby's father as one of

> "the farmer lads who, with the strength of physical and moral manhood that results from living near to nature's heart, go to the cities to make for themselves a place in the commercial world and readily adapt themselves to new conditions, advancing steadily, step by step, to positions of prominence."

This was the stock—the strength of physical and moral manhood—to which son Kirby would be born.

Prior to winning the city clerk position over Harry Sample, one of the foremost businessmen and Republicans in Lafayette, Kirby's father held a variety of jobs. After he left his family's homestead as a teenager, he worked in Danville, Illinois, for the Halloway Transfer Company and the Danville, Olney and Ohio River Railroad.

In the spring of 1882, James Kirby Sr. arrived in Tippecanoe County. He worked as a farmhand until he was twenty-two. Then he moved to Lafayette where he sold farm implements for M. E. Sears. He was a real estate and loan agent, he wrote farm fire insurance, and he was employed with the Vernon Clothing Company. When he married Kirby's mother, Dora Dean Jolly of Sugar Grove, Indiana, which is located north of Crawfordsville, on September 8, 1891, James Kirby

Sr. was twenty-six and was a salesman for Henry Rosenthal's Ullman Clothing House.

In 1898, James Kirby Sr.'s election to the city clerk position was a tip of the hat to his popularity in Lafayette. He was the only Democrat on the ticket to be elected. He won by 57 votes, while other Democrat candidates were defeated by 50 to 240 votes. His election indicated the confidence that his fellow townsmen (*men*, for women could not yet vote) had in his ability.

From 1902 to 1905, James Kirby Sr. collaborated with journalist Leroy Armstrong and lawyer Dan Simms to publish the *Lafayette Daily Democrat*. Later he was affiliated with the North American Life Insurance Company in Chicago. In 1916, he became treasurer and general manager of the Dairy Cream Separator Company in Lebanon, Indiana, a position he would hold for twelve years.

A DOG NAMED JACK

James Kirby Sr. loved his little boy, and that fact is evident in the great strides he took to find the perfect dog for his toddler son. Kirby was two when his father obtained a purebred, sable and white collie from Alloway Lodge Farm in Ontario, Canada. The owner of the farm was Robert McEwen, and he responded to a letter from James Kirby Sr. on January 12, 1903 regarding the dog. James Kirby Sr. had mentioned to McEwen that he wanted the animal as "a companion and protector" for his only child. The Alloway Lodge Farm letterhead featured photos of a collie and a sheep with the words, "Hackney and Saddle Horses, Southdown Sheep, and Collie Dogs." In McEwen's letter, he waxes on about the "exceedingly well-bred" lineage of the collie that the Risks were to receive. He writes, "Last March with a full brother in blood of your pup, in Chicago I won 2 firsts and 4 specials including the $300 American Collie Club Trophy."

Kirby's father must have written McEwen after receiving the pup, which likely traveled by train the great distance from Canada to Lafayette. In a follow-up, McEwen wrote, "I am pleased to hear that the puppy is taking up with his new pack, and you will find that the more you give him the run of the house, the more he will become attached to you. He got the name of Jack here for a pet name." Jack was registered with the American Kennel Club in 1902 at a cost of one dollar. Jack would become Kirby's pal and have a loving and lasting influence. Today, Kirby's son, James Kirby Risk III, said, "My father had a sincere fondness for dogs and had a number throughout his life." Kirby owned bulldogs, one named, appropriately, "Bull," and a schnauzer named "John Purdue" after the founder of Purdue University. The family called the dog "J. P." Through the years, the Risks had a boxer named "Casey," three poodles named "Pogo," "Mindy," and "Ditto," a couple of cocker spaniels, and a gentle stray named "Heidi."

Kirby was born during the last year of his father's four-year term as city clerk. He came along just as his father's political influence was about to make a mark on Lafayette and beyond, and eventually, on all of Kirby's life.

It began when James Kirby Sr. invited his friend William Jennings Bryan, former U. S. Representative and presidential nominee, to come to dinner at 719 Owen.

WILLIAM JENNINGS BRYAN

In 1906, Kirby's father was very active in the Democratic Party as a precinct committee member and chairman of the Democratic City Committee. He was a prominent temperance worker and an executive officer of the Indiana Dry Federation. He also was an executive member of the National Anti-Saloon League and a life member of the Women's Christian Temperance Union. In November of that year, William Jennings Bryan was a guest in the Risk home. Before breakfast, Kirby's mother would pick corn from her backyard garden so it would be fresh for dinner that day. She made spheres of potatoes, similar to melon balls, and fried them crisp and tasty. Bryan did not drink, but he did eat—and he knew he would eat well when he paid a call on the Risk family.

Bryan had already run for president in the intensely fought 1896 and 1900 elections, and he was thinking of running again in 1908. With more than five hundred speeches in 1896, Bryan invented the national stumping tour in an era when other presidential candidates stayed home. It seems Bryan was ahead of his time. A "*stump* speech" is an oration delivered on a campaign tour, coined when a politician stood on a tree stump to speak.

Bryan was a lawyer, an enemy of gold, banks, and railroads, and an opponent of Darwinism on religious grounds (most famously at the 1925 Scopes "Monkey Trial"). A "Silverite," Bryan was a leader in the political movement that favored silver as a monetary standard along with gold. With his deep, commanding voice and wide travels, Bryan was one of the best-known orators and lecturers of the era. His famous "Cross of Gold" speech advocated free coinage of silver. James Kirby Sr. saw an opportunity for Bryan to speak in Lafayette, and perhaps he also saw an opportunity to promote his own political aspirations. At one time, James Kirby Sr. was 10th District Democratic chairman.

While Bryan visited in the Risk home, he confided in James Kirby Sr. that he wanted to declare his candidacy for president in the coming year. His desire was to make the statement in Indiana, perhaps because his running mate, John Kern, was a politician from the Hoosier state. In a first-person typed account of his life, James Kirby Sr. states:

> I asked him [Bryan] to come to Lafayette to make the statement and he with some surprise asked me why I advised his coming to Lafayette instead of going to Indianapolis. I told him there were numerous reasons but the most important one was that we could get more Democrats from all parts of the State, more of the rank and file of the party who would come to Lafayette than could possibly be induced to go to Indianapolis on account of the fear that they would not have opportunity of touching elbows with Mr. Bryan, on account of being crowded out by the large city crowd. This one reason appealed to Mr. Bryan and he told me that he was sure that I could arrange the meeting for Lafayette but to treat the matter confidential until midsummer of 1907 that we might have a further conference on the subject.

Perhaps James Kirby Sr. was thinking of attorney J. Frank Hanly. He lived in the Queen Anne at 739 Owen, down the street from the Risks. Hanly had just been elected governor in 1905. He gave his acceptance speech from the front porch of his home. Why not have Bryan speak in Lafayette?

On November 17, 1907, when Kirby was six years old, Bryan came to Lafayette for what Kirby's father deemed "without question the largest and the most important meeting ever held in the state." Still today, that statement holds true. It was a momentous event not yet surpassed in political pomp and circumstance.

The meeting was under the auspices of the Jackson Club, a Democratic political organization named after Andrew Jackson, and it proved to give the club a national reputation. James Kirby Sr. said, "It brought more people to Lafayette for a two-day stay than I think was ever here before."

Bryan made the rounds, accompanied by James Kirby Sr. In the morning, he addressed students and faculty in Fowler Hall at Purdue University. He ate lunch at the Lafayette Club with prominent Democrats from throughout the state. He addressed Democratic Precinct Committeemen and newspapermen. In the afternoon, a public reception was held at the Hotel Lahr, today the historic Lahr Apartments. Bryan stood in the marble lobby with James Kirby Sr. by his side as throngs entered from North Fifth Street. Risk shook as many hands as Bryan. Music by the Reifers-Floner Orchestra wafted through the downtown air. Popular songs were "Sandy, You're a Dandy" by Hector Grant, "Searchlight Rag" by Scott Joplin, and James Scott's "Kansas City Rag."

A banquet was held that evening in the Coliseum at South and Sixth Streets. James Kirby Sr. acted as toastmaster. Presentations began at seven o'clock with numerous senators, congressmen, politicians, and clergy interested in speaking on everything from local self-government to "The Preacher in Politics." With all the men vying for time on the soapbox and the evening growing late, the crowd became hostile.

Three-time United States presidential candidate William Jennings Bryan, known as the "Great Orator" who originated the "stump speech," was a good friend of James Kirby Risk Sr. Here, Bryan speaks on the campus of Purdue University. Purdue President Winthrop Stone, with the gray hair and dark mustache, is on the left. Young Kirby stands at the front of the crowd, absorbing the historic event.
Courtesy of the Tippecanoe County Historical Association.

As master of ceremonies, James Kirby Sr. asked for order. The *Lafayette Morning Journal* described the scene:

> The crowd yelled for Bryan, hooted and hissed. And then and there Kirby showed fight. Clutching the table, gritting his teeth and hissing, after the manner of the villain in the play, he cried out: "I have been working for thirty days to make this thing a go, and now you fellows have got to give me three minutes."

Finally, at ten o'clock James Kirby Sr. introduced Bryan with a spectacular flourish described by the newspaper:

> A flag that had been suspended above the center of the stage was drawn aside. At the same time, the lights in the hall were extinguished. Lights above the stage were turned on showing a picture

of Mr. Bryan. Standing in the light were J. Kirby Risk [Sr.] and Bryan, a truly impressive tableau. It was just like the spot light in the show.

In the hot Coliseum, Bryan spoke for two hours, mopping his brow continuously. His voice was hoarse when he concluded. "It was certainly a gala day for Lafayette," James Kirby Sr. said later. "The citizens and merchants put politics aside and joined in the spirit of glorious welcome to Mr. Bryan and his hosts of friends from all parts of the state."

Was young Kirby watching his father, Bryan, and the Lafayette masses as they celebrated and shaped history? Did he hear the words of the presidential candidate who because of his faith in the goodness and rightness of the common people was called "The Great Commoner"?

It seems Kirby's way was set in motion.

Letters of Instruction

In September 1911, James Kirby Sr. took a trip to La Moure, North Dakota, to visit his brother, John, who worked for the North American Life Insurance Company as a state manager. John was one of James Kirby Sr.'s five brothers. He had one sister. "Uncle John" had snow-white hair and was one of Kirby's favorite relatives. Kirby's son, Jim, said:

> Uncle John would come to the house when I was a child. My father really had a shine for Uncle John. He was probably forty years older than Dad. They'd play cribbage and banter back and forth. When Uncle John had a fortunate draw, Dad would tease, "If you fell in a privy, you'd come out smelling like a rose!" They had a love for one another.

While visiting John in September 1911 "to get his settlements," James Kirby Sr. wrote a letter on North American Life Insurance letterhead to his ten-year-old son:

I do not know how to find words to express to you my appreciation for the way you have taken care of the lawn and minded Mother and Dora. I am enclosing you another draft for 2.00. . . . Now you will soon be in school and I think you had better come home at noon for your lunch. Come streetcar and go back the same way. . . . Mother will give you 10 cents a day for your rides. . . . Love to all. Much kisses, too.

Yours as ever, James K. Risk

In November of that year, James Kirby Sr. stayed at French Lick Springs Hotel in French Lick, Indiana. Nestled in the Hoosier National Forest, the hotel was an attraction because of the mineral water springs found there. The free-flowing water left a residue of salt, which animals licked off the surrounding rocks. And it smelled like rotten eggs. French fur traders and missionaries were in this area during the time Indiana was part of "New France." In the early 1800s, the first hotel was built and people came to drink the "miracle water" and take baths.

In 1901, Thomas Taggart, the mayor of Indianapolis, along with other investors, formed the French Lick Hotel Company, and the hotel rocketed to international prominence. After Taggart was named Democratic National Chairman, the elite of politics and society discovered French Lick and its luxurious spa. The hotel developed a reputation as the unofficial headquarters of the Democratic Party. In 1931, Franklin D. Roosevelt rounded up support for his presidential nomination there at a Democratic Governor's Conference.

Taggart built a bottling house to bottle "Pluto Water" for national distribution. Pluto Water (named after the Roman god of the underworld) was advertised as "America's Laxative" with the slogan "When Nature Won't, PLUTO Will." The bottle and ads featured an image of a red devil. The mineral water still flows, and the pungent smell wafts from a well house behind the hotel.

Perhaps Pluto Water felt like the work of the devil to those who drank it, including James Kirby Sr., who wrote in a letter to young

Kirby, "I did not get to see Mr. Taggart today. He was quail shooting, and I am about half sick from the water stirring up my system."

The main point of the letter was to encourage ten-year-old Kirby to be a good boy to his mother, for his parents wanted him to be "near perfect":

> I hope you are well and not giving Mother a bit of trouble. You know Mother worries and is troubled about your Grandmother and you must help to comfort her and you best do this by being kind and gentle to her. Kirby, you are an exceptionally good boy and are doing so well in school. You cannot realize how fond we are of you. Be very careful about your playing. Do not get too warm and take cold. . . . God has given you a fine healthy body and you must take every effort to care for it. Mother and father object to you doing some things. This is because we want you to be so near perfect as possible. We want to help you in every way we can and when we are older and you are a shiny clean man you will comfort us. Please remember always how we love you and how we appreciate your love and devotion.

Several words in the above letter are prophetic in describing some of Kirby's idiosyncrasies displayed throughout his life. Kirby liked control, for he wanted his home, business, family, body, and soul to be clean and perfect. Sanitation was almost an obsession. His eldest child, Carol, said, "Cleanliness was really important to Dad. I remember he was really cross with me when I tried to use his towel and washcloth one time. And he used Listerine. If we went by a dead animal in the road, he would hold his breath forever. Clean, clean, clean."

Sherry, Kirby's daughter who is three years younger than Carol, said, "When we were little, we had those purplish fluorescent lights in our bedrooms to kill germs. And we'd sit under a sunlamp set on a timer." When at age ninety-eight Kirby's wife, Caroline, was asked to describe Kirby, she said, "Kind, quiet, unbelievably meticulously clean." It seems Kirby was forever living up to his father's desire for him to be "a shiny clean man" who would comfort his parents.

In April 1913, James Kirby Sr. was staying at the Congress Hotel in Chicago when he wrote Kirby, age twelve, another letter of fatherly direction. It was mailed inside an envelope marked "personal." It appears Kirby's father traveled often, pursuing business and political endeavors. He writes to Kirby, who is on the brink of becoming a teenager:

> allow me to tell you I get a great deal of pleasure out of the time I devote to you, and if I can help you and make you more useful and happy, then my happiness is largely increased. Now Kirby, I want to call your attention to your temper and tell you how wrong it is for you to get mad and use ugly words and names. You should never call anyone a liar. That is such a harsh word and sounds so rough and unmanly. There is no trace of refinement about you when you are in those unpleasant moods. . . . and Kirby, you will never know how it hurts me. I do not want to punish you by whipping you. You are, when you are happy, a perfect boy. . . . I want you to read this letter and remember it is written by one of the best friends you have in the world. There is just one other, and that is Mother. And Kirby, how we want you to be perfect, if you overcome these little faults. . . . Try to think of the things you can do to make everybody around you happy. . . . Try to have a motive in life. . . . Love to all, Father

Again, Kirby is reminded that his father wants him to be "perfect." Refinement is emphasized, along with making others happy. As an adult, Kirby occasionally displayed a bit of a temper. Perhaps the unrealistic expectation of perfection set down by his father bubbled up from time to time. His father stressed respect for others, and Kirby would hand down that teaching to his children. He cautioned his children to never call another person a "liar." Kirby conveyed respect in many ways. When he drove past a cemetery, for example, he removed his hat until he passed the last gravestone.

PLEDGE OF SOBRIETY

When Kirby was fifteen, William Jennings Bryan was at the Risk home for one of his visits when he made the teen a proposal. Would Kirby sign a pledge of intent stating he would not use intoxicating liquor as a beverage?

Bryan was a prohibitionist who had startled the world in 1913 when, as Secretary of State in Woodrow Wilson's administration, he served Welch's grape juice instead of wine at a full-dress diplomatic function honoring the retiring British ambassador. Newspaper columnists and cartoonists made much of it for months, and Welch's grape juice garnered notoriety and popularity with Bryan's powerful endorsement.

By 1916, the year Bryan asked Kirby to sign a pledge of sobriety, more than half of the U.S. states already had statues that prohibited alcohol. Prohibition became effective in Indiana in 1918. The next year, the Eighteenth Amendment to the U.S. Constitution, which prohibited the sale and manufacture of alcohol throughout America, was ratified. Prohibition went into effect on January 16, 1920.

It was at the height of the anti-alcohol movement, which was thought to combat many of society's ills such as crime, debauchery, evil, and the spending of the family paycheck on liquor, when Bryan sat comfortably in the Risk home, enjoying Dora's latest meal. He asked Kirby, on the verge of becoming a man, to sign the pledge. Bryan scrawled the date at the top—November 19, 1916, and penned these words:

> We, the undersigned promise
> God helping us never
> to use intoxicating
> liquor as a beverage.

> William Jennings Bryan

Kirby signed his name below that of Bryan's: "James Kirby Risk Jr."

His father signed below the signature of his only child: "James Kirby Risk Sr."

The "letter of intent" was a mere slip of paper, yet it held the power to affect the span of Kirby's lifetime.

CHAPTER 2

COMMON DENOMINATOR

Governor James P. Goodrich appointed James Kirby Sr. as a member of the board of trustees of the Indiana School for the Deaf in 1920, and succeeding governors reappointed him. O. M. Pittenger, superintendent of the school, said at James Kirby Sr.'s funeral in 1932, "Since 1920 I have been closely associated with Mr. Risk in the work of educating the deaf. He was one of the most faithful public servants I have ever known. Until he was overtaken by his fatal illness [diabetes] he never missed a meeting of the board of trustees and his interest was always genuine and unselfish." Pittenger was a pallbearer at James Kirby Sr.'s funeral.

An article published by the school entitled "A Good Friend Gone" eulogized James Kirby Sr.:

> The cause of temperance and sobriety, the fight for honesty in government, the incessant warfare on political corruption have lost a militant leader. He knew no fear. His exposure of evil without compromise and sometimes without tact made him enemies but even his enemies know and admit that he fought in the open. His wide acquaintance with prominent men, his ability to interpret the

signs of the times, his interest in legislation and his aggressive manner made him a dominant figure in any group. . . .

While he was interested in the material things of the school—the care of the buildings and grounds—his greatest interest was in the boys and girls. He knew many of them by name; he visited them in their work; he attended their games, he attended their summer picnics all over the state, and he won their confidence and love. . . . The deaf throughout the state will miss him.

Kirby was captain of the football and basketball teams at Porter Military Academy in Charleston, South Carolina, when the Porterites won the 1921 state basketball and football championships.

In years to come, many people would bestow the same accolades on James Kirby Sr.'s son, Kirby.

Kirby attended Jefferson High School for a while, but his parents were not happy with his academic efforts, so they sent him to Porter Military Academy in Charleston, South Carolina. One of the primary goals of the school was character development. The Porter crest summarizes that goal with its lexis: "Words, Actions, Thoughts, Character, and Habits."

The school day began with bugle call, breakfast, and chapel. Porter claimed one of the first high school football teams, and Kirby proved to be quite an athlete. He was captain of the football and basketball teams. "The Porterites" were the 1921 state basketball and football champions. Kirby played center on the basketball team and was one of the stars.

James Kirby Sr.'s experiences in the Democratic Party and his ties with Bryan led him to greater political ambitions. While Kirby was at Porter, his father ran unsuccessfully as a candidate for governor on an independent Democratic ticket. He ran a second time four years later, but again, he was not elected.

After he graduated from Porter in 1921, Kirby returned to Lafayette before entering college the following fall. James Kirby Sr. wanted his son to attend Purdue University. He took great strides to connect with the men in power there, so they knew of his son's athletic and scholarly accomplishments at Porter and would welcome Kirby to campus. Yet story has it, Kirby wanted to become an attorney (perhaps because of Bryan's influence) or a minister, and he was accepted into Harvard University. During March of his senior year at Porter, Kirby received letters from Purdue President Winthrop Stone, Director of the Purdue Agricultural Experiment Station G. I. Christie, Head of the School of Mechanical Engineering Gilbert A. Young. President Stone wrote:

> Your father showed me, yesterday, a newspaper clipping calling attention to your success in athletics and this he supplemented by statements as to your general progress in your school. He told me of your intention to enter Purdue next year. I shall be very glad indeed to welcome you here as a member of our next freshman class. Our athletic teams will be glad to have one who has achieved as much distinction as you, but the class work is of still more importance.

Kirby's letter from Young increased the pressure to attend Purdue. Young wrote:

> I was very much pleased to have your father call me up the other night when he had heard about your winning the game, which decided the championship of the state. Congratulations to you. . . . Hope to see you in Purdue next fall.

The letter from Christie emphasized again the expectation that Kirby was to attend Purdue. Christie wrote:

> I learn, with pleasure that you are to be attending Purdue next year. I shall look forward to seeing you in the institution and will be glad to cooperate in every way that your course may be a success.

Yet, in addition to Harvard and Purdue Universities, Kirby also entertained the idea of attending the University of South Carolina, and he wrote Coach Sol Metzger a letter expressing his interest. A letter from Metzger to Kirby dated May 26, 1921 reads in part:

> I recall seeing you play last Thanksgiving Day and I don't mind saying that I believe I can make you into a star football man. . . . You have the drive and grit and the one most necessary quality of all—a love for the game. I certainly hope you do join me at South Carolina this September. We are going to have a very fine eleven, and I'm quite sure the training you get will be all for your best.

Metzger had been a football and basketball coach at several universities, but even while coaching his chief occupation was writing and illustrating for newspapers and magazines, including the *Saturday Evening Post*. He wrote the syndicated column "Touchdown Secrets" that was published by newspapers throughout the United States.

James Kirby Sr. talked the issue over with Williams Jennings Bryan, and they concurred that the future was in agriculture. Kirby's father told him that he was to attend Purdue. Harvard and the University of South Carolina were out.

Kirby's eldest daughter, Carol, said, "It was my sense—just me connecting the dots—that part of the reason Dad had such a wild time at Purdue and never graduated was kind of a rebellion." After all, Kirby had an interest in becoming an attorney, but he was told to follow the compass of William Jennings Bryan, who said the future was in agriculture. Kirby was a city boy, not a farmer. It is possible he felt out of place, for the interurban trolley ran outside his front door, not a horse and plow.

Kirby had fun in a daredevil way—tipping over outhouses, driving fast cars, and zooming speedboats (a trait that lasted his lifetime). He once drove a car down the road, steering only with his feet. Kirby owned both a swanky automobile and a fancy boat he kept at Ydrad (pronounced "e-drad") Power Boat Club located at the foot of Main Street Bridge, today the John T. Myers Pedestrian Bridge, near the

Wabash River in Lafayette. On a dare one January day, he swam across the Wabash River. Kirby did not drink, but life intoxicated him.

MARQUES REITZEL

Kirby was good friends with a boy five years his senior named Marques Reitzel. Marques was born in Fulton, Indiana, in 1896, and was raised in Lafayette. His family was poor, and he made money by selling newspapers in the north end of the city. During World War I, Marques joined the Purdue University Ambulance Corps and saw active duty in France. James Kirby Sr. made it possible for Marques, who displayed an aptitude for painting, to study at the Art Institute of Chicago.

One day, young Kirby was standing in line outside the movie theater in Lafayette waiting to enter, when his friend Marques came by and asked to borrow some money so he and his date could see a motion picture. Kirby handed his friend what money he had and walked home, forgoing the movie. James Kirby Sr.'s tutelage in "making others happy" was taking hold.

While he was in France and later, while attending school in Chicago, Marques wrote Kirby letters. On September 10, 1918, Marques, age twenty-two, wrote Kirby, age seventeen, a letter from the front line. It reads in part:

> our division is always advancing, though not much, but slowly and steadily, we are pushing the "Heir" back. Boy, I have sure seen some sights that would make you sick to see. I know it did me. . . . We are now quartered in what was once a village but what is now a ruin. There is hardly a house left standing. . . .

> Now old man, if anything should ever happen to me and they plant me in the ground and give me the job of pushing up daisies, remember old fellow that I always had a tender spot in my heart for you and that I shall always remember you as being the only chum I ever had.

After World War I ended, Marques began school in Chicago. On November 23, 1919, he wrote Kirby, who was at Porter Military Academy, commenting on his art education:

> I am beginning now to feel the shaping of my work. I am beginning to see results. A couple more years of art training and I ought to just begin to cash in on my training.

> I believe I am indebted to your dad. . . . I don't believe I ever will be able to square the debt with him for his kindness and for his help. I will some day be able to pay the mere money side of it back, but never can I repay the goodness and kindness your family has shown me. If it was not for you folks, I don't know what I would do. . . . Old man, you and I will always stick by each other though thick and thin. Won't we? That's a promise.

Marques lived in Hyde Park and Oak Park while attending school in Chicago. On Kirby's eighteenth birthday, Marques wrote on stationery with letterhead from the Hyde Park Young Men's Christian Association (YMCA) of Chicago. Marques had met a very influential artist of the time.

> I met John T. McCutcheon by means of your father's letter. I showed him some of my sketches, and he liked them. He said I had plenty of natural ability, but I needed training. He advised that I take some intensive training, and then when I was ready to enter the field of commercial art, he would see that I get placed with one of the best firms in Chicago. Wasn't that fine of him?

McCutcheon was known as the "Dean of American Cartoonists." He was a graduate of Purdue University where today a residence hall is named in his honor. McCutcheon worked at the Chicago Tribune from 1903 until his retirement in 1946. He was awarded the Pulitzer Prize for editorial cartooning in 1932.

In subsequent letters from 1920, Marques talks of sending Kirby a painting, asking what "kind" he would like. He writes of having lunch in Chicago with James Kirby Sr., who discussed his candidacy for governor. At the lunch Marques mentioned that his birthday was approaching. Later, Kirby's mother and cousin sent Marques a package with homemade cake and fudge, and a new tie and socks. The Risk family took good care of Marques.

With financial help from James Kirby Sr., Marques received his Bachelor of Fine Arts degree from the Art Institute of Chicago, and later he became an esteemed professor of art at San Jose State University in California.

Marques painted landscapes in vivid hues. In 1935, he entered his oil *Whistling Boy* in the Hoosier Salon. Held in the art gallery of Marshall Field's department store in Chicago, the Hoosier Salon was one of the most competitive exhibitions of the era. *Whistling Boy* is an autobiographical work of Marques's boyhood in Lafayette. Marques said, "I used to carry papers from the *Morning Journal* . . . early in the morning in the winter, I would pass by Greenbush Cemetery making my deliveries of the paper. I used to whistle for company. I am the boy in the picture."

Marques exhibited in the Hoosier Salon for nearly thirty years, from 1925 to 1954. His painting "The Morning Route," an oil of a milkman on his early rounds, is part of the permanent collection of the Art Institute of Chicago. As a nationally known artist, Marques's paintings are highly collectible.

In the late 1950s, former Lafayette art teacher Ben Rifner remembered seeing *Whistling Boy* hanging above the sink in the Jefferson High School art department. After he retired and was photographing art pieces within the school system, he found *Whistling Boy* in a closet at the school. The painting was unframed, dirty, and had two holes in the canvas. He took it to the school corporation's administrative center for safekeeping where it stayed until 1999. That year, a curator at the Art Museum of Greater Lafayette had a chance conversation with Rifner about the painting. Letters from Marques were discovered in the gallery's archives, and it was determined that the painting had been purchased by the museum in 1937 and likely given on loan to the school.

Today, as part of the permanent collection of the museum, the restored and framed *Whistling Boy* captures a blustery winter morning in Lafayette, Indiana, and a lone boy who scurries past a cemetery, whistling to quell his fright.

Renowned artist Marques Reitzel was a childhood friend of Kirby's.
Whistling Boy is an autobiographical work depicting a winter morning
in Lafayette, Indiana, when, as a boy, Marques delivered newspapers.
Courtesy of the Art Museum of Greater Lafayette.

YDRAD POWER BOAT CLUB

The Ydrad Power Boat Club, originally the "Ydrad Rowing and Athletic Club of the City of Lafayette," was organized on October 26, 1871. The constitution announces, "the object of the Club shall be a friendly union of the members, and for the purpose of promoting the healthful exercise of rowing and athletic sports." The by-laws state that there would be "no rowing in Club boats on Sunday, neither shall the athletic hall be opened on Sunday. The uniform for rowing shall consist of white gauze shirt trimmed in blue, white straw hat, blue band with initials of Club on same." Kirby, age sixteen, joined in June 1917.

In 1921, Kirby was elected Ydrad Power Boat Club treasurer. Membership was one dollar per month with twenty-five cents per month charged for boat storage. The clubhouse was in the lower level of the former Main Street Bridge tollhouse, which was in operation before the span was purchased by the county in 1874 and became free to travelers. The clubhouse included an underground "chamber" with batteries of wooden lockers lining two walls where members kept their belongings. The sidewalk and bridge approach ran above the underground room, which was only a few feet from the old Wabash and Erie Canal. The towpath separated the clubhouse and the canal.

The club minutes from June 1922 state that the members "moved and seconded Ydrad Club put on a boat and canoe races 4th of July." Twenty-one-year-old Kirby was on the committee to host the Ydrad Regatta on Independence Day. A Lafayette newspaper story said it was the "first river regatta Lafayette has witnessed in a number of years." Twelve events comprised the program, including a parade of all of the boats participating in the Wabash River spectacle, followed by racing, diving, swimming, and other specialty events. The winners were presented with trophies that, prior to July 4, were displayed at Lodde jewelry store.

Besides the racing contests, there were other events, "such as tilting contest in which one chap tries to tilt the other out of his canoe; a canoe race without paddles, long distance swimming events; a high diving feature and a tandem canoe race." The longest race that day was five miles starting at the Main Street Bridge and "extend[ing] about to the first island, near the Wabash Valley Sanitarium (now River Bend Hospital) and back." Today, as citizens walk across the scenic bridge and look down into the often shallow, muddy Wabash, it is difficult to fathom such fervor for boating, diving, and long-distance swimming.

According to club minutes, the regatta "was a great success in racing." Kirby drove a two-cylinder boat from Main Street Bridge to the "Swimming Beach at West Side Pump House." The Ydrad Power Boat Cub disbanded by the summer of 1925.

PURDUE

While at Purdue, Kirby was a member of Beta Theta Pi, the Purdue football team, and the Dairy Club. Given Kirby's fondness for ice cream and his father's position as treasurer and general manager of the Dairy Cream Separator Company in Lebanon, Indiana, this membership is understandable.

Kirby was good friends with Ralph Claypool. Claypool was one of Purdue's star football players at the time. After graduating from Purdue, Claypool played professional football for the Chicago Cardinals. Prior to school starting, he wrote Kirby a letter on Purdue Department of Physical Education letterhead that rings of a locker room pep talk:

> Jimmy [Purdue Coach Phelan] says we are going to have the best-conditioned team in the conference so it means to start getting ready. He says we have to be ready for heavy work on the 15th when he takes charge. . . . Well, Kirby, there are eleven positions open this fall and lots of competition, so take care of yourself and be ready to rare.

In late February 1925, there was a roof fire in the Risk family's home. James Kirby Sr. and Dora had the house rebuilt to include a basement apartment and a second floor apartment, changing the original lines of the roof. The second floor became a mirror image of the first floor with living room, dining, room, kitchen, and bedrooms in the same layout as the first floor. Mrs. Robert McGrath of McGrath Foundry and her daughter rented one of the apartments for nearly twenty years. Later, the apartment was used to accommodate overnight guests. Eventually, Kirby and Caroline also purchased the houses that flanked 719 Owen and rented those in his initiative to safeguard the Victorian homes in his beloved neighborhood as it began a transition with homeowners passing away or moving.

The fire was big news in Lafayette, and James Kirby Sr. even received a letter from Purdue President Edward Elliott (President Winthrop Stone had died in 1921 in a mountain climbing accident).

> My Dear Mr. Risk:
>
> On returning to Lafayette, after several days' absence, I learn with great sorrow of the fire, which ravaged your home a few days ago. May this carry to you my sympathy for you during this hour of misfortune, which is indeed a test of your recognized courage.

SCOPES "MONKEY TRIAL"

During Kirby's last year at Purdue in 1925, William Jennings Bryan, age sixty-five, agreed to help the prosecution in the now infamous Scopes "Monkey Trial." It began with the passing of the Butler Act in Tennessee, which was the first law in the United States to ban the teaching of evolution. The law prohibited the teaching "of any theory that denies the story of the Divine Creation of man as taught in the Bible, and to teach instead that man has descended from a lower order of animals."

The American Civil Liberties Union (ACLU) ran an advertisement in a Chattanooga newspaper seeking a teacher who would be willing to challenge the Butler Act. A group of economic leaders in Dayton, Tennessee, saw the ad and hatched a plan to bring the case to their town to generate publicity and jump-start the community's economy. They asked a twenty-four-year-old science teacher named John Thomas Scopes if he would be willing to be indicted to bring the case to trial. Scopes agreed, even though he had only taught biology as a substitute teacher. Later he said he wasn't sure if he had covered evolution in his classroom. With Bryan as part of the prosecution, the case was ensured to garner national interest. The most famous criminal defense lawyer in the country, Clarence Darrow, represented Scopes, who was indicted by a grand jury for violating Tennessee's anti-evolution law on May 25.

Dayton prepared for the onslaught of publicity for which the city leaders hoped. Six blocks of Dayton's central road were altered into a pedestrian mall; a speaker's platform was built in front of the Rhea County Courthouse (today a National Historic Landmark); and a "tourist camp" was created. The Scopes trial was a spectacle that included the attendance of a movie performer chimpanzee named Joe Mendi dressed in a suit and hat. Dayton was dubbed "monkeytown." Monkey doll souvenirs were available for sale from locals outside the courthouse.

The courtroom was equipped with the newest technology to transmit the story to the world: telegraph and telephone wiring, movie-newsreel camera platforms, and radio microphones. WGN Radio aired the trial live at a cost of more than $1,000 a day for telephone lines—the first such broadcast of its kind. Did James Kirby Sr., Dora, and Kirby listen to the groundbreaking broadcast from their home on Owen Street in Lafayette as their friend and advisor, the man who was like one of the family, endured the rigors of this staged courtroom clash of science and religion?

The trial lasted just one week in July, and some of the proceedings took place outdoors due to the heat. It was there under a shade tree, as throngs of onlookers crowded around, that the defense asked Bryan to testify as a biblical expert. Darrow drilled Bryan on whether the Bible should be interpreted literally. Bryan accused Darrow of making a "slur at the Bible," and Darrow mocked Bryan for "fool ideas that no intelligent Christian on earth believes." With movie cameras whirring, this outdoor cross-examination, with both men in their long-sleeved, wilting starched shirts, became one of the most famous scenes in American legal history. The next day, the judge ruled that Bryan could not return to the stand and that his testimony should be expunged from the record, declaring that Bryan's testimony "can shed no light upon any issues that will be pending before the higher courts." Darrow then asked the court to bring in the jury and find Scopes guilty. After nine minutes of deliberation, the jury returned a guilty verdict. Scopes was fined $100, which both Bryan and the ACLU offered to pay for him.

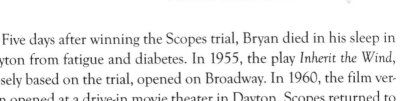

Five days after winning the Scopes trial, Bryan died in his sleep in Dayton from fatigue and diabetes. In 1955, the play *Inherit the Wind*, loosely based on the trial, opened on Broadway. In 1960, the film version opened at a drive-in movie theater in Dayton. Scopes returned to the town for the premiere and was given a key to the city. Neither production used the real names of the trial's participants or location. Today, the movie is criticized as seriously biased and inaccurate, portraying Bryan in an unfavorable light, making him out to be closed-minded, pompous, simple, hypocritical, and gluttonous. Scopes wrote a memoir in 1967 entitled *Center of the Storm*. Also that year, Tennessee repealed the Butler Act, although school boards and legislatures continue to debate how to teach about the origins of life on earth.

What did Kirby think of a movie dishonestly depicting the man who was a good friend of his father's, who had supped on many a meal in his family home and encouraged him to sign a pledge of intent? Kirby's daughter, Sherry, said, "I remember talking about the movie with Mother. I'm not sure Dad was involved, but I think the whole thing made them very uncomfortable. They didn't like it. They didn't want to talk about it. I remember being shut down when I brought it up."

On the day of the funeral of William Jennings Bryan, James Kirby Sr. served as an honorary pallbearer along with senators, representatives, governors, and other dignitaries. At the funeral, Darrow told reporters that he had voted for Bryan twice and respected his "sincerity and devotion." Ruth Bryan Owen presented James Kirby Sr. with a photograph of Bryan along with flowers from his funeral and a card where she wrote:

Sweetheart Roses
The Love Tribute
of
Ruth Meeker
to her
Great-grandfather
William Jennings Bryan

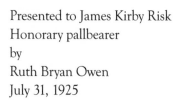

Presented to James Kirby Risk
Honorary pallbearer
by
Ruth Bryan Owen
July 31, 1925

Today, the black and white photograph with the brittle roses and yellowed note is framed and displayed in the home of Julie Pope, Kirby's youngest daughter.

President Calvin Coolidge ordered all American flags on national buildings in Washington, DC, to be displayed at half-mast. Bryan is buried in Arlington National Cemetery. His tombstone reads, "He Kept the Faith."

James Kirby Sr. served as a member of the executive committee of the National Bryan Memorial Association and president of the Indiana Bryan Memorial Association. The national organization's purpose was to erect a permanent memorial to Bryan in the city of Washington, DC. A statue of Bryan was created by Gutzon Borglum, famed sculptor of Mount Rushmore, and originally dedicated by President Theodore Roosevelt on May 3, 1934 in Washington, DC. In 1961, it was moved to Salem, Illinois, where Bryan was born. Another statue of Bryan, given by the Nebraska Memorial Commission in 1937, is part of the Statuary Hall collection at the Capitol.

The year after Bryan's death, Kirby quit school. Perhaps he felt free to do as he pleased without the watchful eye of "The Great Commoner." Kirby borrowed $500 from his father and joined Otto Keiffer to open the Keiffer-Risk Battery Company. It would be the best $500 investment his father ever made.

CHAPTER 3

GIRL FROM OAT FIELDS

"The day I was born—at home—my Papa began cutting oats." Caroline Edna Robinson was born on a farm her Grandparents James Clay and Caroline Victoria Robinson purchased from the government near Wadena, Indiana. Her parents were Edward and Alice Mitten Robinson. Alice had lost a baby boy at birth prior to Caroline's birth. Years later in her journal, Caroline wrote of her mother, "Alice and her sister, Edna, were trying to keep cool in that July heat and wishing Alice's baby would be born. Edna said, 'This baby will never come until you name it.'"

Alice gave birth to Caroline on July 13, 1912 naming her after her mother and sister, who helped her daughter into this world.

Another baby came later. "My brother Russell was born when I was three," said Caroline. "It was long awaited and past due. His arm was broken in the delivery, but I was excited and ran to his basket singing, 'We Shall See the King Some Day.'" Russell was named after his mother's brother.

"The happy times were often at the home of my Grandparent Mitten's in Wadena," Caroline remembered. "Their house was very large with a lovely yard and beautiful flowerbeds. The fence was covered with sweet peas. Grandmother had a box attached to her kitchen window which held goodies like jelly-filled tarts." When she was outside as a child, Caroline wore a gingham sunbonnet.

Caroline was a farm girl with British ancestry. Her maternal Grandfather George Mitten II spoke with an English accent. On November 7, 1874, when he was fifteen, he and his brother, Will, age eighteen, emigrated ahead of their family from England to America aboard the *Indiana*, a steamship from the American Lines that ran between Liverpool and Philadelphia.

Their father, George I, had a cutlery shop and an optician shop in Brighton, England, and the family lived on the first floor of the building that housed the businesses. George I had a nervous breakdown after he lost money due to a dishonest partner, so to help, it was decided that Caroline's grandfather, George II, and his brother would go to America and arrange for the family of seven children to follow. George II and Will, who had never been more than twenty miles from home, headed to the land of opportunity, namely Goodland, Indiana, where their Aunt Martha Verrill lived.

A Goodland newspaper dated November 25, 1934, featured a story with the headline, "Some Memories of Early Goodland, Sixty Years Ago Tuesday, November 27, 1874, Will and George Mitten Arrived in Goodland From England." The story gave George's recount written in the third and first person: "George was very homesick but did not tell Will just how he felt, but as we stood on deck and watched the shores of dear old England fade away, it seemed as if we had lost everything."

Caroline's grandfather wrote:

> In the steerage with hundreds of persons of all nations, locked down below deck in stormy weather, many desperately sick and many on their knees praying and others drinking and cursing—I said to brother Will, "I don't see how hell could be any worse or terrible than this stinking hole." Mother had given us a bottle of whiskey to help us from getting sick, but some of the ruff-tuff men stole it from us the first night out at sea. The rising and falling of waves pitching the boat continued for fourteen days.

Once the one-hundred-foot waves ebbed, optimism prevailed. George II said:

> On November 24, land was sighted and then new hope took a rightful place in our hearts. We began to look forward [to] landing in the country that was to become our home. Big tugboats came to bring us into dock and landed us on Ellis Island. In Philadelphia, Pennsylvania, we were loaded on an immigrant train and came to Goodland via Pittsburg, Fort Wayne and Logansport where we spent the night and arrived in good old Goodland on November 27, 1874.

The teenagers had traveled for twenty days to reach their new American home. They were on their own until the rest of their family arrived seven months later in June 1875. For three years, the Mitten family struggled to adjust with little income before they began to farm.

In 1881, Caroline's grandfather married her grandmother, Mary Alice Fullerton, a neighbor girl. Their daughter, Alice, was Caroline's mother. The Mitten family moved to Wadena, Indiana, and sold coal as a supplement to farming. Later, George II started a farm machinery and hardware business, which became quite successful. As his business grew, George II added groceries, meat, and furniture to his store offerings. Brother Will became a depot agent in Goodland. The brothers who voyaged across the ocean, barely out of childhood, lived the American success story.

Perhaps George II's rough teenage years striving in his new American home were what molded him into a stern yet loving man. Caroline's family attended Sunday school in Wadena where her grandfather was superintendent. When they ate Sunday dinner, he sat at the head of the table, which was covered in a starched, white cloth, and said the blessing. He served the plates and was particular about the children's manners.

Caroline began school at Wadena, but the Robinson family would be forced to move many times because of her father's unemployment and the family's financial challenges. Caroline attended several different schools. Many of her happy times were in the stability of her Grandfather and Grandmother Mitten's home. Yet the moves and hardships would eventually lead to a man named Kirby.

SCHOOL DAYS

Caroline began school in Miss Peckham's first grade class at Wadena School. It was a red brick building with the school bell perched in the roof's cupola. A lightning rod reached skyward from the apex. Caroline traveled to school by horse-drawn buggy. There was a pump organ in her classroom of students in three grade levels. When the school staged the play *Uncle Tom's Cabin*, Caroline portrayed Little Eva. She said of her role, "I felt important."

At age ninety-eight, Caroline remembered the day she was the first in her class to count to one hundred. "The teacher wrote my name on the chalkboard," she said. "Miss Peckham wore a black dress with a white apron."

Around 1920, after Caroline's second grade year, her family moved to a farm near Ade, Indiana. There, the school building was large, but because of low enrollment, only one room was used for teaching. There was no third grade. Miss Peckham had sent a note to the new school indicating that Caroline was ready for the fourth grade. Caroline was never a third grader.

The Robinson family moved again to Columbia City, where Caroline's father farmed for a short while. The land was too rocky, so the family was forced to relocate yet again, and they struggled financially. Caroline remembered, "My mother was so embarrassed."

This time, they moved to a city—Fort Wayne—where Caroline's father worked for the Pennsylvania Railroad. Life was different there. Accustomed to eating the meat and vegetables from the family farm, young Caroline was fascinated with the Piggly Wiggly grocery store and its array of offerings at-the-ready. She took piano lessons downtown at the European School of Music and Art. She eventually played advanced music and performed in the auditorium of the Wolf & Dessauer Department Store—at the time the largest retail store in northern Indiana. Wolf & Dessauer was known for its customer service and elaborate Christmas displays and lights.

Caroline was happy in Fort Wayne with her first city-living experience, music, and friends who lived close by in "big houses." After two years in Fort Wayne, the family moved to Goodland. Caroline's father worked for her Grandfather Mitten's farm implement store.

Caroline attended high school directly across the road from her grandparents' home. She loved school and played the piano in the orchestra and for the boys' Glee Club. They performed an operetta each year, and Caroline was the accompanist. Her best friend was Marceline Parks, a darling redhead. She also played piano; often, the two sat side-by-side at the piano bench.

During Caroline's first year of high school, she was stricken with appendicitis. Her appendix ruptured, which was a grave condition in the 1920s. A doctor from Rensselaer was called to the house. Caroline underwent surgery on the dining room table. Drainage tubes were placed in her abdomen, a registered nurse was employed, and a makeshift hospital room was set up in their home. Her stitches broke, so the doctor paid a daily visit. It was a long, difficult healing process. With no antibiotics at that time, Caroline sat in the sun to heal. She missed most of her first semester of high school.

When Caroline returned to school for the second semester, her friend Clarence Thise tutored her in what she had missed in chemistry and physics.

Caroline's father, Edward, and his brother, Bill, opened an International Harvester store in Boswell after their father passed away and left them an inheritance. Her mother "kept the books" for the business. So in January of Caroline's senior year in high school, her family moved again. In her last semester before graduation, Caroline had to adjust to a new school and new friends.

Caroline remembered, "Boswell never made me happy. No one there danced or played bridge. I did get the lead in the senior play, but that only made it worse."

Caroline graduated from a very different school than that which she had been accustomed. The Boswell school had only eighteen students in grades first through twelfth. Caroline summed up the stark differences between her previous and new educational environments in this way: "The principal at my former school wore suits, while the principal at the Boswell school wore high-top boots and sweaters."

When Caroline was almost seventeen, she attended the Goodland July Fourth Fair. There, she bought a dollar raffle ticket for a chance to win a car—and won a green Whippet Overland convertible with red wire wheels and a rumble seat. Caroline's new sports car became her ticket to Purdue University. Caroline's Uncle Russell had been the one to convince her mother that his niece should go to Purdue.

Caroline sold the Whippet for $600 in order to pay for college. Her Uncle Thomas E. Mitten gave her an additional $500. Mitten was the president of the Mitten Bank Securities Corporation in Philadelphia and the Philadelphia Rapid Transit Company (also in Buffalo and Chicago). His "Mitten Men" operated the trolley lines. Their nickname was a play on Mitten's moniker and on the fact that the trolley staff wore thick work gloves. John Philip Sousa wrote the "March of the Mitten Men" in 1923, dedicating the song to "Thomas Mitten and the men of the Philadelphia Rapid Transit Company." The march incorporates the tune of "Onward, Christian Soldiers," one of Thomas Mitten's favorite hymns.

In the fall of 1929, Caroline entered Purdue with just enough money for one year of education. She packed as many experiences as possible into that year. She took chemistry, biology, and French, among other subjects. She sang in the girls' Glee Club, the predecessor to the Purduettes, and was elected secretary of her freshman class. She pledged Zeta Tau Alpha. She lived with Catherine Trainor at the home of Captain Finney, a French professor. "[Purdue] was a great experience with so much new knowledge," Caroline said. She finished her freshman year in the spring of 1930. Then singing led her to new experiences.

"In Boswell, I sang in our church choir and, often, with the band. I sang solos wherever they played," Caroline wrote in her journal. Fowler, Hoopeston, and Boswell had bandstands in the center of town, and Caroline sang the popular tunes of the time, which spoke of the Depression and President Franklin Roosevelt. Caroline was fond of this melody: "So let's have another cup of coffee, and let's have another piece of pie." These words were from a 1932 Irving Berlin song filled with hope for the time. The song ended with this timely verse: "Mr. Herbert Hoover / Says that now's the time to buy, / So let's have another cup o' coffee, / And let's have another piece o' pie!"

Caroline's mother, Alice, belonged to a club that held a state meeting in Indianapolis. Caroline was asked to sing at the gathering. After the program, a young man named Bob Kettrick approached Caroline and asked her if she would be interested in singing with his dance band. It was an opportunity.

Caroline lived in Indianapolis with her Aunt Edna, attended shorthand school, and sang with Bob's band. There was a weekly rehearsal with performances in Tudor Hall and the Indianapolis Athletic Club. She was paid five dollars a show. "It was exciting and I could use my evening dresses from Purdue," Caroline said.

Years later, Caroline wrote in her journal about a world event that made headlines at the time: "The kidnapping of the Lindbergh baby happened that fall [actually, it was spring]. Such tragic news—and Bruno Hauptman's [sic] name is still etched in my mind. His trial was large news. He was condemned to death."

Caroline was referring to the March 1932 kidnapping of Charles and Anne Morrow Lindbergh's infant son. Lindbergh was the famed 1927 aviator who flew solo, nonstop from New York to Paris in the single-seat, single-engine *Spirit of St. Louis*. A $50,000 ransom was paid to kidnapper Bruno Hauptmann, but the baby was found dead. The case was considered the crime of the century. It was yet another reason the world needed hope for the time, and Irving Berlin's song provided solace with a cup of coffee and a piece of pie.

CHAPTER 4

KIRBY'S CHARGE

After he borrowed startup money from his father, Kirby and his partner Otto Keiffer opened Keiffer-Risk Battery Company in an abandoned blacksmith shop at 209 North Second Street in downtown Lafayette, just a couple of blocks from the Wabash River. The business sold, rented, and recharged automobile batteries. While the company was recharging a battery, a "loaner" battery was provided to the customer for use in the meantime. The reason Kirby started a battery business isn't officially known. Perhaps Kirby, who was always inventive and on the cusp of trends, saw that the future, with the new automobile and advancing industrial technologies of the time, required more batteries, battery recharging, and repair.

This was June 1926, the era of the Ford Model T. Automobile sales were booming. The fact that Kirby's automobile battery company began in a former blacksmith shop is a bit of irony. The "horseless carriage" had put blacksmiths out of business. With Kirby's new battery business and Caroline's sale of the Whippet to attend Purdue, the automobile was the linchpin of change for both, as they led their separate lives in different Indiana towns.

Keiffer-Risk was a small but active business that also provided generator repair. The garage sat next door to Pottlitzer and Sons Fresh Produce and nearby was the brick Monon Railroad freight depot. It was a bustling block. In the air, the scent of ripening produce mixed with the metallic perfume of coal-fed locomotive engines.

An invoice from Keiffer-Risk Battery Company to Quick Service Garage dated September 1, 1926, includes this byline: "Starting, Lighting, Ignition Experts." It also states on the invoice, "All kinds of starters, generators and magnetoes [sic] repaired. All makes of batteries repaired and recharged." A magneto is an electrical generator that uses permanent magnets to produce alternating current. Hand-cranked magneto generators were used to provide ringing current in early telephone systems. Magnetos are used in the ignition systems of some gasoline-powered internal combustion engines to provide power to the spark plugs. The magneto is now mainly used in engines where there is no available electrical supply, such as lawn mowers and chain saws. Another popular and common use of magnetos today is to power lights on bicycles. Usually, a small magneto rubs against the tire of the bicycle and generates power as the wheel spins.

In the fall of 1926, Keiffer withdrew from the company due to illness. George Tweedie, a rusty-haired Scotchman, became Kirby's new partner, and the name of the business changed to Risk-Tweedie Electric Service. With Tweedie's knowledge of motor repair and rewinding, the business expanded. Kirby was able to repay his $500 debt to his father.

Kirby enlarged his business to include electrical supplies and contracting just as more homes and businesses were wired for electricity. In 1920, only about 25 percent of American dwellings had electricity; by 1930, nearly 70 percent would have electric power. It was 1925 when Northern Indiana Public Service Company finished construction of Lake Freeman just north of Lafayette in Carroll and White Counties by opening the Oakdale Dam on the Tippecanoe River. Norway Dam, which formed Lake Shafer, had been completed in 1923. Electricity was flowing, and Kirby saw his opportunity.

In 1926, George Tweedie, pictured far right, became Kirby's business partner. Risk-Tweedie Electric Service was at 209 North Second Street in downtown Lafayette, Indiana. The establishment formerly had been a blacksmith shop.

Another fortunate turn was the hiring of an additional employee, Glenn Buschman, known as "Bud." With only an eighth-grade education, Bud was taught the rewinding and repairing of electric motors. He was a steady, dependable, and highly regarded employee who continued with the company, eventually serving as an officer of the corporation until his death.

They Meet

With the stock market crash of 1929, banks closed, including the Fowler Bank, patronized by Risk and Tweedie. Yet this was the year Caroline won the Whippet she sold to attend college, and her uncle gave her the additional funds for her education. For Caroline, the toughest times were in the past.

In 1931, when Caroline was nineteen, she worked for an attorney in Boswell. One summer evening during her walk home, she ran into Paul Calvert, a Phi Gamma Delta and football player she had known at Purdue University. He was with another fellow in a pickup truck parked on Main Street.

Paul leaned out the window and said, "Hello, Caroline. Can we give you a lift home? This is my friend, Kirby Risk."

Kirby had asked Paul to accompany him to help repair a motor at the Boswell grain elevator.

As the three rode to Caroline's house, Paul asked, "Want to go to a movie in Lafayette tonight with Kirby and his date?"

"I can go right after choir practice," Caroline said.

Later, however, Paul phoned Caroline with an apology—the movie plans had to be cancelled. Kirby had not found a date.

A few days later, the wall phone rang again at the Robinson home. Caroline picked up the receiver and said, "Hello."

The voice at the other end responded, "This is Kirby Risk, but you don't know who that is from the man in the moon!"

Caroline remembered Kirby. He was much older than she—ten years older—and he had his own battery and electrical supply business in Lafayette. Kirby was calling to invite Caroline to a movie.

The evening of their first date, they climbed into Kirby's open convertible. On the drive from Boswell to Lafayette, the couple zoomed by cornfields, silos, cattle, and drifts of orange tiger lilies waving in the wake of Kirby's car. Caroline would soon learn that Kirby liked fast cars and speedboats.

After the movie, they made a stop at Kirby's home, and Caroline met Mrs. Risk. James Kirby Sr. had died a few months earlier on February 27, at the age of sixty-six, after a long illness due to diabetes and Bright's disease.

In the months to come, Kirby returned to Caroline's home in Boswell several times for visits. It was a thirty-mile trip from Lafayette. Kirby was meticulous about his clothing, and when he dressed to go out, he always wore a bow tie. Sometimes he would bring ice cream.

Kirby loved ice cream; it was his indulgence. Perhaps since he had signed William Jennings Bryan's letter of intent vowing never to consume alcohol as a beverage, ice cream became his "substitute" pleasure. Ice cream was his "after-dinner drink" or "celebratory cocktail," so to speak. Specifically, he loved frozen custard. Yet on a few occasions, he consumed alcohol in other ways. His daughter, Carol, said, "Dad didn't drink, but he would put liquor on certain foods. You know, sherry in chili." Technically, when he "ate" alcohol with foods, he was not "consuming alcohol as a beverage," as was stated in Bryan's pledge of intent that Kirby signed at age sixteen.

Kirby's father ran the Dairy Cream Separator Company in Lebanon, Indiana. As a young man, Kirby spent summers working there. Kirby became good friends with Charles Kirkhoff, who opened the Frozen Custard at Main Street and Wallace Avenue in Lafayette in 1932, the year James Kirby Sr. passed away. The Frozen Custard was a customer of the Dairy Cream Separator Company. Kirkhoff developed his own formula for his delicious frozen custard that still melts like silk on the tongue.

Frozen custard would always play a part in Caroline's life with this dapper man, as they would one day raise a family together and host friends and business associates. Little did she know at the time, bits and pieces of their future swirled about them.

Later that year, Kirby invited Caroline to travel to Detroit with him to pick up his mother, who was visiting her niece, Dodie, the girl who had lived with the Risk family when she was younger. Caroline's parents weren't sure about letting their young daughter travel to the big city alone with a man ten years her senior. Therefore, Kirby invited twelve-year-old Johnnie Moran, a neighbor boy who lived at 723 Owen, to go along as chaperone. The three took off for Detroit to see sights Caroline wrote about in her journal: "It was a wonderful trip. Detroit! The zoo, the Harmsworth Trophy Races, the theater where Rudy Vallee was singing! I fell in love. We went to Canada, ate Dodie's delicious food with all of her silver shining."

This small-town girl dreamily recorded her list of Detroit experiences, gently slipping in the sentence that summed up the trip and her feelings for Kirby: "I fell in love."

CHAPTER 5

WORLD'S FAIR WEDDING

"Science and show biz come together to revive a city worn weary by Depression." That was how the *Chicago Tribune* described the "Chicago World's Fair: A Century of Progress International Exposition," held from 1933 to 1934. The Chicago World's Fair's luminous art deco buildings were constructed on new land created by filling in Lake Michigan. The structures were multicolored, designed to create a "Rainbow City" as opposed to the "White City" of the World's Columbian Exposition held in 1893. For an admission price of fifty cents, fairgoers wandered among eighty-two miles of displays that ranged from scholarly—the chemistry of sulfur in the Hall of Science—to quirky—trained fleas on the Midway. The children's play area featured giant characters from the book *The Wonderful Wizard of Oz* (it would not be made into a movie until 1939). The "straw man" loomed high above the entrance of "Enchanted Island." The fair would prove supremely enchanting for a young country girl from Boswell, Indiana.

A Century of Progress International Exposition opened on Saturday, May 27, 1933, with the pomp and pageantry of a parade, including marching bands, spiffily uniformed mounted police, and a queen

---

TRANSMITTAL COUPON

"QUEEN" COMPETITION, CHICAGO TRIBUNE
POST OFFICE BOX 1539, CHICAGO, ILLINOIS

I submit the attached photograph to be entered in your offer of $20,000.00 in Cash Prizes to find a "Queen" and her "Court of Honor" to dedicate the Century of Progress International Exposition at Chicago and agree to abide by the rules published by you. I also grant to you the right to publish this photograph in any manner you may determine.

The name of the person in this photograph is...... *Caroline Robinson*

Her street address is...

City...... *Boswell* .... State.... *Ind.*

Her occupation is...... *home girl*
(State whether stenographer, clerk, school girl, home girl, factory girl, etc.)

The color of her hair is ☒ Blonde   ☐ Brunette   ☐ Titian

The color of her eyes is *Blue* .... Weight. *108* ... Height. *5'3"*

Submitted by.... *Mr. Thomas Thompson*
(Signature of person submitting photograph)

This is the entry form Caroline Risk pasted into a scrapbook of memories of the 1933 Chicago World's Fair queen competition. Caroline's Grandmother Mitten submitted her photo and this "Transmittal Coupon" to the Chicago Tribune, the contest sponsor.

and her court of honor, who dedicated the Chicago World's Fair. One of the beauties selected by a panel of judges to be on the queen's court of honor was Caroline Robinson.

The *Chicago Sunday Tribune* ran a full-page ad on January 29, 1933, announcing the "Century of Progress 'Queen' Competition." The *San Antonio Express and Evening News*, together with the *Tribune*, cosponsored the photographic contest seeking "charming" girls from across the globe who would formally dedicate the Exposition in Chicago on June 1. Sixteen other newspapers participated in the event, including the *Tribune's* Paris edition. In the *Tribune*, a drawing of a queen with her scepter pointed to the headline that read, "The Chicago Tribune will pay $20,000 to find the 51 most charming girls in the World to become QUEEN and Her Court of Honor to Dedicate the Triumphal Century of Progress International Exposition at Chicago." The piece went on to say:

Girls! Have You Sent in Your Photograph?

The Chicago Tribune presents this opportunity to girls everywhere—without one cent of cost. All that is necessary is to send a photograph to the Chicago Tribune. Ten photographs are published each Sunday in this Section. To each of the girls whose photographs are so published the Chicago Tribune will pay $100.00 in cash. In addition, three Grand Prizes of $5,000.00, $3,000.00 and $2,000.00 will be awarded at the end of the competition. . . . Unmarried girls everywhere are eligible—excepting professionals, such as stage girls and artists' models.

The fifty-one winners would be awarded a two-week trip to Chicago, all expenses paid, including transportation, hotels, meals, and entertainment, plus the gowns for the events at the Exposition. The *Tribune* would provide "proper chaperonage for such girls." The money prizes were over-the-top for the Great Depression—$100 in 1933 is equivalent to about $1,700 today. The $5,000 that was to be awarded to the queen would be worth more than $85,000 in 2012.

Caroline's Grandmother Mitten saw the *Tribune* call for contestants, and she submitted her granddaughter's photograph along with the "Transmittal Coupon" that accompanied the advertisement. Caroline kept a memory book of the event. The cover is in black and white polka dots with crayon-hued, three-inch letters that shout "SCRAPBOOK." It looks of the 1930s in a very "Betty Boop" style of the day. The ad and coupon are preserved in the scrapbook. Caroline's address written on the entry is simply "Boswell, Indiana." No street or county road was included or necessary back then. Where the coupon states, "Her occupation is," Caroline's grandmother wrote, "home girl." (The occupation examples given in the newspaper were "stenographer, clerk, school girl, home girl, factory girl, etc.") The

Caroline Risk's Grandmother Mitten submitted this photograph to the Chicago Tribune for the 1933 Chicago World's Fair queen competition. Caroline was twenty years old when she was selected to be a member of the queen's court with fifty other women.

responses continue: "The color of hair: blonde. The color of her eyes is: blue. Weight: 108. Height 5' 2"." There was no age restriction.

One of the eight judges for the queen competition was John T. McCutcheon, the Purdue graduate and Pulitzer-Prize winning cartoonist from the *Chicago Tribune*, who had met with Kirby's artist friend Marques Reitzel to critique his work back in 1919. Regarding the judge's criteria, the newspaper states, "Judgments will be based upon charm, loveliness and personality." The young, female entrants came from all over the world and all lifestyles. Kathleen McLaughlin wrote a *Chicago Daily Tribune* story on May 20, 1933, which read, "Contrast the sweet faced little factory girl from Chicago's west side, ecstatic over acquiring the first real party dress she ever owned, with the Philadelphia debutante, daughter of a Bethlehem Steel company official, who is dropping her Junior league activities to join the fun as Chicago inaugurates its 1933 World's Fair."

In April, Eleanor Nangle, director of fashion and beauty for the *Tribune,* visited the small town of Boswell to meet and talk to Caroline. Nangle had covered other charm contests sponsored by the newspaper. The next year, she would start her famous "Thru the Looking Glass" beauty column that would run through the 1960s. Soon after Nangle visited the Robinson home, Caroline received a special delivery letter inviting her to the queen competition as one of the fifty-one young female finalists from Europe and many other cities in America. Before she left for a week of majestic splendor, she purchased and borrowed new clothes. She received a check from the Tribune Company for five dollars. The memorandum typed on the check stub that Caroline saved in her scrapbook explains the purpose of the money, "To cover expenses to be incurred by you on your way to Chicago to participate in the Chicago Tribune's 'QUEEN' contest." Caroline wrote years later in a journal, "I was invited to go to the Chicago Tribune's Queen contest for the 1933 Century of Progress. What a thrill!"

But that thrill worried her beau Kirby.

When Kirby heard that Caroline was selected to spend nearly two weeks in Chicago with the possibility of becoming queen of the World's Fair, he feared he would lose his girl amidst the starry enchantment. He did not want to take any chances. Years later, Caroline wrote, "The night before I was to leave via the New York Central, Kirby gave me a lovely solitaire [diamond ring] purchased from a family on Owen Street, jeweler friend, Mr. Eisenbach. How I survived all the excitement, I don't now know." The year before, Eisenbach who owned Eisenbach Jewelers in downtown Lafayette, had been a pallbearer at the funeral of Kirby's father.

The next day, an escort arrived at Caroline's door to accompany the newly engaged queen contestant on the train to Chicago. By the end of the following week, Caroline and Kirby would be married at the Century of Progress International Exposition. The two weeks of waiting at home in Lafayette was agonizing for Kirby, while Caroline was floating along in Chicago, gilded in the wrappings of near royalty. Kirby wrote letters to his fiancée nearly every day.

On May 25, 1933, Kirby wrote the first of five letters to Caroline on Risk-Tweedie Electric Service letterhead. Printed at the bottom of the business stationery is this statement: "Lafayette's only complete electric repair shop." A drawing of a motor in muted green is featured in the center of the writing paper, and Kirby's handwriting is scrawled across the image. He writes, in part:

> Dearest—I do hope they don't mention our engagement, although I don't care who knows it. You know I just can't do any good talking to you, so I'll have to write what I feel, and that is "I love you—I love you—I love you." Be sure to call me tonight or in the morning. With all my love and kisses, and I do want you now and all the time. With all my love, Kirby.

In 2001, when Caroline was eighty-nine, she wrote of that week, "As I think about it now, it is like a beautiful dream. Marshal Field made to order each girl's gown, which we wore as we rode on floats down Michigan Avenue to open the Century of Progress. The girls were housed in seven different hotels, with each hotel using its own special autos. I was at the Sherman and we used one white, one blue and one red Dodge."

Kirby's handwritten letters arrived each day addressed to Caroline Robinson, room 1606, Sherman Hotel. His letter on May 26, the day before the opening of the World's Fair, is four pages long. He tells Caroline that he talked to her mother and she was coming to Lafayette to shop at The Fashion (a clothing store on the Courthouse Square) to buy Caroline something to wear.

> Dearest Caroline—She [Caroline's mother] saw your picture this morning in the Tribune. Jane said she has never seen that expression on your face, and I agree. We also agree on the other girls. After looking at the picture a dozen times, I have become reconciled

to it. Although, I'll confess there was a question in my heart after the first look. . . . I haven't the slightest wish for you to win a prize, excepting for the pleasure it might give you. None of the judges could possibly subject you to the critical standard that you passed in my mind, and that is all that matters to me.

Jane, mentioned in the above letter, was an aunt of Kirby's. Kirby's son, Jim, said of her, "Aunt Jane was kind of scary to all of us. Off the wall." It is telling that "scary" Aunt Jane would say that she had never seen the expression Caroline displayed in her queen contestant photo. Perhaps Aunt Jane was rather critical. At age ninety-eight in 2010, Caroline said, "Nobody liked her."

More than sixty years later, Caroline wrote in her journal about her World's Fair experience: "It was an 'out of this world' week with many special delivery letters and phone calls from J. K. R."

Kirby was lonesome for his bride-to-be and perhaps a bit worried about their ten-year age difference. He continued;

> I believe I have adjusted myself to your being away, I miss you terribly, but don't worry the least bit. I think we had better wait until the end to see each other. . . . Steve spent an hour telling about why our ages were ideal. I hope he is right.

Kirby tells Caroline to let him know if she needs money and that "anything and everything I have is yours." Kirby ends his letter with:

> Honey, remember I love you, and the old prize doesn't appeal to me in the least. In fact, I would rather you would look sort of mean when they are judging you. The responsibility of trying to satisfy a queen is more than I would attempt.

Caroline cut out each finalist's photo from the *Chicago Tribune* and pasted it into her scrapbook. She wrote comments near many of the pictures. Under the photo of gorgeous Julia Rose Weideman from Kansas City who later must have gone to Hollywood, she scrawled, "My roommate gave me white roses when I left. [She was] at the wedding as maid of honor. Movie contract." Under other photos of girls, most with hair in the "finger wave" style that was so popular then, she wrote, "very sweet girl," "beauty operator," "rather large, but beautiful," "exceptionally tall, bobbed hair," "a little coarse," and "pretty, but so quick, you couldn't talk to her." Next to Ruth Joyce Hardie's photo, Caroline wrote, "Played my wedding march. Very accomplished musician."

As the *Tribune* stated, the girls were "representative of the finest feminine charm from all parts of the world." Caroline preserved two stories about a girl from London, England, and another from Paris, France. The first story, titled "Foreign Queens Sail for the U.S. Next Thursday," is written by Kathleen McLaughlin and begins, "Beyond the Atlantic this morning a petite English miss and a slim French mademoiselle, wild with excitement, are packing their bags for as thrilling a journey as either have conjured in their dreams." The girls sailed to Canada and then took a train to Chicago. The story is filled with poetic prose about the young women's journey to America. In contrast, the second story, dated June 6, bares a startling headline: "French Entrant for Queen of Fair Dies." The copy reads, "The French representative in the competition for queen of the Chicago's world's fair—Mlle Lyette Teppaz, of Paris, died in a hospital early today. Physicians said acute peritonitis following an attack of colitis was the cause of death. She was 29 years old."

The story goes on to say that Teppaz was able to attend only two days of the queen contest festivities before she was admitted to the hospital with a slight fever. Her condition had not been considered critical until a few hours before her death. She "had been indisposed on her ocean voyage to America, but it was considered only a slight illness due to the ocean trip." Caroline wrote next to the Paris beauty's photo: "Stenographer. Ate her last meal with the group next to me at the Pabst Casino."

The contest schedule was moved up after President Franklin Roosevelt announced he could open the Exposition on May 27 rather than June 1. This change resulted in the transportation of the girls to be rearranged, and the fittings of the gowns to transpire in one day instead of four. The selection of the queen took place the afternoon of May 26. Each girl was escorted by an honor student from Northwestern University or the University of Chicago. The queen and her court were chosen after the contestants promenaded before the judges in the Bal Tabarin (a bar and lounge) of the Hotel Sherman. The girls wore white taffeta, red hats, muffs, and slippers. They were identified by numbers on their arms and judged on poise, carriage, speaking voice, beauty, and figure.

A May 26 article in the *Chicago Daily Tribune* described how the announcement of the queen would be made at a formal dinner. It reads, "The decision, however, is to be kept a dark secret until this evening when trumpets sound and doors on either side of the great stairway in the grand ballroom of the Hotel Sherman are thrown open and the queen and her court march down. Rufus C. Dawes, president of A Century of Progress will perform the coronation ceremony to a medley of 'God Save the King,' the 'Marseillaise,' and 'The Star Spangled Banner.' Dawes announced the winners over a nationwide radio broadcast on NBC-WJZ.

Lillian Anderson from Racine, Wisconsin, was "picked as the victor" to be the queen of the World's Fair. In her scrapbook, Caroline wrote next to Anderson's photo, "Cashier in tea room. All of the girls loved her and everyone was so happy for her. A deserving girl—marvelous personality—poise, etc." A full-page photo of Anderson in her queen attire appeared in the *Tribune*. Her gown was trimmed in tiny jewels and was complete with a train that trailed well behind her and bore a foot-high, stand-up collar that framed her face. Anderson's crown was of the same jewels as her frock and gloves that nearly covered her arms. Her hefty scepter was also decorated in matching jewels. But Lillian Anderson would not be the only queen at the fair. After all, there was a wedding in the works.

OPENING DAY

On May 27, the day the fair opened, Kirby wrote:

> Honey, please, please get a little rest. Even if you have to give up calling me. You sound so tired. It is awfully hard for me to sleep

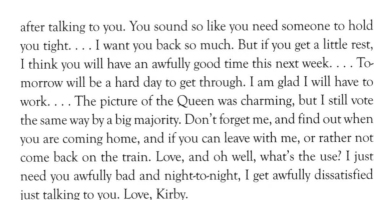

after talking to you. You sound so like you need someone to hold you tight. . . . I want you back so much. But if you get a little rest, I think you will have an awfully good time this next week. . . . Tomorrow will be a hard day to get through. I am glad I will have to work. . . . The picture of the Queen was charming, but I still vote the same way by a big majority. Don't forget me, and find out when you are coming home, and if you can leave with me, or rather not come back on the train. Love, and oh well, what's the use? I just need you awfully bad and night-to-night, I get awfully dissatisfied just talking to you. Love, Kirby.

The queen and her court rode down Michigan Avenue on six colorful floats that were created by the *Chicago Tribune's* art department. Spectacular sights swirled around the chosen beauties. The architectural symbol of the Exposition was the Sky Ride. Ten double-decker scarlet and silver "rocket cars" were suspended on steel cables between two six-hundred-foot towers perpendicular to the shore. Each hour, up to five thousand passengers rode from one side of the fair to the other. The Sky Ride booklet beckoned, "See the fair from the air." When night fell on opening day, the occasion took on an otherworldly glow. Rays from the star Arcturus were harnessed to spark floodlights that illuminated the sky. This star was chosen because its light takes about forty years to reach the earth, and forty years had passed since the previous Chicago World's Fair. As Kirby Risk rode the current of electricity to build his business, the Century of Progress International Exposition harnessed that wonder and splashed it across the sky like an oil painting above the rolling waves of Lake Michigan.

The afternoon of the opening day, the women participated in the inaugural ceremonies at Soldier Field. The week after was filled with formal dinners in the "city's smartest spots" and events featuring renowned dignitaries and stars with music by famous bands. Caroline wrote in 2001, "Every detail was carefully handled and the 'queens' met Mayor Kelly, George Burns and Gracie Allen, etc. We dined at the Palmer House 'Empire Room' and with Buddy Rogers' band at the Sherman Hotel, and at the Drake." The women were slated to meet President Franklin Roosevelt, but even after all the last-minute schedule changes on his behalf, he was unable to attend the fair.

On May 28, Kirby related a story in his letter that referred to the decade age difference between he and his fiancée:

> Now I'll really tell you one. The superintendent from Brown Rubber [a factory in Lafayette, Indiana] was down to see about the job this noon. His five or six year old son was with him. His dad was complimenting me about your picture. The little fellow looked up and said, "Gee, is that your daughter Dad was talking about at dinner?"

In Kirby's letter from Tuesday, May 30, it sounds as if he is referring to a request made by Kathleen McLaughlin of the *Tribune* to help plan their wedding, which was to take place on the last day of the queens' festivities.

> When I woke up after an hour's sleep your suggestion was upper most in my mind. It made me so weak that it was after ten o'clock before I could hold my head steady. I am perfectly willing to talk it over with you or the woman you mentioned. . . . If there was absolutely no publicity before hand it would not be objectionable. After all that is your party. Only we don't want to cheapen it any. . . . All my love and kisses dear and I want to do what ever will make you happy as long as it won't hurt us later on. . . . I hope you can manage to see me tomorrow night after your party at the Drake.

Years later, Caroline wrote in her journal, "Unbelievably and magically we had our wedding planned with Kirby and Mother consulted. Kathleen McLaughlin (of the *Trib*) went with me to buy my gown and veil and shoes at Stevens, and then to the Stop and Shop for the cake and ordered white orchid bouquet."

During the Jazz Age, the Charles A. Stevens Department Store, Mandel Brothers, Carson Pirie Scott, and Marshall Field's formed a group of the largest department stores in the world on North State Street in Chicago. Promoting elegance, Stevens put on Chicago's first fashion shows, had a doorman to welcome customers on a red carpet, and featured "dark rooms" where women could examine gowns under dim ballroom light. Caroline's wedding gown from Stevens was made of "mousseline de soie" with a floor-length, full skirt and ruffled bodice. The veil was of white tulle and held in place with orange blossoms. Caroline must have felt that she was the queen.

Stop and Shop was a gourmet grocer in the Chicago Loop. It closed in the 1980s. The upscale store offered beautiful produce and the finest meats, plus imported candy. A locked glass case held canned, chocolate-covered ants and chocolate-covered bees imported from Asia. Caroline's wedding bouquet from the Stop and Shop consisted of white sweet peas, gardenias, and orchids tied with white satin ribbons.

WEDDING

The *Chicago Tribune* orchestrated the Robinson-Risk wedding, which was held on the last day of festivities for the queen and her court, June 3, 1933. Years later, Caroline wrote in her journal, "Mother came up that a.m. and we purchased lingerie and extras." The marriage took place in the Rose Room of the Hotel Sherman. The eight women of the court who also stayed at the Sherman were Caroline's bridesmaids. Kirby's best man was his friend and Lafayette attorney Charles McCabe.

Kirby was notoriously late for many events throughout his life, including his own wedding. He traveled from Lafayette to Chicago, accompanied by Reverend Fred Williams, the minister of Trinity United Methodist Church. Caroline remembered in her diary, "The wedding was at 8:00 p.m. with no rehearsal!! As Kirby was late!" This Kirby trait was one Caroline would learn to accept throughout their marriage. In Lafayette circles, Kirby came to be called "The Late Mr. Risk."

About thirty of Caroline and Kirby's relatives were in attendance, including Caroline's parents and brother, Russell, her grandparents, aunts, uncles, and cousins, and Kirby's mother, along with many Risk cousins. Caroline wrote of the ceremony, "It was in a lovely grey and

James Kirby Risk Jr. and Caroline Edna Robinson were married at the 1933 Chicago World's Fair. Caroline's bridesmaids were other women who had been selected to reign on the queen's court and take part in the fair's opening ceremonies.

gold room. 'I Love You Truly' was played." On their wedding day Caroline was twenty and Kirby was thirty-one.

Following the nuptials, the guests were treated to a "beautiful sit down supper." A newspaper clipping from Caroline's scrapbook bears the headline, "Boswell Beauty Weds in Chicago." The story ends with, "Just ten days ago Miss Robinson became a member of the court of honor, and her marriage Saturday night preceded the formal disbanding of the court.

Incidentally, it was just ten days ago that Miss Robinson became formally engaged."

The couple spent their first night at the Hotel Shoreland along Lake Michigan in Chicago. Caroline kept a postcard with a painting of the hotel depicted. A dirt trail meanders in front of the Shoreland along the water's edge, and people on horseback are enjoying the path as sailboats dance in the breeze and waves. Years later, Caroline placed a yellow note under the postcard and wrote, "Where *we* spent our first night. Also: Had beautiful Sunday brunch in Crystal Dining Room with Dora and Ralph Smith and Edith and Charles McCabe. That afternoon, we left in Kirby's new black Chevrolet convertible for Michigan. We spent several days on Lake Michigan at Dora and Ralph's cottage—then to Detroit to Smiths." Caroline would pay many visits to the Smiths in the years to come. Dora Fidler Smith was the cousin who Kirby's parents had raised.

One of the wedding gifts that the Risks received was from Marques Reitzel, the now nationally famous artist who attended art school with the financial assistance of Kirby's father. Marques gave Kirby and Caroline a painting. On the back Caroline wrote, "Scene near Rockford, Illinois. Wedding gift from M. Reitzel to Carolyn Robinson and Kirby Risk Jr., June 2, 1933." The vibrant painting is of a stream with a hint of autumn. One tree along the water's edge is auburn; others are shades of emerald. Marques had given several paintings to Kirby's parents as a thank-you. All were displayed on the walls at 719 Owen.

Marques received a gold medal for landscape painting at the Century of Progress International Exposition. In 1941, he became the third American to "paint his way to a Ph.D. degree." Marques earned his doctorate from The Ohio State University through the merits of his painting alone. He did not write a dissertation; instead, he submitted twenty-seven paintings to his examining board.

On the Risk's first anniversary, the Shoreland Hotel sent them flowers. Also, the following spring, the *Chicago Tribune* invited Caroline and her fellow "queens" to help reopen the 1934 World's Fair. They stayed for a week at the Drake Hotel.

On June 1, 2001, Caroline, then eighty-nine, wrote a letter to the *Chicago Tribune* recounting the events of the summer of 1933. Had he been living, Kirby would have turned one hundred that year. Caroline's handwritten letter began, "As my 68th wedding anniversary and the 68th anniversary of the 1933 Century of Progress approaches, I felt I should again thank you for the *unbelievably fantastic* week you gave me and 48 other young women!" She ended the two-page letter with:

> As I retell this, I can scarcely believe the great excitement and plea-
> sure all 49 young women shared—such beautiful and great and last-
> ing memories!! My husband and I raised four great children, and we
> were married for over 60 years before he died. Thank you ever so
> much, again and again, for such beautiful and exciting memories.
> Most Sincerely, Caroline Robinson Risk (Mrs. J. Kirby).

Caroline kept a copy of her letter in an envelope. She wrote on the envelope, "No answer."

CHAPTER 6

OFF TO WORK THEY GO

When Kirby and Caroline returned to Lafayette after their honeymoon, they moved in with Kirby's mother on Owen Street. Dora Risk instructed her new daughter-in-law to, "Sit up straight, hold your head high, you're a Risk now." From that day forward, Caroline would refer to her mother-in-law as "Mrs. Risk." She was never Dora, or mother.

Decades later, Caroline wrote, "I was a young, unsophisticated, green small-town bride who came in 1933 to live in *The* Risk home—already their home for more than 40 years. Dora Risk's house was immaculate, and besides, she was a splendid cook—for those days, perhaps, 'gourmet.' I didn't even know how to poach an egg." Mrs. Risk taught Caroline to be a fabulous cook. She would be called upon to prepare dinners for numerous guests throughout her married life, often "at the drop of a hat" when Kirby brought home business associates, Purdue students—many who were from foreign countries—and people in need.

Caroline smoked cigarettes, which was socially acceptable in the 1930s and often was depicted as glamorous in motion pictures.

Cigarette ads of the day featured movie stars and even Santa Claus smoking Camels or Lucky Strikes with headlines like, "Luckies are always kind to your throat." Caroline quit smoking after she moved into the Risk's "sophisticated" home. Caroline said of smoking, "Well, it's not much fun when your husband and mother-in-law are glaring at you." Caroline, the queen contestant, arrived at her new home from the pageantry of the World's Fair and a whirlwind, fairytale wedding to live in someone else's court.

One night after dinner when they were newlyweds, Caroline said to Kirby, "It's your turn to do the dishes." Kirby gathered the dishes from the table and threw them in the sink. When he finished breaking the dinner plates and cups, he said, "There. That's done." Caroline watched in shock. One can only imagine what Mrs. Risk thought of her only child and what looked like a temper tantrum at the age of thirty-two. Ironically, after the night he "ditched" the dishes, Kirby voluntarily stepped to the kitchen sink and washed the pots, pans, and plates after many a meal throughout his marriage. One may deduce that Kirby was making a point: no one could tell him it was his turn to do the dishes; he would decide if he wanted to scrub the china, and then proceed to do just that. Perhaps, too, he was sending a message to his mother that his wife did not tell him what to do.

Also at this time, Kirby decided to change the spelling of Caroline's name. She was born "Caroline," said with a long "i," the way her mother, Alice, pronounced it. Kirby wanted to call his wife "Carolyn" with a short "i," so she altered the spelling and the pronunciation. Their daughter, Sherry, said, "Years ago, mother told me she was sorry she ever changed it." So after she married, Caroline Edna Robinson became Carolyn Edna Risk. (For this book, to honor her preference, the woman who married James Kirby Risk II will be referenced as her parents christened her. She is Caroline.)

Caroline learned that her new husband had some quirky ways of expressing himself, yet she also learned he knelt by his bedside nightly to pray. Down on his knees next to his bed, Kirby said prayers for family, friends, and business. Without fail, Kirby was committed to his faith and nightly connection with the divine. Again, when Kirby made a promise, he followed through to the end. He was a stickler for doing things right, and right meant you prayed and honored the One who granted you breath and bread. He garnered his unwavering faith from his parents, who were devout Presbyterians, and from the influence of family friend William Jennings Bryan, also a Presbyterian, who, after his retirement, crossed America giving what were known as "Bryan Bible Talks" in defense of a literal interruption of the Bible and against evolution.

WORKING TOGETHER

Soon after her marriage, Caroline began to accompany Kirby to his office at Risk-Tweedie Electric Service to help with the phone, cash drawer, and correspondence. Kirby always wanted to "keep things private," so many files were kept at home. For confidentiality with his legal matters, he hired an attorney from Indianapolis rather than employing one of his lawyer-friends in Lafayette.

On February 10, 1934, John M. Tweedie, the son of Kirby's partner, George Tweedie, was killed in an automobile accident when he hit a telephone pole near Stockwell, Indiana, while driving Kirby's black Chevrolet coup. An article in the Lafayette *Journal and Courier* stated that the car overturned, "was demolished," and "the youth's skull was crushed." When the accident occurred, Kirby was on a service call in Stockwell. While Kirby was tending to a client's needs, John Tweedie drove two girls from Stockwell to the town of Monitor. The girls were thrown out of the car but survived. After losing their only child, Mr. and Mrs. George Tweedie were overcome with grief and felt they needed to distance themselves from all that reminded them of the tragedy. Consequently, the Risk-Tweedie partnership was dissolved. Kirby's sports car, the color of stoker coal, the one in which he and his bride had zoomed into their future from their magical wedding, was destroyed. For some time after, Kirby and Caroline used the company pickup truck for transportation.

Kirby's firm relocated to a larger building adjacent to the original buildings on North Second Street in Lafayette and became Kirby Risk Electric Company. Kirby discontinued automotive electrical repair, battery service, and electrical contracting. Instead, he concentrated on wholesale distribution of electrical supplies, motor sales, and service. Kirby's son, Jim, explained his father's business shift: "It was a natural progression. Tweedie was the one who had the expertise and interest in automotive and motor repair. Dad leaned more toward the distribution of electrical supplies."

Occasionally at this time, Caroline would drive to Indianapolis to pick up parts at Westinghouse or Graybar. Kirby Risk Electric was a small company, so Caroline's help was a necessity. Graybar is an electrical and telecommunications supplier that was incorporated in 1925 and, today, stocks and sells hundreds of thousands of electrical needs from thousands of manufacturers. Now, Graybar is one of Kirby Risk Corporation's competitors.

Motor repair was big back then. Motors were not replaced, because they were not readily available. Instead, they were refurbished, and often a customer's motor was better repaired than it had been new. Kirby Risk Electric repaired motors found in industry and in homes. Brown Rubber Company in Lafayette produced rubber auto parts, and Kirby Risk Electric maintained the motors that powered the production line. Another booming area for business in the agricultural belt was grain elevator motor repair. Electrical supplies were not readily available in Lafayette in the 1920s and 1930s. Kirby bought supplies from what would later be his competitors—big distributors in Indianapolis or Chicago, like Graybar. Later, the business grew large enough to warrant buying directly from electrical supply manufacturers.

A requisition form, dated 1931, indicates that Kirby Risk Electric supplied the automobile repair shop of Jefferson High School with sixteen standard size battery plates, positive. In 1932, a purchase order from the Indiana Lock-Joint Concrete Pipe Company in Lafayette is scrawled in pencil with the words, "Recharge and Rental on Battery—$2.45." Kirby Risk Electric's clients ran the gamut, and Kirby worked hard to assist every one with the utmost in service, no matter the company, no matter the size. His work ethic never changed.

In 1934, after the Chicago World's Fair closed for its second summer run, there was a massive dismantling and moving of equipment, architectural parts, displays, and more. It was an opportunity for Kirby Risk Electric to make hay while the Chicago sun shone. There was a vast amount of used wire, conduit, electric motors, and more available for purchase. An electrical dealer in south Chicago, David Goodon, helped Kirby obtain the World's Fair castoffs. Kirby borrowed the truck Caroline's father used for his farm implement dealership to haul his finds from Chicago to Lafayette and add to the Kirby Risk Electric sales inventory. Kirby knew how to negotiate to obtain goods inexpensively and sell them to companies who were in dire need of the merchandise. This is how he would later attract big industries like the Aluminum Company of America (Alcoa). Kirby always looked for and found products that were scarce to help others obtain what they needed and grease the gears of his relationships. Others loved him for it, and throughout his life, Kirby's wheeling and dealing took him and his family far in business and in pleasure.

Another opportunity for growth in Kirby's business came about with the changes in electrical service throughout the country. Years later, Caroline wrote:

> A small community south of Lafayette determined the electric service needed to be changed from direct to alternating current. This would necessitate the rewiring [rewinding] of electric motors to accommodate the new current. This change gave Kirby Risk Electric Company an opportunity to offer their services. It was a good amount of business for the electric company and a real help in the early stages.

During the development of commercial electric power systems at the turn of the twentieth century, many different frequencies (and voltages) were used. When a power company made a large investment in equipment in a different frequency than that of their competitors, it made standardization a slow process. Motors may not operate efficiently or even safely if used on anything other than the intended frequency. The move toward a standard 60 hertz kept Kirby Risk Electric Company very busy "rewinding." It was another windfall for Kirby's business.

DEPRESSION YEARS

This was the time of the Great Depression, and money was scarce. A customer of Kirby Risk Electric was George Potter. He owned many properties and a dairy in Lafayette. Kirby's company worked on motors at the dairy, and Potter insisted on paying his bill with ten-cent milk coupons. The Great Depression changed the habit of coupon clipping for families from an infrequent, voluntary activity to an everyday, mandatory endeavor. People looked for coupons that offered them a penny or two off a quart of milk so they could then afford to purchase flour or eggs. Evidently, Potter thought the milk coupons were as valuable as money.

Caroline said of the time, "This was Depression with a capital 'D.' At our home, where there were three, we budgeted $10 per week for groceries."

People earned money any way they could. Children stopped by Kirby Risk Electric to sell apples or candy. Friends of Kirby's, who lived on nearby farms, frequented the office to sell honey, chickens, butter, or eggs. To help with his cash flow, Kirby and his staff carefully saved all copper and iron to resell.

As the perfect world thought possible by the temperance movement failed to materialize, the stock market crashed in 1929, and the Great Depression took hold, the American people's attitudes regarding Prohibition changed. If alcohol were legal again, more jobs would be available and additional sales taxes would help the government.

Five months after Kirby and Caroline were married, on December 5, 1933, the Twenty-first Amendment to the U. S. Constitution was ratified, which repealed the Eighteenth Amendment, making alcohol once again legal. But, of course, Kirby still honored his pledge of intent to never drink alcohol as a beverage.

Downtown Lafayette was a close hamlet with shops, businesses, services, and offices shoulder-to-shoulder in the bustling hub of the community. Caroline wrote in her journal, "Welfare Loan was located just around the corner on Main Street. Ella Osterhauf was employed there and was very helpful many times. The Osterhaufs were 'neighbors' and friends. We purchased a large, heavy easy chair from them, as 'Kirby and Carolyn' did not have furniture of their own. The chair was a great buy and large and comfortable."

It is telling that years later Caroline would record her memory of the purchase of a secondhand piece of furniture that she had her husband bought together. Caroline did not "set up housekeeping" in the traditional way after her marriage. Instead, she moved into her mother-in-law's home. Kirby and Caroline did not purchase or rent their own place to live or buy furniture, new or used. The purchase of a used easy chair must have felt like a small nod to a private life for Caroline—a symbol of her own turf.

The Risks kept the chair for years, eventually giving it to their daughter Carol after her marriage in 1957.

In 1935, President Franklin Roosevelt's "New Deal" legislation was passed to regulate public utilities and bring electricity to rural America. As electricity reached the American countryside, Kirby Risk Electric rode the current of change and serviced the needs of new electrical customers. Kirby's business was in the right place at the right time as electricity transformed the day-to-day home and work lives of thousands of Hoosiers. When Kirby started his business in 1926, 58 percent of American homes were wired for electricity and only 5 percent of farms were wired. By 1935, 68 percent of homes were wired and 13 percent of farms had electricity. It would not be until the 1950s when nearly 100 percent of both homes and farms in America would be glowing with current.

By 1936, a company invoice bore these words:

KIRBY RISK

209-213 NORTH SECOND STREET

Phone 7875—Night 2658—76235

Kirby included his home telephone number for nighttime service. The twenty-four-hour service that Kirby offered would continue in an even grander and more inventive form in the future. Technically at the time, the hours of operation for the company were 7:00 a.m. to 5:30 p.m., but Kirby's business and home doors were always open. Serving the customer's needs no matter the hour was his company mainstay. The invoice also included a rundown of what Kirby Risk Electric supplied to its customers: "Rockwood Pulleys, V-Drives, Electric Supplies, Retail – Wholesale, Black & Decker, Sales & Service, Motor Rewinding and Industrial Wiring." Centered like an emblem of pride was the GE logo of the time, a sort of medallion, which read, "General Electric Motor Dealer."

PURDUE SPORTS

Kirby was a staunch supporter of Purdue and attended every football game, home and away. From the early 1930s, Kirby was in the stands cheering the Boilermakers. He would not miss a game for his entire adult life until his health prevented him from attending. This is another example of Kirby's faithfulness to every pledge he made, personal or otherwise, and his "excessive" nature. Almost anything Kirby did, he did to the extreme, which prompted Caroline to say many times, "Good thing he *didn't* drink alcohol!" So when Caroline married Kirby, she, too, attended all Purdue pigskin matches. When he gave money to help with the expansion of Ross-

From the early 1930s, Kirby was true to his commitment to attend every Purdue University football game, home and away. He and Caroline are shown here at Purdue's Ross-Ade Stadium.

Ade Stadium in the 1940s, he was given two free football tickets every year for twenty-five years.

Each season, Kirby ordered more than two hundred football tickets for friends, customers, staff, and vendors. He helped Purdue raise money for athletics by buying and selling tickets for football games, often "eating" the tickets that weren't claimed, especially on rainy football Saturdays when people failed to show. Kirby's buying and selling of tickets, almost like an agent, helped start what is known today as the John Purdue Club, a large group of supporters who are responsible for raising all funds necessary to cover the tuition, room, board, and books of Purdue's student-athletes. In 1958, the Big Ten announced that member schools could raise money for athletic grants-in-aid. Athletic Director Guy "Red" Mackey cofounded the John Purdue Club that same year. Kirby and Caroline were good friends with Red and Goldie Mackey. Mackey started at Purdue as an assistant football coach in 1929. He became Purdue's athletic director in 1942. Purdue's basketball arena was named after the red-haired, sometimes fiery, kind, congenial gentleman in 1972.

Kirby's son, Jim, said:

> We [Kirby Risk Corporation] were always one of the larger if not the largest procurer of football tickets. I started handling the tickets in the 1960s. We were purchasing 252 season tickets. Today, much of the communication is done electronically. Back then, there was a great deal of personal contact. Almost every football Friday, I'd go with Dad, and we'd go into the athletic offices to visit with the ticket manager, Pop Doan, later Dick Kindig. There was a wooden gate we walked through, and Red Mackey was there, too. Dad occasionally had some tickets on consignment to sell, might be returning some, or picking up. Dad was really one of the leads in starting the Quarterback Club [Downtown Gridiron Club] that still continues today. So he was just immersed in that whole activity, and Red and Dad were dear friends.

Members of the Downtown Gridiron Club (DGC) support Purdue football during lunch meetings held every Monday following a game, with the coach as guest speaker. The coach shows game footage and offers commentary and insights while members network and ask questions.

Years later, Caroline wrote (in the third person), "Risks always found time and money to attend all Purdue football games . . . and often drove all night to avoid hotel bills for the away games. Risks had before-game luncheons for customers and friends, including out-of-town guests." As the years progressed, the "business" of Kirby Risk Electric's Purdue football ticket sales grew. Caroline continued, "Sometimes for game-day parties, furniture, including Kirby and Caroline's bed, had to be moved to the garage to make room for the guests and the food and drink bar. Sometimes the crowds were so large, guests sat and ate on the stairway to the upper floor. We served shrimp often and ham loafs—even turkey; one time it took both ovens, an electric roaster and the basement apartment oven to roast enough turkey."

Caroline and Kirby traveled with the team in 1936 to New York City to see Purdue play Fordham. Tucked inside her Chicago World's Fair queen scrapbook is a pocket-sized, tri-fold brochure with the headline, "Amusements in New York for Week Ending November 7, 1936." The brochure lists the Broadway plays of the time: Jimmy Durante, Ethel Merman, Bob Hope in "Red, Hot and Blue," Helen Hayes in "Victoria Regina," and Tallulah Bankhead in" Reflected Glory," to name a few. Caroline also kept the palm-sized, fifteen-page "Directory of the Vanderbilt Hotel," where the Risks stayed with the team. The mini booklet in steel blue is as austere and understated as the gracious art deco hotel itself.

Daughter Carol explains how her parents hosted friends before she was born. "They did really unusual things by today's standards. Like for parties, they would get a panel truck or bigger and set up tables inside and take people out to Oxford [Indiana] for the twin swimming pools." Kirby and Caroline also took their friends, staff, and business associates to away Purdue games on passenger buses.

GLENN SAFFORD

In 1937, a gentlemen by the name of Glenn Safford approached Kirby about a job. Safford had been selling magazines door-to-door, which was quite common back then. Kirby liked Glenn, who was originally from the nearby, small town of Wolcott, Indiana, but he felt he did not have a place for him in his company. Instead, he made a phone call to Curtis Crook in the maintenance department at Fairfield Manufacturing in Lafayette, and Crook offered Glenn a job. It was in 1919 that the management of Ross Gear and Tool Company, which was founded by David Ross who became a Purdue University trustee and dedicated benefactor (Ross-Ade Stadium is one of his legacies), separated the company's rear axle and transmission gear business and named it Fairfield Manufacturing. Known to generations of employees as "The Gear," Ross Gear continued to operate, concentrating on developing and producing steering gears. In its beginning, Ross Gear manufactured differential gears for the new automotive industry.

Ross Gear would become a part of the Thompson Ramo Wooldridge (TRW) manufacturing empire in the 1960s. Lafayette remains headquarters of the modern-day Commercial Steering Systems of TRW Automotive.

A yellowed purchase order from Ross Gear and Tool Company to Risk-Tweedie Electric Service dated October 18, 1930, indicates that a 7 ½ horsepower motor was repaired by Risk-Tweedie (a coil shorted). Kirby Risk had a close business relationship with Ross Gear and later with another David Ross company, Fairfield Manufacturing. That Kirby Risk relationship continues today with Fairfield, now known as Oerlikon, which is part of Oerlikon Drive Systems global engineering, manufacturing, sales, and support for gear and drive solutions.

By the 1930s, Fairfield expanded from a small gear shop to a highly regarded producer of all types of gears with customers like John Deere and Clark Equipment Company. The morning after Kirby's phone call and Glenn's job offer from Fairfield, Kirby arrived at work and found Glenn sweeping the company driveway. When Kirby asked about the Fairfield job, Glenn said, "I want to work for you, and I'll stay for $8 per week." Caroline wrote, decades later, "Kirby had a long discussion [with Safford] about the pros and cons and did Safford have knowledge about electric repairs, etc.? Glenn assured Kirby he could learn and would be dependable and 'honorable.' (He talked about his new redheaded baby boy.) He was hired and began at once and stayed loyal to his word until his death in 2000."

The day Kirby saw Safford sweeping the Kirby Risk Electric driveway was the beginning of a long business relationship and friendship between the two men. Glenn became a top-notch salesman for the company, and in 1947 he was named vice president, followed by president in 1966. For decades to come, Kirby and Glenn would conduct countless lunch meetings at the Risk's kitchen table, and Caroline would cook their noontime meal. Caroline wrote, "Glenn proved to be a tireless and ambitious employee even earning the nickname of 'Sure-Grip.' New items were gradually added to the inventory. It was one of Safford's best talents to SELL. He was talented at selling and raising money for good causes."

Glenn's nickname of "Sure-Grip" came about by way of a colossal practical joke. Jim said, "Folks at Alcoa got together and took this big five-hundred-watt incandescent lightbulb used to light warehouses and factories, and with heat they put little indents where your fingers could grip the lamp on the glass bulb. When Glenn made a call on Alcoa, they told him they needed a case of these 'Sure Grip' lightbulbs. It was a joke. It wasn't really a product. They just had the one bulb made up in the factory."

The prank really worked on Glenn, because the lightbulb manufacturer was also in on the charade.

Jim continued, "Then the lighting manufacturer was in cahoots and said, 'Well, you have to have a minimum order of five hundred.' So Glenn went about taking this Sure Grip lightbulb out to his clients and showing the 'features' until he sold five hundred."

The joke went on for months as the workers at Alcoa, the manufacturer representatives of the pseudo lightbulb, and the staff at Kirby

Risk Electric stood back and watched Glenn take preorders of the fictitious "Sure Grip."

"So it finally had to come to light that it was a joke. He really got taken," said Jim.

"Even to his grave, he was furious about it because he spent days, weeks, and months selling. So they called him "Sure Grip" and teased him because he bit on the joke hook, line, and sinker."

After the sham was revealed, Glenn had to return to his customers who "bought" the Sure Grip, look them in the eye, and tell them there was no such product.

"It was just part of the way things happened back then. Just goofing around. Having fun," Jim said. "But think about it. Going out . . ." Jim's voice trailed off as he commiserated with Glenn at the memory.

BABIES

The year 1937 was a good one for Kirby and Caroline in business and in their home life with the hire of Kirby's right-hand man, Glenn Safford, and the birth of their first child. Years later Caroline wrote in her journal, "Our first born, Carol was born Sunday, July 11, 1937 at 1:55 p.m. Dr. Oliver Griest delivered her. I stayed two weeks in the Home Hospital! It had been a hot summer. My mother made most of my 'wrap-around' maternity dresses. Carol's arrival was a special and happy event—our first—the first grandchild, and the first babe in quite awhile among our group of friends."

Because Kirby was ten years older than Caroline, most of the couple's friends were also much older than his wife. Her friendships had been made in Benton County. When she moved to Lafayette after her marriage, she and Kirby socialized with his circle, so most of their friends had older children. Carol's birth was a novelty among the Risk's peers. Sharon (nicknamed "Sherry") came along three years later on May 22, 1940—the same day Kirby purchased a new building. Caroline, age ninety-eight, said in 2011, "I thought it was more important that Sherry was born. We had waited so long. She was late. But he was buying the building at the time she was delivered." Caroline also said, "Grandmother Risk was still living and not too well, but she really enjoyed the two little girls."

Caroline and Kirby had a kind of love that transcended the every day. That love is evident in a letter Caroline wrote to Kirby on the occasion of their seventh wedding anniversary in 1940. Carol was three and Sherry was just a few weeks old when she wrote:

My Dearest,

I don't suppose there is another person in this town as happy as I. I love you so dearly, and I can't tell you how I appreciate all the wonderful things you are forever doing for me. Then we have Carol—who couldn't be sweeter—and now our dear babe—and she's healthy and I'm ok. And your business is growing and then we had just hundreds of wonderful times together that I'll never forget. The Lord couldn't have been kinder to us, and I sincerely thank him for all his blessings, and pray that I may be a worthy wife and a wise mother.

Thank you, darling, for the beautiful flowers that you sent. You always do so much that it leaves me speechless, and I don't thank you properly. I did enjoy them so and shall press the orchid and put it in Sharon's book so she'll know how good to her mother her father was when she was a tiny new thing. I love you seven times as much as I did seven years ago. I just love you as much as I can possibly love.

Kirby purchased at auction the red brick Lafayette Milling Company building at Third and Ferry Streets in Lafayette. Kirby felt the structure that once housed grain and seed was excellent for his needs, and he liked its spaciousness. Because the structure had been a mill, for years to come, flour seeped from the building's pores, dusting desks, shelves, and all within. Even when wiped clean, a surface would quickly become sprinkled again with a powdery memento of the building's past. Kirby Risk Electric moved to the new location in 1941, the year son James "Jim" Kirby Risk III was born.

Caroline wrote in her journal, "Sixteen months after Sherry, our son arrived. Wheeee! Everyone was happy and he easily slipped right into the family. Grandmother Risk was delighted to have a *boy* and especially to have him named for her husband and her son!! Mary Sloan lived in our lower apartment and helped with the children. (She named her only child, later, 'Carol!')"

Because Jim was just over a year younger than Sherry, when they were small, people often mistook them for twins. They had the same smile and eyes.

A Risk tradition began with the birth of Carol and continued with each addition to the household. On the way home from the hospital, the newly expanded family made a stop at the Frozen Custard, which was owned by Kirby and Caroline's friends Charles and Florence Kirkhoff. Today, the stand is still located on Wallace Avenue across from Columbian Park, a few blocks from where Home Hospital stood. Kirby loved frozen custard, and he served it, ate it, and gifted it throughout his life. The Frozen Custard was the first business of its kind. Previously, Charles Kirkhoff had been the general manager and mixmaster of the Frankfort Ice Cream Company.

Kirkhoff obtained mixing machines and then developed the formula for the frozen custard he sold, a formula that hasn't changed. Since his original lease forbade carbonated drinks, Charles developed his now popular "Fruit Drink," which was originally called "Hawaiian Frozen Drink," a golden blend of refreshing secret ingredients.

Another new-baby tradition that Kirby instigated was a serenade by a group from the Purdue Glee Club. He asked the clean-cut gents to stand under Caroline's hospital window and sing her favorite songs. The Risks were supporters and fans of Purdue Musical Organizations throughout their marriage.

REVVING UP

As time progressed, many changes were necessary as Kirby Risk Electric serviced larger motors. The work became more complex and required more expertise and equipment. "Ovens" were installed for "burning out" and "baking" motors. Caroline explained it in this manner: "Arrangements needed to be made for 'dipping' larger motors. Before and after rewinding, they would be put in 'to bake.'"

Caroline was referring to "burn-off ovens." These are heat-cleaning ovens that have been used for years in the motor rewind industry. Alternating current motors have copper wire coils, which are insulated with a coating of varnish that dries to a hard consistency. Prior to rewinding, the insulating resin must be removed from the copper winding, and the coil softened so that it can be easily removed and the motor can be rebuilt.

As Kirby developed his business, he believed in quietly giving back to his community. With all of his philanthropy, good works, and time spent aiding this fellow man, in the back of his mind ran his favorite Bible passage, Matthew 6:3, "But when you do a kindness to someone, do it secretly." Kirby was at the center of many civic activities, including the Red Feather Campaign, a precursor to what today is the United Way. The United Way movement began in 1887 in Denver, Colorado, when religious leaders founded the Charity Organizations Society, which planned and coordinated local services and conducted a single fundraising campaign for twenty-two agencies. In 1913, the nation's first modern Community Chest was created in Cleveland where a program for allocating campaign funds was developed. From 1919 to 1929, communities across America began establishing Community Chests, which would later be known as United Funds, and now the United Way.

The Red Feather drive for charity was an annual October campaign that began in 1928 when New Orleans added the red feather as the symbol of united giving ("a feather in your cap"). Kirby actively sought out donations to the campaign that helped such services as the YMCA, YWCA, Boy Scouts, Girl Scouts, Salvation Army, settlement houses, neighborhood centers, and more. Caroline wrote in a brief history she created in the 1990s, "Kirby was always at the center of most civic activities."

That was an understatement.

This photo from 1955 shows Caroline Risk (right of sign) holding the
"Community Fund Night" banner. Kirby stands at the right of the group
wearing his signature bow tie. The Kirby Risk staff is in the "motor shop"
working after-hours to contribute to the United Way Community Chest.

Each October, Kirby and Caroline held "Community Fund Night"
at their shop with food and entertainment for their employees as they
worked after hours. All money made that night was donated to the
United Way Community Chest. Photos from the 1950s show Caroline in her beaded cardigan serving mountains of fried chicken,
mashed potatoes, and slices of pie next to the shop's tool-laden work-
bench holding a tall, silver metal coffee urn. Each staff member wears
a nametag. The shop floor is stained with motor oil. A sign on the wall
says "Kirby Risk Supply Co., Kirby Risk Electric Motors Community
Fund Night." Flanking the words are images of two red feathers.

Kirby joined trade associations, the National Association of Manufacturers (NAM), the Electrical Apparatus Service Association (EASA), and the National Association of Electrical Distributors (NAED). Kirby's and Caroline's community and church activities and professional affiliations added layers to their life, not just in Lafayette, Indiana, but also throughout the United States and the world. Creating goodwill created good business. As their family expanded and their relationships with friends, staff, and professional associates increased and deepened, their business continued to prosper. Kirby and Caroline's credo to help others and treat all persons as they would want to be treated was a natural part of their being. Growth and new beginnings were abundant, and all aspects of their shared life interconnected and moved forward with high voltage.

CHAPTER 7

FLORIDA CIRCUS

In the winter of 1942, Caroline took four-year-old Carol, nineteen-month-old Sherry, and baby Jim to live for the winter in Fort Lauderdale. Kirby stayed in Lafayette to work. Caroline's Florida winter stays with her three children occurred for several years because of Sherry's medical condition.

When Sherry was a toddler, she was diagnosed with an enlarged thymus gland. The thymus gland lies underneath the top of the breastbone in the middle of the chest. In 2011, Sherry, age seventy-one, explained, "They did radiation on my throat to try to shrink it. The thought was that if I were to get a cold, I could possibly die. So that is why we wintered in Florida."

Until the 1960s, infants and toddlers who had enlarged thymus glands were irradiated to shrink the gland with the belief that it would prevent sudden infant death syndrome. This treatment was used in hospitals and pediatricians' offices across America. Now it is known that it is not unusual for an infant's thymus gland to be larger than it will be later in the child's life.

Sherry said, "I read several books, long before the Internet, and found out that it was really a kind of old wives' tale. When you do Xrays, the thymus gland looks large. And it turns out that's the way you are born, and it doesn't continue to grow inside, but your body grows and it becomes proportional over time."

It is now known that the thymus gland is essential for the proper function of the lymphatic system, and the gland carries out its major purpose during the first few years of a person's life. Sherry said, "As an adult, I read some new studies that advised anybody who had radiation in this area to look for thyroid cancer. I went to a new internist, and, in fact, I had a nodule on my thyroid. They biopsied it and couldn't decide what it was, so my thyroid was removed. Turns out it was benign. Those years that Mother had us down in Florida and Dad was in Lafayette—I think that was quite a sacrifice in many ways, but we had wonderful adventures. It worked out in some ways, but I'm sure it wasn't easy for her."

Carol said of her sister's misdiagnosed condition, "I've had some people in the medical community say an enlarged thymus gland is a healthy thing. Times change. Sherry and I both had our thyroids removed because we had too much Xray therapy. But that was what was best at the time. So, we went to Florida. I always wondered if partially it was so Mother could be away from Mrs. Risk (our grandmother) for a while, because I don't think that was totally easy."

Most years, Caroline and her children stayed at a guesthouse behind the main house owned by the Crockers on Northeast Third Street, just a few blocks off of Osceola, the main thoroughfare to the beach in Fort Lauderdale. It was before the time of condos and cloud-high hotels. Little white-framed cottages sat in clusters like patches of daisies.

Caroline and her children became close to their landlords. "The people who had the main house were lovely people from Cleveland," Carol said of the Fort Lauderdale homeowners. "He had been a golf pro and had some kind of terrible accident and was paralyzed. And so he was in bed. We called them 'Mom and Pop Crocker.' We got to be like family to them—like grandchildren. He had like a rope ladder on the side of the bed. He could get hold of a rung and pull himself up."

For the first few winters when the three children were very young, Caroline had a helper named Ester Baker who tagged along for the stay. Carol said, "That little house had twin beds, and Mother slept between Sherry and me on the crack. Ester slept on a studio couch, and Jimmy was in there. There was just one bedroom and a dining room. I don't know if there was a separate kitchen or if it was just part of the dining area, and a sunroom with jalousie windows."

Caroline and her daughters, Carol and Sherry, enjoy the beach in Fort Lauderdale, Florida, 1942. For several years, Caroline and her children lived in Florida during the winter months because of Sherry's medical condition.

Soon after the group arrived for their first winter, Ester took baby Jimmy out for a walk. Carol said, "Mother tells that Jimmy came back and the next day he had blisters all over his body. Ester had been collecting cactus, and the needles were in Jimmy's skin. She had to get all those out."

Perhaps for Caroline her Florida sojourns did not feel much like a vacation.

Good friend Nancy Neubert also accompanied Caroline to Florida on several occasions. Her husband, Len, was the purchasing agent for Alcoa. The couple had no children. Nancy helped Caroline with hers. Kirby was the best man at the Neubert's wedding. Jim said, "The Neuberts became close family friends. Len taught me to walk in 1942. He had a towel, and he held on to one end, and I held the other as I took some steps. Then Len let it go, and I kept walking."

WORLD WAR II

For Americans, World War II started on December 7, 1941, when Japan attacked Pearl Harbor. Jim was born just two months prior, on October 4. Caroline and her pint-sized entourage traveled to the seaside community of Fort Lauderdale at the height of America's fear of attack in their own waters, as men marched off, leaving their families and the country solidified in the common aim to conserve for the war industry. Kirby was not drafted because his company was identified as necessary to the war effort.

Carol said:

> I still have terrible feelings about World War II. And some of it, I'm sure, comes from living in Florida at that point. And I was old enough to know. It was blackout every night. It wasn't brown out; it was black out. There would be sirens when they thought they spotted German submarines on the horizon. On the beach were built big towers—almost like scaffolding—grey two-by-fours where the Navy looked out. Mother took us out to Port Everglades to see the German prisoner of warship where they marched the German soldiers on the deck. I said to her years later, "Why would you take a five-year-old out to see that?" And she said, "Well, it was part of history."

Some of Carol's World War II fears and recollections as a young child came about from the newsreels that ran prior to theater movies. With only radio and no television at that time, black-and-white theater

In the 1990s, Caroline and Carol visited the Fort Lauderdale, Florida, house where they stayed during the winter months in the 1940s. The Risks paid $500 for five month's rent. On the back of the photo Caroline wrote, "We lived here when the bleachers collapsed at a Purdue basketball game, and we heard the news report as Carol dressed for first grade that morning. I worried about Daddy."

newsreels were how Americans "saw" the news. She said, "Maybe we went to see *Snow White*. She's my age exactly. I remember seeing all the newsreels of the prisoner of war camps and the Nazi soldiers and 'Heil Hitlers!' and him talking. I knew some of what was going on."

With the backdrop of her elementary school years painted with images of the war, Carol attended her second semester of first grade in Florida, as well as portions of third and fourth grades. She said of her first-grade year:

> We had to go down on the train that year, so we had no car. I had to get on the bus with the high school kids to go to school. I went to Central, which was first grade through high school. And so I was there all day. There were kids that weren't nice to me that were older. I just remember it being a terrifying experience. I think that

was the year I had something wrong—I have no idea what—and was in the hospital for a while. Of course, Mother couldn't get there easily because she didn't have a car.

Sherry, who is three years younger than Carol, has few memories of the World War II years. "I can just vaguely remember closing curtains," she said. "I can remember talking about submarines. I remember mother stamping on tin cans to get them flat to give as metal for the war effort." Recycling was born with the government's encouragement. Saving tin cans meant more ammunition for the soldiers.

Food was scarce during the war years. Caroline served Spam with a diamond pattern she cut in the top, studded with cloves and brushed with mustard and brown sugar. Spam is a canned, precooked meat product that has been made by the Hormel Foods Corporation since 1937 in Austin, Minnesota, aptly nicknamed "Spamtown, USA." Production of Spam began the same year Carol was born. Fresh meat was difficult to get to the soldiers on the front, so Spam was the perfect provision. GI's ate Spam for breakfast, lunch, and dinner. (Some soldiers referred to Spam as "ham that didn't pass its physical" and "meatloaf without basic training.") For Americans today, the "mystery meat" has become the brunt of many jokes and part of pop culture.

When America entered World War II, the federal government confiscated silk and nylon for the nation's defense needs. Overnight, women's stockings became hard to find. Nylon was important to the war effort because it was used in parachutes and tires. On the home front, the popular press presented nylon as a miracle of technology that Americans could again enjoy when the war ended. But Kirby played Santa, and he found stockings to give before the war was over. Carol remembered, "At Christmastime, Dad would have Santa Claus come in, and they would have couples over who had no children. And I remember him giving the women nylons."

Kirby obtained the stockings from Sargent's 5 & 10 variety store in Cloverdale, Indiana. In a letter Kirby wrote many years later, he recalled, "During World War II days, Sargent's kept me supplied with nylons for Carolyn, rubber pants for our babies, strainers for my tea, and fly swatters for my peace of mind."

Kirby often surprised Caroline. Carol remembered, "One year we went home on the train, and we were in a drawing room. I was standing in the doorway, probably around Atlanta, and I saw Dad coming down the hall. I said to Mother, 'There's Dad! Daddy!' And she said, 'Well, whose daddy?' And I can remember thinking, 'How dumb can you be? Who else would I say is daddy?' But why would she think he was on the train? He'd come to meet her part way to come home with us. That was typical."

One can imagine the challenges that Caroline confronted as she cared for three children away from home with no car and no husband at the height of World War II on America's coastline. The worry of having a child with what was perceived as a chronic medical condition and her inability to see her eldest as frequently as she would have liked during a hospital stay compounded Caroline's trials. But there were so many fun times.

ENTER KIRBY

Kirby traveled down to Florida for visits. Sherry explained, "When he was around, life was like a circus. Adventures and excitement and silliness. We would go to the *Las Olas* Boulevard Bakery and get chocolate éclairs." A vintage 1940s postcard depicts Las Olas Boulevard in muted hues and contains this caption: "Las Olas Boulevard, a beautiful palm-studded highway between Fort Lauderdale and Fort Lauderdale beach, has many little bridges running from it to small islands where there are hundreds of small beautiful tropical homes."

"And Swanky Franks," Sherry said. "My father loved to find kind of obscure places and go over and over again so that people would know him there. He enjoyed being recognized and having relationships. And Swanky Franks was a new place that opened up. It was called 'the hotdog with an attitude.' As I recall, they made continuous diagonal slices along the top of the hotdog to present a 'swanky' appearance."

"I can remember going to the Pioneer Inn on Las Olas Boulevard for a big meal, maybe it was for Sunday meal," Sherry added. Today, the Pioneer House Restaurant is the Stranahan House and Museum, located on the banks of New River. Built by Frank Stranahan as a trading post for settlers and the Seminole Native Americans in 1901, it evolved into the post office, community center, and town hall, as Frank became Fort Lauderdale's first postmaster, banker, and businessman. He married another pioneer, Ivy Julia Cromartie, the area's first schoolteacher. Following Frank's suicide during the Great Depression, Ivy leased the first floor of the house for use as the Pioneer House Restaurant, while she lived upstairs. In 1979, the restaurant closed and the Fort Lauderdale Historical Society took possession.

"And Jungle Queen," Sherry continued. "The boat was the one that would take you back into the deep Florida waters where the Seminoles still lived. We'd take the river ride on the Jungle Queen and see the Seminoles wrestle alligators."

The Seminoles of Florida call themselves the "Unconquered People," descendants of just three hundred Native Americans who managed to elude capture by the US army in the nineteenth century. They began the twentieth century where they had been left at the conclusion of the Seminole Wars—in abject poverty, hiding out in remote camps in the wet wilderness areas of South Florida. In 1928, the Tamiami Trail opened, the southernmost section of US Highway 41 between Tampa and Miami, fueling the boom in South Florida tourism. Seminoles begin to sell crafts and wrestle alligators for show. The Jungle Queen still carries tourists along the New River to see a Native American village.

"I remember one time my father came down to visit, and we had gone fishing with Uncle John and caught a blowfish and put it in the bathtub to save it," Sherry said. "And my father was an absolute stickler, fanatic about hygiene and cleanliness. You don't share towels; you don't share this, that, and everything. And when he took one look at the blowfish in the bathtub, I can remember him just being horrified."

One year, the Risks spent a Florida winter as neighbors to a circus. Carol said, "Our next-door neighbor behind us was the Clyde Beatty Circus. They had wild animals in the circus. It was their winter quarters. And we'd go visit. I remember the elephant eating my grandmother's hat at one time. She had a straw hat with flowers on it, and the elephant just took it off."

Clyde Raymond Beatty was a true "lion tamer." Armed with a whip, chair, and a pistol strapped to his side, he entered a circus cage filled with "man-eating jungle cats." Through the 1930s and 1940s, Beatty became one of the most celebrated circus performers in the world, appearing under the big top and on the radio. He also appeared in movies like Abbott and Costello's *Africa Screams*. Later, he was on television. In 1939, he purchased a lion-breeding farm located in Fort Lauderdale at Northeast Tenth Street near Federal Highway. Beatty turned it into a winter home for his circus and a tourist attraction. Clyde Beatty's Jungle Zoo operated from 1939 to 1945, the timeframe the Risks wintered in Florida.

"Before you went to the circus, there were the elephants and other animals out just behind ropes that you walked through before you went under the big top," Carol said. "And we bought peanuts to feed them. Well, today, they wouldn't let a child hold their hand out and feed an elephant."

Thanks to Kirby, there was a Florida Easter that turned "zooy." Carol said, "He kept saying to mother, 'There's going to be a big surprise at Easter.' And she thought he was coming. She was stuck there with three kids under five. Maybe he was coming to surprise her. Maybe he was sending her a gift."

A large box arrived. Caroline and the children opened the lid, and inside were twenty-four dyed chicks and two ducklings, all chirping an Easter hello. "That was not a good surprise," said Carol, laughing. "Donald was the only one who survived. He came home. He got so nasty. He bit us on the arms. I can remember Mother in the parking lot. We had a big, black Studebaker, and she had all three of us kids. She'd get us in the car, and Donald the duck would run under the car, and she'd try to catch him. His feathers were almost white then. We had him in Lafayette until the middle of summer. Then mother gave him to someone on a farm."

Another year, when Caroline returned to Lafayette from Florida with the children, she arrived back at 719 Owen to discover Kirby had enclosed the veranda that extended across the front of their Victorian home. Carol said, "We were in Florida, and Dad kept writing mother, again, you know, like with the 'chickies'—'You're going to be surprised. There's going to be a surprise when you come home.' He had redone the house. He closed in those porches. They were open if you look at old pictures. I guess I might have been in preschool when he did that."

In the 1940s, Kirby enclosed the front porch at 719 Owen. Caroline used that space as her office, keeping Kirby Risk Company files there.

At that time, Caroline handled the company payroll at home. She kept her files and desk on the front porch that Kirby had enclosed. Perhaps in his mind, when he turned their open veranda into a closed vestibule, he was surprising Caroline with an "office." After the arrival of two-dozen chicks and a couple of ducks tinted like Easter eggs, and seeing her open-air veranda sealed as tight as Tupperware, Caroline may have had her guard up whenever Kirby said, "There's going to be a surprise."

TWO DORAS

Carol, as the oldest, has more memories than her siblings of their Grandmother Dora Dean Jolly Risk, called "Mrs. Risk" even by her grandchildren. "She took me downtown on the bus to drink water in the artesian well. They all thought it was healthy. It was a fun thing to do. Mrs. Risk expected perfection, and so I was expected to behave." Carol is referring to a statue of the Marquis de Lafayette that stands above an artesian well on the northeast side of the Tippecanoe County Courthouse in Lafayette. The well could discharge almost 2,000 gallons of water a day through eight faucets. The water was thought to be a tonic. In later years, the well was sealed, and the fountain was connected to city water where it still flows today.

Mrs. Risk had been in failing health throughout most of Carol's young life. She passed away on Easter Sunday 1943, after suffering a stroke. Her obituary in a Lafayette newspaper states, "Surviving is an only child, J. Kirby Risk, of this city, and a niece, Mrs. Ralph Smith of Detroit, who was formerly Dora Fidler of this city and who was reared by Mr. And Mrs. Risk." Kirby was forty-two when he lost his mother.

Less than one month later, Dora Fidler's husband, Ralph Smith, who was an engineer for Chrysler Corporation, passed away. From that day forward, Kirby would look after his cousin, Dora, who may have felt like a big sister. After her husband died, Dora lived in Detroit with her eccentric mother, Jane.

Carol gave her theory on why Kirby's parents raised Dora, the woman the Risk children called "Aunt Dodie" or "Aunt Dode." "I think Dora's mother, Jane, was kind of the black sheep of the family," she said. "She had several marriages and was probably not wanting to be home with Dora all of the time. She wore black dresses with sequins, even in the daytime when she came to visit. She would tell me I had to cut my hair by the moonlight, and she was kind of like a witch. She'd tell me all these potions you should do, and she had short, grey, tightly curled hair. She was just exotic in a strange kind of way, kind of like in the fairy tales."

"Aunt Dodie never remarried and she was not employed, and so Dad felt a closeness to her and a responsibility to care for her," Jim said. "Dad knew the porters on the trains very well, and I can remember getting on the train in Lafayette to go visit Aunt Dodie in Detroit. The porters really provided special service." Once at his cousin's home, Kirby did not want anyone inconvenienced. Jim continued, "Dad was a polite but stubborn guest and insisted on sleeping on their dining room table. They'd try to get him to take one of the few beds, and he wouldn't do it."

As much as Jane was spooky, Dora was spunky.

"Dodie was full of life and a party girl," Jim said. "She lost her husband early and never had much income, but she always tried to act like she did. She'd have a drink and dress up. I'd take her out with my high school friends when she was probably in her sixties. They'd call her 'Aunt Dode.'"

Over the years, Kirby was the glue in the Risk family, keeping the lines of communication open and paying visits to relatives. Some, like Aunt Dodie, he took care of financially.

Carol said, "Aunt Dodie was real energetic, and kind of hyper. She made fabulous noodles and pies. When we went up there, she would serve huge meals. I don't think we went real often. She came to visit us more. I don't think she had much family. I can remember even when I was in college, going up and spending a weekend with her. Jimmy and his friends would meet her at the train. They'd play poker together or cards, and they loved to tease her. We were probably the only family that paid much attention."

In later years, Kirby encouraged Dora to move from Detroit to Lafayette, where he rented her an apartment on Ninth Street. When she died, she lived in Comfort Care Nursing Home on Ferry Street, a few blocks from the offices of Kirby Risk Electric.

DIPHTHERIA

When Jimmy was about a year old, he contracted diphtheria. Diphtheria was known as "the plague among children." Since the introduction of effective immunization, starting in the 1920s, diphtheria rates have dropped dramatically in the United States and other countries. Diphtheria is a respiratory disease that is transmitted from person to person. Patients are kept in isolation until they are no longer capable of infecting others.

Carol was five at the time. "So Mother, Sherry, and Jim stayed at home. They were quarantined. And I moved out with Dad. We lived at the Fowler Hotel, and he sent me to the beauty shop downstairs to have my hair braided in the morning. We would go to the driveway of the house and talk to Mother through the window. But I couldn't go in the house."

Kirby had an opening installed under the kitchen sink that led to a small outside door that the milkman opened to deliver glass bottles of milk. Kirby used the milkman's door to pass food and other items to Caroline. It was summertime, and Kirby delivered garden-fresh produce to his wife who was caring for two children, one sick with diphtheria. Carol said, "Mother canned or froze food during that time. And she froze a lot of chicken. That was back when you had to clean the chickens by pulling the feathers out. I don't know if he was thinking that putting up food would keep her busy."

In the early 1940s, a new type of business swept across America—locker plants. Families rented a frozen food storage locker to keep large quantities of meat, vegetables, and fruit. A *Time* magazine article from

Caroline, Kirby, and their right-hand man Glenn Safford pose at Kirby Risk Supply in 1957. This was the year Kirby and Caroline purchased the Lafayette Locker Plant at First and Smith Streets in Lafayette, Indiana, to house Kirby Risk Electric Motors.

April 1, 1940, entitled "Food: Public Iceboxes," states: ". . . today thousands of farmers go to cold-storage locker plants, rent lockers big enough to hold 250 Ibs. of meat . . . for $10 a year. The plants quick-freeze their meat. Seventy-five per cent of the plants are situated in rural areas, but lockermen have their eyes on the big city markets."

Carol remembers her parents freezing their family food. "They had a locker in the locker plant that was way out near Klondike. I suspect the beef they froze was from my grandparents' farm. We'd go out and get the meat and bring it home. You know it was harder to get things in the 1940s during the war."

Jim has fond memories of the Lafayette Locker Plant that was downtown. "I enjoyed going there as a child," he said. "The whole building was freezing cold. People rented lockers for their meat, before people had freezers at home. In 1957, Kirby encouraged Caroline to agree to purchase the Lafayette Locker Plant building, and Kirby Risk

Electric moved to that location. In a leather-bound, steel blue "personal record and reference book for 1957" published by Hilton Hotels, Caroline recorded her family's calendar of events. On February 20, she wrote of the Lafayette Locker Plant, "THE Day. Purchased First and Smith Street Building."

Years later, she wrote more, "The Lafayette Frozen Food Locker at First and Smith Streets, which flourished during the rationing period, had closed. Carolyn borrowed money and purchased the building where subsequently the service portion of the business was moved. Property across First Street was purchased for parking space." Today, Kirby Risk Mechanical Solutions and Service is at 715 South First Street.

Kirby and Caroline also bought more property on North Third Street, filling out the half block with Kirby Risk Electric commerce. Their First Street building and North Third Street properties sat many blocks apart, yet all a stone's throw from the Wabash River.

CHAPTER 8

SURPLUS MAN

Kirby continued to build his company from his tiny office on Ferry Street. In 1940, he added mill supplies and light machinery items to his line. His motor repair department kept the company in close contact with their industrial customers, and the business was a member of the National Industrial Service Association (NISA).

Carol, Kirby's eldest child, described the office:

> In the building, you went up a few steps, it certainly was not a glamorous building. There was a modest lighting showroom. And early on, there were small appliances. Dad handled Sunbeam appliances when the first hand mixers and electric skillets came out. He enjoyed selling unusual items that didn't relate to his business. Like he stocked Kicksteps, toys like a talking parrot and the first little Christmas lights.

Through the years, large photographs of the Purdue University Varsity Glee Club hung on the walls in the Kirby Risk Electric offices. One photograph was taken at the Purdue University Airport, as the choral group was about to take their first European tour, which Kirby helped facilitate through fundraising. The year was 1950, and the Varsity Glee Club's six-week trip was sponsored by the US State Department. The trip was designed to turn the singers into overseas ambassadors—instruments in the rebuilding of friendly relations between the United States and Germany after World War II. Another poster-sized photo depicted the Glee Club in their signature black tuxedo tails and white gloves standing on the steps of what would one day be named the Frederick L. Hovde Hall of Administration, or Hovde Hall.

Kirby's business grew after Alcoa opened a plant in Lafayette in 1937, the same year Carol was born. Within six years, Alcoa employed three thousand people and would become one of Kirby Risk Corporation's best customers. Alcoa originally opened in 1888 in Pittsburgh, Pennsylvania. It "took off" in 1903 when the Wright brothers flew an airplane with an engine that had a block and crankcase made from an exotic new material—aluminum, a metal from Alcoa.

During World War II, aluminum became one of the most important materials in the war effort. Alcoa met wartime challenges at an astounding pace. In three years, it built more than twenty plants. Kirby Risk Electric serviced Alcoa's needs in Lafayette and rode on the coattails of aluminum's success. Kirby also took advantage of war surplus finds.

Kirby had the energy and eagle eye for finding and purchasing what he could resell, reuse, or trade to better his business and his relationships with others. Kirby's son, Jim, said, "He'd go to a mothballed plant and find machinery and equipment to sell to customers, such as Fairfield, providing an opportunity to make a dollar while offering a service to the customer." Fairfield made significant contributions in the production of war materials during World War II.

Jim said, "Ross Gear, which is now TRW, Fairfield, Rostone, and Brown Rubber were some of my father's early customers. Brown Rubber and Rostone are no longer in business, and Fairfield is now owned by the Swiss. The exterior of some homes in Lafayette is made from Rostone (synthetic stone). It's remarkable all the subtle connections."

When he signed the Surplus Property Act in 1944, President Franklin Roosevelt said, "Our surplus property should speedily be placed into channels of disposition which should provide the most jobs and the greatest good for the greatest number." Kirby was all about the greatest good for the greatest number. Companies were required to apply to the Reconstruction Finance Corporation's Surplus Property Division to become an "MT-Approved Dealer." MT stood for "Machine Tools."

Kirby wrote a letter to the Surplus Property Division in Chicago on headed paper that reads: "Kirby Risk Electric Company, Wholesale Electric and Mill Supplies," January 2, 1946. Kirby stated:

> We sincerely trust that the application will receive your favorable attention and that in event of favorable action by the Reconstruction Finance Corporation that we will be able to get two of our clients, the Ross Gear and Tool company and the Fairfield Manufacturing Company, into the Chicago Dodge plant on January fifteenth, the day we were informed by you that the plant would be thrown open.

Kirby attached a page listing the "reasons why we feel qualified to aid our customers in obtaining needed equipment and at the same time, help the Surplus Property Division of the Reconstruction Finance Corporation move some of their surplus material." He listed a brief history of the evolution of his company to that point and wrote several paragraphs that tell of the fact that his company assisted all customers, both large and small, with a high level of service:

> Our territory is made up of small cities and towns, and we feel we can be of real service to any of our small accounts who may have requirements for one or more tools and who would never think that their particular needs could be satisfied through your organization.

> We were asked by one of our largest accounts, the Fairfield Manufacturing Company, to make application for an Approved Dealership and Mr. A. J. McAllister, President of the Fairfield Manufacturing Company, felt we could be of real service to his company.

> We do not want to make a misrepresentation that we are experi-
> enced heavy machinery dealers. Our importance as a dealer to your
> corporation is in the close and very friendly relationship that exists
> between all of our industrial accounts and our company and their
> confidence in our organization.

The last sentence sums up Kirby and how he ran his company and his
life: relationships. Kirby knew how to form them and make them last.
He was the king of *quid pro quo*, the Latin legal term that means "something for something." Yet do not misunderstand the man; Kirby did
not see building associations as a callous tit for tat sort of living, but
as the natural, enjoyable reciprocity that develops within true relationships. Today his approach may be called "networking," but Kirby took
his encounters much deeper. With Kirby, it was real friendship. Most
people with whom he did business or made repeated transactions
became lifelong pals, from a maître d' in Chicago to A. J. McAllister,
president of Fairfield.

During the 1920s, Fairfield's business grew steadily, but the Great
Depression took its toll, and founder David Ross was forced to reor-
ganize. He surprised his associates by appointing McAllister, a recent
Purdue graduate, as the general manager. Ross's reason for placing the
young man in such a high position was "his mind won't be all set. He'll
still be open to new ideas, to seeing new ways of doing things."

In the 1930s, Ross added the role of treasurer to McAllister's du-
ties, and the young man fulfilled all of his boss's expectations by making Fairfield a remarkable success. A. J. and Dorothy McAllister had
no children. They donated to many endeavors. McAllister Recreation
Center in Lafayette is named in their honor. The McAllister and Risk
families shared many a meal and good times through the years.

According to the four-page smudged agreement on legal-sized paper signed by Kirby in 1946, Kirby Risk Electric was granted a license
by the Reconstruction Finance Corporation to be an MT-Approved
Dealer "to solicit and negotiate sales of surplus equipment declared
by government owning agencies to RFC for disposal." The agreement
stated that "Approved Dealer shall be paid a commission by RFC with

respect to each sales contract or order for equipment negotiated by Approved Dealer equal to 12 ½% of established government sales price." Claims for commissions due were made to the War Assets Administration regional office, which was located on LaSalle Street in Chicago.

Carol remembered her father's excursions to find surplus he could utilize:

> He had a big parka he wore when he went to army base facilities. They weren't heated. They were huge acres of warehouses where the army stored stuff. Dad was kind of a wheeler and dealer. He was looking for anything that was not easy to get. That was one of the reasons he got Alcoa as a client, because he was able to supply things that other people couldn't. Anyway, he had a big army-colored parka; I'm sure very stiff. And mother had written in her writing, which is always beautiful, "If lost, return to Carolyn Risk."

Kirby donned that same parka when he cheered in the stands during cold-weather Purdue football games.

There were all types of creative ways the military surplus was used by many American businesses. For instance, gas masks were taken apart and the rubber tubes on the masks were made into bicycle handlebar covers; the glass lenses became workshop goggles; the canisters were painted and sold as powder puff holders. What was left was made into toy gas masks. Kirby, who was a scavenger and forward thinker, had a heyday buying and selling for his particular niche in the postwar economy.

Some of the machinery and production equipment covered by the MT-Approved Dealers agreement that Kirby signed were conveyor systems, cranes, hoists, winches, baking ovens, industry furnaces, kilns, foundry equipment, lathes, jointers, die casting machines, gear cutting and finishing machines, bending machines, hydraulic presses, wire forming machines, welding machinery, and more.

Most of the other companies that were MT-Approved Dealers were from large cities like Chicago, Dallas, Detroit, Charlotte, Philadelphia, St. Louis, Boston, and Los Angeles.

It was around this time that Kirby bought a switchboard. The Kirby Risk Electric switchboard was revolutionary and transformed the ease with which Kirby could do business.

Jim said, "Dad acquired an old plug-in switchboard from an army surplus store. The sophisticated switchboard allowed conference calls to as many people as he wanted. It was unique for the time."

The only thing more original than the switchboard was the switchboard operator, Peggy Bennett. Jim said, "Peggy was the face of the company. She could anticipate whom you wanted to reach, almost before you told her. She was friendly, known far and wide. She had a feel-good style and voice. She kept notes and remembered names. There was an editorial in the *Journal and Courier* that read, 'If you're having a bad day, call Kirby Risk and talk to Peggy Bennett.' She was absolutely the best. She was with Kirby Risk for more than thirty years. She started out of high school. For many years a plaque paying tribute to Peggy hung in the lobby."

Switchboards were originally used in telephone company offices to connect subscribers so they could talk. A switchboard was a desk with a tall backboard dotted with hundreds of small holes, known as "jacks." Each opening led to a different telephone. With a cable connecting the two

Peggy Bennett was the friendly switchboard operator—the "face of the company"—for Kirby Risk Electric.

channels, the operator patched together the parties who would talk to each other. When businesses began installing multiple phones within their buildings, an on-site switchboard was used to connect a particular phone to an outside line. The switchboard also provided an intercom, where the operator could connect one phone to another in a different part of the building by "plugging in."

Kirby's switchboard enabled him to make conference calls with as many as eight or more people, which was groundbreaking at the time. Additionally, he had several telephones in his home, which also was innovative. Jim said, "Dad had a phone in the garage and in the bathroom with multiple buttons—a direct line to the office and an extra outside line. People wouldn't know he wasn't at the office. It helped with fundraising and in getting customers what they needed. He would have the customer, trucking company, manufacturer all patched in at the same time on a call. It also helped with community projects."

Kirby's home telephone system was the next best thing to a cell phone. Kirby kept odd hours; he was a night owl. Many days he slept late and then worked in the late afternoons and evenings. He frequented Mary Lou Donuts, a bakery housed in an A-frame building that is still in business on Fourth Street, not far from his home. He loved doughnuts and often gave a box to whomever he would have a meeting, or to the secretary or receptionist at an office he visited. Because Kirby slept late, his breakfast might be at lunchtime. With the company switchboard patched into his home telephone, it was possible for him to still take calls from customers and vendors, even when he was not at the company. He also had a great staff at the office, particularly his right-hand man, Glenn Safford, who consistently arrived at the office well before eight o'clock in the morning. Kirby surrounded himself with good people like Safford, who exuded common sense, responsive customer service, and vendor loyalty.

Carol said, "I remember as a little child not seeing him a lot. He slept while we were in school, and he would work late. I guess he came home for dinner, but that was about it. He would be asleep when I got up. He wouldn't be at home when I went to bed. He'd be at the office. He lived an erratic lifestyle."

What did Caroline think of Kirby's odd hours?

Her daughter, Carol, answered:

They had a really good, happy marriage. He adored her, and she adored him. They teased each other unmercifully. He would sleep late, and she'd go roaming through the room making all kind of noises, pulling up the window shades. We did eat a lot of meals together. We often ate in the dining room when I was young. We had our own places set by protocol. I was at Dad's right, because that's the guest of honor, and I was the oldest. Jimmy would have been at Mother's right because he was the only boy. Mother was at one end; Dad was at one end.

All three of the Risk daughters (Julie would be born ten years after Jim) ran the switchboard during summers when Peggy was on vacation. Carol remembered:

I thought the switchboard was huge. It was a couple of feet high. It was the kind you've seen in the movies that have the cords that pull out and go in. Peggy was fantastic. She knew everybody who called by name. She'd recognize their voice. I would relieve her in the summer when I was in high school. And it was scary because Dad was kind of a tough taskmaster when you were working. He was a softy in a lot of ways, but in that way he definitely was not. He expected you to be able to operate just like Peggy did. And there was no way I was going to be able to perform at Peggy's level. Anyway, it was fun. I remember it as being fun mostly, except when he would walk by.

Julie has fond memories of working the switchboard. She recalled:

I just knew Peggy enough to know how cheery and upbeat and awesome she was. I mean incredible and positive without being overly gushy. I worked for her on the switchboard a lot when I was in high school and college as a summer job. I always tried to emulate her. It was a remarkable switchboard with up and down switch buttons, just hundreds. So it was quite exciting to learn how to use it. That was a plum job. I just remember watching her as a youngster and just being in awe. So, if you got your chance to work the switchboard, that was quite the coup.

Because the switchboard patched directly into the Risk home, Kirby instructed his children on how to answer the phone. Julie said:

> What I will never forget is, without question, customer service was number one in anything you did as an employee or as a family member. And if somebody called at night that was calling about the office, you dropped everything. It didn't matter what you were doing—entertaining, whatever. You served the customer. You didn't have to be an employee to have to do that. Dad would go out in the middle of the night to service, to satisfy customer needs. At home, it's always, "Risk residence" or "Risk residence, may I help you?" Always. Always. It was *never* "Hello."

Carol echoed this memory:

> You know the customer is first. He drilled into us that you never take a phone call where you don't help the person who is calling. You made sure you connected them with somebody who could pick up the item in need or get it or open the door or whatever. We had a list of backup numbers and our number was always first—pick up motors, lights, generators, whatever. So at night, the factory would call, or a contractor would call and say, "I'm in need of some electrical supply." Our number was listed in the classified pages.

Kirby also wanted his children to be proficient with using the phone in other areas of their lives. Carol said, "He would have us phone and make reservations for dinner and figure out maps on how to get places. He said he always wished that if we were dropped anywhere, we could get ourselves home."

Kirby valued good behavior and honesty, and he rewarded his children when they displayed those attributes. Carol recalled, "When I was about ten, I broke a plate while doing the dishes. I was so scared, and when I went to confess to him in the living room, he gave me money for telling him. That made me feel better. He also paid us for our grades, but we got double pay for conduct."

FLUORESCENT

On March 8, 1945, Kirby received a letter from G. M. Basford Company, an advertising firm out of New York and Cleveland. It states:

> We are handling the advertising for the Spero Electric Corporation. Mr. H. I. Spero told us that you have made some installations of Spero Fluorescent fixtures in your territory, which would make good advertising material. We are very anxious to get photographs of good installations, and Mr. Spero suggested that I write to you to ask if you could arrange to get pictures of one or more of those in your territory.

German scientist Edmund Germer is recognized as the father of the fluorescent lamp. In 1926, the year Kirby started his company, Germer applied for a patent. General Electric (GE) later purchased the patent. General Electric began offering fluorescent bulbs for sale in 1938. As one of the country's largest electrical companies, GE was well equipped to promote this new technology. GE showcased the fluorescent bulb and its improved efficiency over other lighting sources at the 1939 New York World's Fair. Many businesses and organizations began using these fluorescent lights, and the increased need for manufacturing and industry during World War II amplified the demand. By the end of the war, fluorescent bulbs had replaced incandescent technology for use in commercial applications.

The 1945 letter that Kirby received from G. M. Basford Company asking for photographs of Spero Fluorescent fixture installations is on onionskin paper and is now dingy from age. Attached by paperclip is an ad for the Spero LVR 448 fluorescent light. The rust and white promotional sheet shows a photo of the "egg crate louvers" ("for shielding the light" and "ease of removal for cleaning") fixture that "combines outstanding design features and striking appearance." The copy reads, "Good lighting in the office is now essential with the increasing amount of exacting work involved in the administration of our 'Victory' program. A shielded fixture, giving sufficient light of low surface brightness, is needed to do such a job. The Spero LVR was designed especially for this purpose."

The fluorescent light fixture of 1945 looks stark and utilitarian by today's standards. It sold for $65.90, less tubes.

Perhaps Kirby had a photographer take shots of the Spero Fluorescent fixtures for Basford at Ross Gear and Tool Company. In a letter to the Spero Electric Corporation a few weeks later, dated March 28, he wrote of his client Ross Gear: "We have received an inquiry from the Ross Gear and Tool Company for between sixty and seventy fluorescent fixtures. The Ross Gear and Tool Company intends to hang the fixtures individually in their general office."

ELECTRIC FRIENDS

In 1946, the electrical supply and electric motor sales and repair segments of Kirby's business were incorporated as two separate companies—Kirby Risk Supply Company, Inc. and Kirby Risk Electric Motors, Inc. When Kirby incorporated, Glenn Safford and Arnold Smith, who had been hired in 1938, were named vice presidents. On her timeline written years later, Caroline records a list of some happenings in 1946:

> Kirby Risk incorporated.
> Mary Kiddon of Bull Dog—Detroit—very helpful
> Mary Kiddon came from Detroit for the weekend at 719 Owen
> Frequent guests at Owen Street:
> Fat Bass—Westinghouse
> Dick Jacobs—Economy Fuse
> Earl Nelson—National Electrical Products (urged for incorporation).

Earl "Swede" Nelson of Pittsburgh National Electric Wire Products was a mentor and business advisor for Kirby. Kirby Risk Electric purchased Romex from National Electric. The word "Romex" is often used as a generic term to refer to any type of non-metallic ("NM") sheathed electrical cable. Fundamentally, Romex is electrical wiring sheathed in a plastic coating. The Romex brand originated in 1922 with its development by the former Rome Wire Company of Rome, New York (thus, the name Romex), a predecessor to General Cable Corporation. Later, Southwire purchased the company. Nelson, in his starched white shirt and tie, encouraged Kirby to incorporate his business. He also advised Kirby to "buy things direct—not through other distributors."

Mary Kiddon was the secretary for Bulldog Electric Products out of Detroit, Michigan, their regional office. Jim said, "Dad would set up meetings through her or get products with her help. He befriended her with hard-to-find items at the time—nylons stockings and butter. She became a dear friend and was helpful in getting products in short supply and in expediting delivery."

Caroline Risk, Julie Risk, and Mary Kiddon stand outside of Kirby Risk Supply in October 1955. Kiddon was a secretary for Bulldog Electric Products in Detroit, Michigan, who became a close friend of the Risk family and helped Kirby obtain hard-to-find products during World War II.

Jim continued, "Bulldog was a major brand—an electrical equipment company. Many homes around town had Bulldog breaker panels
with 'pushmatic' breakers. There was a red bulldog printed on the
panel box. We put Bulldog panels in our National Homes Electrical
packages." National Homes Corporation was a manufacturer of prefabricated housing and buildings that was founded in 1940 and headquartered in Lafayette. It was owned by brothers Jim and George Price,
who became Kirby's good friends.

"As I remember, Bulldog was sold to ITE [originally Inverse Time
Element] then ITE sold to Gould, then to Siemens, a very large, global
company headquartered in Germany," Jim said. "They no longer manufacture products under the Bulldog brand. Siemens continues to be
one of our most important vendors." Siemens, which is no longer
affiliated with ITE, is a German engineering conglomerate, the largest
of its kind in Europe, with international headquarters located in Berlin, Munich, and Erlangen.

A toggle switch breaker has replaced pushmatic breakers. The in-
structions on the Bulldog panel box were printed on a silver metal
plate with a center image of a thickset bulldog surrounded by a red
background. The sign read, "Pushmatic ELECTRI-CENTER, Auto-
matic Protection, Push Button Control." A Bulldog Electric Products
invoice sent to Kirby Risk Electric and dated March 7, 1946, greyed
with age and still wafting a faint scent of motor oil, bears this sentence
describing Bulldog: "Originators of flexible electrical distribution systems for light and power." Jim said, "The Bulldog line was a big deal,
and Siemens continues to be important. Bulldog was a great name to
be associated with." In his lifetime, Kirby owned bulldogs as pets.
Perhaps it was his nod to irony. Today, a ceramic china bulldog figu-
rine, a service award, stands out next to numerous other traditionally
designed plaques and Lucite awards in a display case in the lobby of
the Kirby Risk headquarters in Lafayette.

"Fat" Bass was Kirby's connection with Westinghouse Electric Supply Company. Jim recalled:

He was a character—big, obviously. Dad bought things from him, before we were a fully recognized distributor. He purchased from Westinghouse and Graybar and resold the products in Lafayette. Today, Westinghouse is viewed as a competitor, and they would have been then, but distributors were located in large metropolitan areas such as Chicago and Indianapolis. We'd buy from these other distributors until we could develop our own relationships with the manufacturers.

When out-of-town business associates and friends came to visit the Risk home, they were often invited to spend the night. Kirby's and Caroline's home was large. There was always room for visitors, and the Risk children grew up with a constant swirl of faces, personalities, connections, and those in need sitting at their dinner table and sleeping in a spare room, treated like family, or regarded better than family, no matter their station in life, simply because they were guests.

CHAPTER 9

WHEN PREFAB WAS FAB

The year is 1940. A young couple can achieve what was once impossible for newlyweds—they can afford to purchase their own home. The fresh-faced pair fans open a catalog and orders their hearts' desire. A new house—complete with windows, doors, trim, roofing, and electrical necessities—arrives on their property, ready for assembly in one convenient package. Builders can erect the couple's new abode in a single day and finish it in a week or so. Such a house, wrapped and ready, complete with the pretty little bow of an affordable price, began in Lafayette, Indiana, and put the "fab" in "prefab."

The prefabricated house offered the first glorious glow of homeownership for thousands of American families who previously, during the Great Depression, could only afford to live with extended family or rent an apartment when they "set up housekeeping." This is when brothers Jim and George Price began National Homes Corporation in Lafayette. During their revolutionary company's beginning arose the interweaving of the lives and work of the Price family with that of the Risk family.

National Homes Corporation officially started in 1940, but the idea of the company sparked a few months before. In a 1990 Lafayette *Journal and Courier* interview, George Price said, "I got out of college in 1939. . . . I graduated on a Sunday and I was on the erection crew putting up a house on Lingle Avenue [in Lafayette] on Monday or Tuesday." The house was the latest in home construction where the components were built in a factory and then assembled on site. Price continued, "I was working with my brother. He said, 'You know, we ought to look into this housing. It's going to go.'"

That was an understatement. For nearly fifty years, National Homes Corporation was the leading prefabricated home manufacturer in America.

Jim Price quit Indiana University's business school during the Great Depression. In 1937, he worked for Prudential Life and sold houses on the side. "Somebody asked if I could sell him a prefabricated house," Price said in a 1954 interview. "I'd never seen a prefab, but I said yes."

The Price brothers became dealers for Gunnison Housing Corporation in Lafayette, which were manufactured in New Albany, Indiana. In the spring of 1940, John King and two of his Purdue University engineering buddies left Gunnison and arrived in Lafayette to start their own prefabricated housing company. They wanted to produce a less-expensive house than Gunnison and tap into the demand for homes created by the Great Depression and by generous New Deal finance programs. But they needed money.

They found capital with the help of two Lafayette Gunnison home dealers, Frank Tedford and Jim Price. Price was described as "impatient," "frugal," "practical," and as "a heavy-set man who wore a bowler hat." He led the charge and raised $12,000 in startup investments. Among the first stakeholders was George Price and Roger Branigin.

On June 25, 1940, National Homes Corporation was born, changing not only the lives of the Prices, but also the lives of millions of Americans for the next fifty years. National Homes Corporation became a "housing empire." Kirby Risk Electric was a component of that kingdom. The company supplied the electrical needs for thousands of houses manufactured by National Homes, becoming one of the cogs in the wheel of the evolution of suburban American living that sprouted from the prefabricated house boom.

The designs for the company's first home were drawn on a drafting table in the front window of Tedford and Price's office where Tedford's company, the Mitchell Agency, was located at 217 North Fourth Street in downtown Lafayette—just a block away from Kirby Risk Electric at Third and Ferry. The Mitchell Agency still operates in the original location. Characteristically impatient, Price was eager to deliver, and at his insistence, the first panels of a home were constructed in a shed behind his office on North Fourth Street and later transported to the new factory once it was completed. Construction of a 7,500-square-foot factory began on July 1, 1940 on Earl Avenue, near Ferry Street—where Von Tobel Lumber and Hardware now stands.

The first National homes cost about $3,200, including the lot. Mortgage payments averaged $20 per month. National homes featured a single picture window in the living room, one of the characteristics that still makes it easy to identify an early "National." Essentially, prefabricated homes are made the same way today as they were then. The walls, called panels, are constructed in the factory with the windows and doors in place. The panels are erected on the home's foundation and fastened together. Until the mid-1950s, roofs were made of panels. Today, prefabricated trusses are employed. During the company's second year, the United States entered World War II, and contracts with the American government increased National's home production tenfold.

An article in the Lafayette *Journal and Courier* dated August 11, 1990, entitled "The Rise and Fall of National Homes," includes a story about a couple who purchased their National home for $3,200 in 1941. "Sam and Mary Hockstra's house was erected at 1631 N. 16th Street [in Lafayette]. The Federal Housing Administration backed the mortgage. Hockstra, who was 21 at the time, was making $36 a month as a Ross Gear machine operator. He paid $50 down and $26 a month."

More than likely, Mary Hockstra's work was "housewife," as was the norm for women of the day. It was an understood "given" that she would not have an income to contribute to the financing of the home.

"The main thing we did during that whole period was make it possible for just about anybody who had a job to own a home of their own," said John King, a founding National Homes officer who resigned to join the US Army during World War II. "They weren't big, but it was ownership, and it was responsibility."

After Japan's attack on Pearl Harbor, the government ordered an end to all private housing starts, so National Homes switched gears and worked for the government, which needed housing around defense plants. In a 1985 interview conducted by John Norberg and printed in the Lafayette *Journal and Courier*, George Price said, "We had jobs in Ohio and Michigan, and our reputation with Washington DC was top, top, top."

In 1944, the National Homes plant on Earl Avenue burned, so the company rebuilt a few blocks south on US 52, what is today Sagamore Parkway. Price said, "During the war we had one customer, the US government. But the worry was, what we were going to do when the war comes to an end? Manufacturing is what we learned during the war. Merchandising is what we learned after."

When World War II ended, an entire generation was armed with FHA and VA loans and could, for the first time, purchase a home. There were five million people caught in the worst housing shortage in American history. National Homes set up dealers and taught them how to merchandise and sell and help families obtain financing. The company also set up their own financing company, National Homes Acceptance Corporation. During peak years, National Homes could produce up to 100 homes a day and by 1985, the company had manufactured some 700,000 homes.

In 1954, Vice President Glenn Safford hired Roger Swindle to lead assembly of the electrical and fixture packages for National Homes.

Today, Swindle is a fit man who walks four miles a day wearing his affable grin. He still works part time, marking fifty-eight years with Kirby Risk in 2012. Safford died in 2000.

Kirby's son, Jim, said, "Our company's biggest customer in those days would have been National Homes, especially when they were manufacturing 100 homes a day. Roger managed all of the inventory, including the wire, panels, boxes, fixtures, and more to assemble electrical and fixture packages. They would go on a semi with the National Homes panels and everything needed to make prefab homes."

As National Homes flourished, Kirby Risk Electric grew. Kirby expanded the inventory dedicated for National Homes to supply the electrical needs of the prefabricated homes that hummed off the assembly line on Earl Avenue.

The business of assembling the "fixture package" and "universal electrical package" was housed in a former Dr. Pepper distribution center directly behind the Kirby Risk offices at Third and Ferry. Swindle worked in this warehouse, which the staff called "the Dr. Pepper." "I almost immediately moved into this packaging business," he said. "That was pretty much what I did for a long time. A lot of other things thrown in, but that was my primary function."

In 1954, Swindle was only the sixteenth employee to be hired since Kirby began his company in 1926. "Roger joined Kirby Risk the year the company initiated a profit-sharing plan for its employees," Jim said. "Very few companies had profit-sharing plans in that era. We were one of the first in our industry. Roger witnessed the company's growth over the years from $1 million to $400 million. He also watched the employee count go from sixteen to more than a thousand."

There's a photo of the "universal electrical packaging" display that Swindle and Safford took to trade exhibits they attended. The display shows the individual pieces that fit like a brainteaser puzzle into a box about three-feet wide by two-feet long and eighteen-inches deep. The National Homes dealer paid $86 and received light fixtures (with the "atomic" decorator look of the day), switches, outlets, a circuit panel box, wiring, and more for each room and the exterior of the house.

Each piece of the package fit snugly into a box. The display sign on the universal electrical package exhibit that Swindle and Safford toted across the country read, "With NEW 100 Amp Twin Breaker Panel."

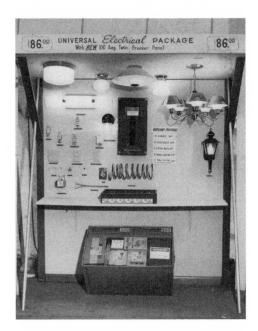

"When I started, National Homes only had the plant in Lafayette, and then they started to expand," Swindle said. "They added plants in Illinois, Mississippi, Georgia, New York, and Texas. National Homes grew dramatically. Meetings were held at the different plants. Dealers from the surrounding areas would attend to view the new model homes and inspect the products displayed by the vendors. We would set up a display at each meeting so the dealer could see what he was getting for his $86."

In the 1950s and 1960s, Glenn Safford and Roger Swindle took this universal electrical package to display at meetings held at National Homes Corporation manufacturing plants across the United States. Dealers could purchase all of the electrical needs to install in one house for $86.

Swindle made the dealer trips part of his family vacations. "Usually, I drove. Glenn flew. They would arrange it so I could take my family along for a vacation at the same time. It worked out real well. I could have my wife and kids with me. We had two children who were pretty young at the time."

Ultimately, it was the homebuilder's choice whether to purchase the universal electrical package assembled by Kirby Risk Electric, or have the equipment furnished by a local electrical contractor in whatever state the house was landing—Texas, New York, Ohio, anywhere in the country.

In 2011, as Jim and Swindle looked back on the growth of the Kirby Risk Corporation, Jim said to his coworker, "We thought we were a significant business in the 1960s, didn't we?"

"Yes, sure did. Didn't have any idea where it was going."

"And National Homes—I suppose it was 35 percent of our business. It was really impressive what Roger was a part of. When system selling was introduced twenty-five years ago, we had already been providing the service back in the 1950s for National Homes. Later, we were the first just-in-time supplier to Caterpillar [a manufacturing company]."

With just-in-time delivery, a manufacturer or distributor supplies inventory "just in time" for the need. The customer keeps costs and storage needs down with no requirement to accumulate inventory in a warehouse. Jim continued, "Roger was providing just-in-time delivery as one of the first in the industry because he was developing these packages for National Homes, maintaining a couple of days' worth of inventory for them and delivering daily to the plant."

Swindle said, "Today, they call it VMI, vendor managed inventory. The vendors ship us what they predict we are going to need and periodically, if things don't sell, we return it. National Homes never called up and ordered anything. We just kept the products in stock for a few days, based on their need, of course."

On October 11, 1954, *Time* magazine ran an article about Jim Price, then forty-three, titled "Housing: King of the Builders." It states:

> One secret of Jim Price's success is that he never starts a house down his assembly line before it is sold, thus keeps inventories of finished units down to zero. Another secret is his fleet of 255 huge trailers to deliver houses to building sites within 400 miles of his plant, thus licking the transportation costs that ruined many other prefabbers. Price sells his houses through some 550 builder-dealers around the country, some of whom gross upwards of $500,000 a

year. Biggest cluster of National Homes: a development of 2,000 units in Fort Wayne, Indiana.

The number of "Nationals" in Lafayette grew dramatically in the 1950s and 1960s. The company built schools and churches within the neighborhoods. Price's daughter, Anne Price McKenzie Goodnight, said, "Dad always gave land to build a church. Like at Edgelea it's the Methodist Church and down at Vinton it's the Bethany Presbyterian."

The National Homes products dotted the perfectly planned neighborhoods like cracker boxes on the Piggly Wiggly shelf. They stood along winding streets and cul-de-sacs, all located a short walk to a school, church, and a neighborhood pool. The tract of front lawn, newly planted elms, and sense of secure sameness made for a microcosm of 1950s to 1960s living. Dad drove off to work in the only car the family owned. Mom stayed home. The kids walked from school to home each day for lunch and then returned to class after eating a bologna sandwich on white bread.

"The 1950s were golden years," Price's daughter said. "My Dad listened to Paul Harvey, and Paul Harvey said, 'What this world needs is a $6,000 house.' The next thing you knew, we had the 'Thrift Home,' a $6,000 house. I can remember pictures of me on Greenbush Street in the Vinton addition toward the railroad tracks handing out pamphlets. The open houses had tons of people."

Paul Harvey was an American radio broadcaster who died in 2009. He was known for his segment *The Rest of the Story*. His folksy delivery was peppered with dramatic pauses and quirky intonations. He ended his show with his signature, "Good day."

An article about Jim Price and National Homes appeared in the *Indianapolis Star Magazine* in 1956. It states, "Jim Price of Lafayette became the Henry Ford of the building industry, putting the construction of houses on an assembly line basis, like autos." It also described National Homes as a "Hoosier giant that started out as a midget." At that time, National Homes had more than five hundred builder-dealers in forty-one states, and the company claimed that one out of every forty-eight homes built in the country at that point was a National.

During this time, Swindle and an assistant at Kirby Risk Supply assembled approximately two hundred electrical packages a week. "They would send us one of their trailers and we would load it with packages. They would take it out to their plant at Horseheads, New York. It was a pretty big deal."

Roger Swindle, Norm Butler, and Joe Gress worked for Kirby Risk Supply on a United Way Community Chest fund-raiser night in October 1955. Swindle was in charge of assembling the universal electrical packages for use in houses manufactured by National Homes Corporation, at that time headquartered in Lafayette, Indiana.

For decades, National's red trucks were a famous, familiar sight tooling across the United States. In the prime years of the late 1950s, the truck was painted with the "nh" logo, the word "National" in friendly lowercase cursive, and the word "Homes" in a solid, all-caps font. The tagline across the side of the truck commanded with pride,

"Watch the Nationals go up." And you could. Right before your eyes, a house was unloaded, set upon a cement slab foundation, and nailed together like a Christmas day gingerbread house.

In the 1950s, the red trucks of National Homes Corporation, headquartered in Lafayette, Indiana, were a familiar sight across the United States. New homeowners could literally "Watch the Nationals go up" in a matter of days.
Courtesy of the Wabash Valley Trust for Historic Preservation.

By 1985, the side of a National Homes truck was painted with this statement: "More people live in National Homes than in any other homes in the world."

The 1950s exploded with prefabricated housing, shopping centers, and suburbia. Passenger air travel, a prewar novelty, became common-place. Early on, National Homes owned a Lockheed Lodestar twin-engine airplane to transport Jim, George, their staff, and others from their headquarters in Lafayette to the company's other factories across the country. The plane, based out of the Purdue University Airport, was used for transportation to meetings, as well as the Price's private pursuits, which often coupled with business.

In the early, overcast morning of Sunday, October 7, 1951, the National Homes plane hurtled into a soybean field and burst into flames. Jim and George, along with Dr. Thomas Graham, Karl H. Kettelhut, Cecil Clark, and Ralph Shurmeyer, were returning to Lafayette from a hunting trip. A Lafayette *Journal and Courier* article from October 8, 1951, reads, "A game-laden plane returning a Lafayette hunting party from an expedition into the Canadian North Woods skimmed through treetops and crashed in a field southeast of West Point early Sunday, claiming three lives and injuring three others."

C. Kenneth August had been a World War II US Air Force pilot and was hired as the National Homes company pilot a year earlier. He was killed instantly. Graham, age forty-two, also died immediately. He was a prominent Lafayette surgeon who was president of the staff of Home Hospital. He was one of the initial National Homes investors back in 1940. Graham was a licensed pilot who owned his own airplane, and he often flew as a copilot in the National Homes plane, as he did on this flight from Canada. He and his wife, Martha, lived on Wea Avenue, a street that runs perpendicular to Owen and Central in the Highland Park neighborhood, very near the Risk and Jim Price homes. George Price lived in the neighborhood as well, at 1008 Highland Avenue, a block behind his brother. Martha was a distant relative of the Price brothers.

In 2011, Jim Price's daughter, Anne, said, "Tom Graham was my Dad's very best friend, and that was a huge loss."

Clark, a painting contractor from Crawfordsville, was fatally injured. Shurmeyer was a National Homes representative from Fort Wayne who sustained injuries but survived. Kettelhut was thrown clear of the wreckage and was unharmed. A state police officer drove him home from the accident that morning. The newspaper reported that Kettelhut described the trip as "typical" and said, "'There was no engine or structural failure. And then came a 'Ke-bang, Ke-bang.' And the next thing he knew he was sitting in the mud several feet from the burning plane."

Kettelhut and his wife, Marietta, both Purdue University graduates, founded Kettelhut Construction, and their company built numerous landmark buildings on the West Lafayette campus and in Greater Lafayette. A distinguished professorship of structural engineering is named in their honor, as is a structural engineering laboratory on campus.

George Price, age thirty-three, secretary of National Homes, was listed in fair condition in Home Hospital with head injuries and cuts and burns on his hands and face. Jim Price, age forty, president of National Homes, was in critical condition in St. Elizabeth Hospital with a broken leg and internal injuries. Upon hearing of the crash, Kirby rushed to the bedside of his good friend. Years later, Caroline wrote in a timeline of her life, "James Price hospitalized. Kirby sat with him many nights guarding his hospital door against newspaper people."

Jim Price's daughter was fourteen when her father and uncle were injured in the accident. Her brother, David, was eleven. She recalled, "My dad was critical for maybe ten days. Really, really critical. My dad was thrown through a table that folded down. So he had a lot of internal injuries."

The night of the accident was Lafayette Jefferson High School's annual girl-ask-boy dance called "The Gallop," an apropos name for a school with a "Broncho" as a mascot. Price's daughter said, "I'd asked a boy and he turned me down, so I didn't go to the Gallop. And I'm so glad I didn't. It would have been terrible for my mother if somebody had to go pick me up. I just knew there were people coming in and out of my house. Probably Kirby and Caroline were some of them. But I just knew something bad had happened. I just didn't know what."

Years later, at Anne's fiftieth high school class reunion, she saw the boy who had turned her down for the dance. "Dave Jones came up to me, and I could never remember who I'd asked. And he said, 'Anne,

I feel so bad.' I said, 'Dave, don't worry about it. I needed to be home. My dad was in a really bad accident that night.'"

When Dave Jones turned Anne down, she felt bad and Kirby knew it. Anne said, "When the boy said, 'No,' I thought this is really bad, and so Kirby had a surprise birthday party on September 26 to make me feel better. He was just like a little angel to me. He was very nice. He was just very, very thoughtful. Then a week and a half later was the plane accident."

Kirby took care of Anne after the plane crash, too. "Kirby would take Carol and me to school. We were freshmen. He would pick up applesauce doughnuts, and then we'd go up to my dad's room in St. Elizabeth. I don't know if my dad could eat a donut, but we went up, which was really neat to be able to see my dad before school started. Because it was a scary time."

Jim Risk said, "When Jim and George were in the airplane accident, I remember Dad going to the hospital and just willing, scolding Jim to live. Cheerleading. Challenging him."

Jim Price's daughter continued:

> My Dad and George were in two different hospitals. And they finally had to put up communications between them because they weren't' sure if they were telling them the truth about their brother. They were so worried. They had to know. My Dad got home by Christmas because they built a room onto the kitchen that later could be used as an eating area. He came home with a full-time nurse. He was in a hospital bed. He wanted to come home.

The National Homes plane crash was big news across the country. The photos taken in the Indiana field that accompanied the *Journal and Courier* story show a mutilated deer carcass and numerous lifeless ducks and fish, remnants of the prominent entourage's hunting vacation scattered amid singed, contorted metal.

Also strewn over four acres of farmland were "charred guns and cases of hunters' ammunition which escaped exploding."

Still Home

National Homes rose to the top of home manufactures after the war, gaining 25 percent of the prefabrication market by 1959. At that time, the plant pulsated with 2,500 workers generating 50 to 100 houses a day around the clock. Factory workers wore white T-shirts with the National Homes logo and the phrase, "For a lifetime of pleasant living."

In 2012, Roger Swindle still lives in the house he and his wife bought from National Homes in 1956. Of course, his home included a Kirby Risk electrical fixture package that he packed and shipped himself. National Homes named all of its models, like additions to the family. Swindle's home is the "Finley," originally 900 square feet, with three bedrooms and no garage. Over the years, Swindle and his wife, who has passed away, doubled their home's size by adding a family room, fireplace, laundry room, bath, walk-in closet, and garage. A maple tree, decades old, trunk too big for one man to wrap his arms around, towers above Swindle's fifty-five-year-old National.

CHAPTER 10

CAMP KIRBY

Kirby, Caroline, Carol, Sherry, Jim, and Julie Risk became close friends with Jim, Roberta, Anne, and David Price. During their children's growing years, the Price family lived at 620 Central Avenue in a home built by Henry Poor, who owned a lumber company in Lafayette. Poor was one of the original investors in National Homes. The Risk and Price homes, both two-stories tall and decades old, sat a couple of blocks apart in the shady Highland Park neighborhood. The Risks were also friends with Jim Price's brother, George, and his wife, Eleanor, who lived nearby at 1008 Highland Avenue.

Anne Price McKenzie Goodnight was Carol's best friend, and Dave Price, who was Sherry's age, was Jim's best friend beginning when they were in the first and second grades at Highland Elementary School. Dave passed away in 2008. The families shared vacations, work, and lives. Anne said of Carol Risk, "She will always be my best friend. I don't really remember Carol until first grade because my Dad was building houses. And he was building them for government housing for the military. So I came back to Lafayette to get ready to go to school."

Like his sisters, Anne still refers to Jim Risk as "Jimmy." She said, "Jimmy and David were best friends all the way through. They were on the same teams, and then David married Jane Hovde. She was in Jimmy's class. All of us circle right there together."

Jane Hovde Price is the daughter of the late Frederick Hovde, president of Purdue University from 1946 to 1971. President Hovde was the University's longest-serving president, and during his twenty-five-year tenure, Purdue experienced its greatest period of growth, leading to its emergence as a top research institution. President Hovde was married to Priscilla Boyd, and they had three children: Frederick "Boyd," Jane, and Linda. The family lived in the "President's Home," then located at 515 South Seventh Street in Lafayette. Hovde's predecessor, Edward Elliott, had been the first Purdue president to reside there.

The grey stucco, Spanish Eclectic-style mansion with arched windows and entrance canopy stands a couple blocks from the Highland Park neighborhood. Today, the home is a private residence. Roger Branigin, an attorney who served as governor of Indiana from 1965 to 1969, lived about a block away in a Colonial brick home at 611 South Seventh Street. Branigin was one of the first investors in National Homes back when Jim Price hustled startup capital in 1940. The area, Highland Park and the surrounding boulevards sheltered by oaks, maples, and catalpas, housed the families of mighty midwesterners who hobnobbed in the same sphere.

Jim Risk's wife, Mary Jo Mohlman, also grew up in Highland at 602 Cherokee, the house next door to Highland School. Her grandfather and father owned Gerry Mohlman and Son Jewelers. She was friends with Sherry Risk at an early age and played at the Risk home. Mary Jo's family was Catholic, so she attended St. Mary's School until she entered Sunnyside Junior High. Her parents, Robert and Margaret (Bob and Marg), knew Kirby and Caroline well. Mary Jo's best friend was Jane Hovde. Their group of high school girlfriends was diverse and close. Jane married David Price, Jim Risk's best friend. The Risk family's friendships are interwoven like the warp and weft of a weaver's loom.

"I still see a lot of our gang of girls from high school," Mary Jo said. "Our backgrounds were very different. One's father was a bus driver. Another was president of Purdue. One's father was a detective; another father was gone. It didn't make any difference. We all went to each other's houses, knew each other's parents real well."

Jane Hovde Price said, "I would have most of the slumber parties at my house, so my mother would *think* she could chaperone. We had what we called the 'card room' that was off of the sunroom in the back. It had French doors. My friends would sneak out. We had a fence in the back alley. They would go back there and smoke."

"And then we had a laundry shoot from the second floor all the way down to the basement," Jane continued. "They loved to mess with that. Throw stuff down it. We had a lot of the events at my house. We all slumbered in the sunroom, way away from Mother and Dad."

Jane's father, Frederick Hovde—a Rhodes scholar, Oxford University rugby star, chemical engineer, educator, and seventh president of Purdue University—was the father sleeping upstairs while, downstairs, his daughter and her giggling friends schemed harmless mischief during their slumber parties. This was the same man who gave Winston Churchill some important information.

Jane said, "My Dad delivered the message to Winston Churchill that we were going to drop the atomic bomb. He was in London. He was with the Navel Rocket Ordinance Research Committee in Washington DC, so that's where we lived before we came to Lafayette."

During World War II, Hovde worked for the National Defense Research Committee, which later became part of the wartime Office of Scientific Research and Development (OSRD). He was appointed head of the OSRD London Mission. While in England, he received his master's degree from Oxford University.

Later, Hovde was assigned to be chief of Division 3, Rocket Ordnance Research, of the National Defense Research Committee. In honor of his war services, he was presented with the Presidential Medal for Merit and the King's Medal for Service in the Cause of

Freedom by the British Government. Hovde became president of Purdue University after World War II ended.

Jane was four when the Hovde family moved to Lafayette. Seventh Street, Highland Elementary, Sunnyside Junior High, Jefferson High School, the Lafayette Country Club, and Central Presbyterian Church were her stomping grounds. And there, too, amidst the idyllic turf of the post-World War II environment, were the Risk and the Price families, Kirby Risk Electric, National Homes, and Purdue University.

Many in the Risk fold were from the Benton County area, small towns that wrought rural upbringings of down-to-earth people. This included the widow of Dr. Thomas Graham, who had died in the 1951 National Homes airplane accident. Martha Graham remained a lifelong friend of the Risk and the Price families. They all attended Central Presbyterian Church at Columbia and Seventh Streets in Lafayette.

Anne remembered, "Martha was a distant relative on my Dad's side. She had lived in Otterbein. My mother, Roberta, was from Otterbein; my dad was from Fowler. Caroline Risk was from Boswell. They are all Benton County people. We said Benton County sure produced sturdy people." Caroline's mother, Alice Robinson, lived in Boswell until the later part of her life. In the summertime, Anne would go with Carol to visit her grandmother, who they called "Germsie." "Carol and I painted a playhouse in the back," Anne said. "All those years we knew all those people. It was fun."

Anne's brother, David, was born in 1940, the same year their father and uncle began National Homes. The Price family lived on Tenth Street at the time. Then they moved to a National Home in Highland Park, which had come from their father's brand new business. Anne said, "I lived on Shawnee from age three to seven. And I think it was the third National Home built. I remember my mother pushing me over there in a stroller to look at the house when they were building."

The early National owned by the Price family still stands across from the neighborhood's famous "Bicycle Bridge," a pedestrian span where Risk and Price kids pedaled and ran across a ravine. Early twentieth-century Craftsman bungalows and Colonial Revivals surround the one-story, rectangular house. In 1940, the third National to be built was Highland Park's "odd man out," but it laid claim to the future with a lone, knowing nod.

SUMMER DAYS

The Price family had a cottage on Lake Freeman, near Lafayette, and Jim Risk spent time with his friend's family there. Anne said, "My Dad wanted to garden or be at the lake. He spent time with his family or his company."

Jim Risk said, "Jim Price enjoyed and related very well with kids. We were very close family friends, and in fact Jim Price bought the Risk family our first TV."

Kirby loved new gadgets—his company switchboard, for example. He purchased some of the first bicycles with handbrakes, and he could ride one backward. Yet he boycotted some new offerings. Carol said, "We were the last people in the world to get a television and a dishwasher. I was fifteen, and Jim Price bought a TV and gave it to us for Christmas because Dad wouldn't buy one." The year would have been 1952, the same year Kirby and Caroline's youngest child, Julie, was born.

When the Risks finally obtained a dishwasher, Kirby discouraged his family from using it. He helped wash the dishes, though. Carol said, "He was critical about the way we did dishes. You had to use the clean water, the rinse water, and the soap water. You scrape them. They were so clean before you washed them."

The Risk and Price children attended summer camp together. Beginning in 1950, Jim attended Camp Pemigewassett in Wentworth, New Hampshire, and Carol and Sherry spent time with Anne Price at Ogontz White Mountain Camp in Lyman, New Hampshire. George Price's children also attended. "It was a wonderful camp," Anne said. "My mother and Caroline would come out to visit, and then they would go antiquing. And then the families would always come back at the end of camp, and we'd take a family vacation together. One year we went to Maine, and we went to New York. That was really, really fun."

Jim said, "Now think about this. You're the mother and you put your eight-year-old son on a train in Chicago to go to New Hampshire to camp for eight weeks. Mostly eastern people attended. When the train reached Cleveland, a counselor and campers got on."

Jim said he was not excited, but rather a bit nervous about going; however, he enjoyed the experience, and it expanded his horizons at a young age. "I was exposed to many new opportunities—mountain climbing, sailing, canoeing, nature, crafts, and more," he said.

Caroline said, "Jim had a cold when we sent him. And we made him promise not to enjoy the lake for a while. Then as soon as he arrived, he swam clear across the great big lake."

Jim continued, "I wasn't much of a swimmer at the time, but in order to go out on a boat by yourself, you had to swim from junior camp to senior camp, which was three-quarters of a mile or so. After the first few days, I just dove in and swam, and the counselor followed in the boat. So I qualified to boat alone, and I also joined the swim team. I played other sports, too. Professor Dyke from the University of Rhode Island ran the nature cabin. He fascinated me, and I enjoyed collecting and learning about cecropias, lunas [types of moths], ferns, grasses, and butterflies. It was a great experience."

Ogontz White Mountain Camp, which the girls attended, was a couple of hours by car from Camp Pemigewassett. "During the summer, Ogontz campers would visit Pemigewassett—one time," Jim said. "And so my parents knew I'd get to see family once." Jim laughed at the thought. "Carol and Sherry were embarrassed to come over to the boys' camp, and they didn't visit!"

Camp Pemigewassett, referred to as "Pemi," was founded in 1908 and still operates today. The website reads, "For over 100 years . . . boys ages 8-15 make friends from around the world as they explore sports, nature, music and art, and trips."

Ogontz is also still in business. The camp's homepage reads, "Formerly an elite girls camp, Ogontz, a 350-acre private retreat center . . . (is) . . . located beside a mountain stream and nestled deep within the forests of New Hampshire's White Mountains, the camp rests above its own lake complete with mountain view!"

FUN

The Risk and Price families took many vacations together. Anne would travel with the Risks on their holidays. Anne said, "I can remember we drove back from Florida, and it was nothing to drive in the middle of the night for Kirby. He wouldn't start until evening."

Carol recalled her father's late-night starts also:

> When we were taking family trips, we had to stop at the office for him to do a few things before we would leave. And we'd all be out in the car waiting for up to an hour or more. We would get restless. Sometimes we would accidently hit the car horn, and Mother would say, "Don't do that!" You knew if you did that, it would mean we would wait even longer. So we were often leaving right after school to go to Florida, and end up leaving at three in the morning. But then he'd always make it wonderful fun.

How did Caroline feel about waiting in the car for hours, in the dark, with four children?

"It was what worked for them," Carol said. "It worked really well. They had a wonderful relationship. I think they both were strong individuals. And Mom was pretty spunky. I said to her, 'I know what attracted him to you. Because you really are spunky.' He was really strong and controlling. They had a way of managing that worked for them. She said to me once after he was gone, 'You're going to think it's terrible, but I never even filled up the car without asking him.' And I said, 'I don't think it's terrible at all. It worked. You were happy.'"

Youngest daughter Julie said, "Dad was always late. I don't know how Mother stayed married to him. I didn't appreciate it at the time. We'd be getting ready to go to an away football game, and Mother and

I would have the car packed—all the rain gear in it, food in it, sitting in the car, in the driveway. And an hour to an hour and a half later we would leave. And then we would always stop by the office and he would do things before you got out of town."

Kirby surprised his family with trips. When she was ten, Carol came home from school one day and her mother was packing her suitcase. "Dad came home and took me with him on a trip to New York. We flew there, and he took me to see all kinds of plays."

Julie said, "Sometimes we would come home, and he'd say, 'Pack. We're going to Florida tomorrow.' Pull you out of school. He had already made all the arrangements with the teachers."

Kirby knew how to make any event fun. He was the great instigator, planner, and orchestrator. He enjoyed fine hotels and the amenities found there. Anne Price said:

> When I was in junior high, the Risks and Prices all went to New York for Thanksgiving and the Macy's Day Parade. We went to Chicago together to see the Cubs and to go to the Empire Room, and Kirby always wanted the dessert to be chocolate ice cream with raspberry sherbet. We did lots of fun things. When I look back, they were so smart. They kept us so busy having fun family things. We maybe missed some other stuff, but we really didn't miss anything. We were kept very, very busy. Kirby spent a lot of time thinking about what to keep doing.

The Empire Room is the opulent dining hall at the Palmer House, a Hilton Hotel in downtown Chicago billed as the longest continuously operating hotel in North America. Caroline had dined here when she was part of the Chicago World's Fair queen's court. Crystal chandeliers dripped from ceilings that sparkled with gold leaf. Marble walls surrounded French tables and chairs, and thick, luxurious drapes dressed windows as part of the French Empire motif. The Empire room opened for dining and dancing in 1925 after the aging Palmer House was torn down and rebuilt on the same property. In 1933, the year Kirby and Caroline married during the Chicago World's Fair, the

Empire Room's Gaslight Club began with weekly performances by stars of stage and screen.

The Risk and Price families enjoy a rink-side view of an ice show in the Boulevard Room at the Conrad Hilton Hotel in Chicago in the early 1950s. From left to right: Jim Risk, Carol Risk holding Julie Risk, Roberta Price, Kirby Risk, Caroline Risk, maître d' Phil Ida (standing), Laura Wolf, Jim Price, Anne Price, Eleanor Diamond (friend), and Sherry Risk.

Maurice Chevalier, Jimmy Durante, Eartha Kitt, Carol Channing, Liberace, Harry Belafonte, Peggy Lee, and Phyllis Diller performed on the dance floor of the Empire Room. For many years, and particularly during the zenith of the Empire Room in the 1950s and 1960s, Kirby reveled in taking Caroline, his family, and friends to the Empire at the Palmer, one of the first hotels in the world to boast electricity. One can imagine Kirby holding court at a lengthy table covered in white linen and fine china, as the Price and Risk families dip silver spoons into chocolate ice cream bejeweled with raspberry sherbet.

Kirby also relished taking his family to the Boulevard Room in what was then called the Conrad Hilton Hotel in Chicago, originally the Stevens Hotel. Conrad Hilton purchased the hotel in 1945. The board of directors changed the name of the hotel, branding it after Conrad Hilton himself in November 1951. Hilton used his Hollywood connections to attract film stars, politicians, and royalty to the hotel. This occurred in a time when big city hotels were majestic havens, where couples dined with panache, the men in suits or tuxedos, the women in full-skirted cocktail dresses, gloves, and pearls. Diners were fussed over by the waiter who walked from table to table with a white towel draped over his arm as a famous crooner or a woman dressed in a sequined "formal" stood at a carbon microphone and offered a melodic backdrop. In 1948, a sizable, shimmering ice stage was created in the Boulevard Room, which featured luxurious ice shows. It was promoted as the largest hotel ice rink in the country.

"We'd go to the ice show in Chicago at the Boulevard Room," Jim said. "Dad befriended the maître d' Phil Ida who would get us a table next to the rink."

Ice shows featured opulent chorus numbers and variety acts, with the entertainers all donning ice skates as they performed arabesques, backflips, and graceful spins just a few feet from the people dining in front row seats. Ice shows dominated live entertainment for decades. They included glitzy costumes, swooping music, and enormous production numbers enjoyed by the whole family.

"Dad could be extremely demanding," Jim said. "On an occasion, he'd get up and leave if the service was not as expected or if the New York strip steak wasn't cut the way he wanted it. Then Phil Ida would send an 'I'm sorry' cake up to our room to reestablish Dad's respect."

Jim Price was Kirby's friend, but he was also a major client, so when the Risks and Prices went out to dinner, Kirby always wanted to pick up the check. Anne Price remembered a meal where her father turned the tables. Anne said, "We were out to eat at Teibel's, and Kirby had the check. My Dad said, 'I want the check.' Kirby said, 'No.' My dad picked up a cup of coffee and said, 'If you don't give me that check, I'm going to throw this on you.' Kirby looked at him and let him have the check."

Teibel's is a family-owned restaurant that's been open since 1929 in Schererville, Indiana, a town between Lafayette and Chicago. Carol also remembered the check "standoff" between her father and Jim Price. She said, "It taught me a lesson that you need to be able to receive and not just give."

PLEASANT SURPRISE

Caroline wrote in her memory book about the birth of her fourth child. "I am forty-years-old. Carol is a high-school senior, and we have a precious new baby to watch, to teach, to educate—and all of us—to *love*." Julia, also known as Julie, was born July 17, 1952.

Anne Price said, "I remember December 1951, we all went to the Fort Lauderdale Biltmore after Christmas. Then they told us that Caroline was going to have a baby. We were all mortified. We just couldn't believe it." The Price and Risk children and Jane Hovde were between the ages of nine and fourteen when Kirby and Caroline made their announcement that a new baby was on the way.

Jane said, "We were snickering. Kirby was fifty years old when Julie was born. And back then, people at fifty weren't as young as the fifties today."

"Julie was the most loved baby there ever was," Anne said. "My dad wanted to steal her. He loved her so much. All the kids did. I remember, we were in New York, and Dad wanted to kidnap Julie and take her home with him. Kirby said, 'This isn't funny, Jim.' We had a lot of fun."

Caroline wrote in her journal, "Julie brought many joys to the family. She shared her brother's bedroom for a while. He loved showing her off and taking care of her." Brother Jimmy was ten.

Caroline continued, "A new doctor, Frank Peyton, delivered Julie—caesarian section. I stayed in the Home Hospital two weeks and Carol shopped for the little things we needed. Julie used pink, blue and green baby diapers. Her siblings used only white!! Lollypop came to interview and stayed five or six years, adoring Julie."

"Lollypop" was the affectionate name Julie gave to Laura Wolf, a member of the German Baptist Brethren, sometimes known as the Dunkard Brethren, who took care of her and lived in the Risk family's basement apartment.

Laura was a teenager when she came to live in the Risk home. Caroline had to train her in the kitchen and with child care. Laura became part of the family and made everyday tasks and traveling easier on Caroline, providing help with the house, cooking, and care of Julie, both at home and on the road.

Mary Jo said, "We all knew Laura growing up, because if you knew the Risks, you knew Laura. She was at all of our weddings. The Risks took Laura everywhere with them."

Laura's kitchen help was greatly needed as the Risks held work-related or volunteer organization lunches and dinners in their home several times a week, often on back-to-back days. In addition, they hosted meals for Purdue home football games. The schedule they kept, feeding friends, staff, business associates, church groups, and philanthropic societies, seems herculean in the context of today's typical family lifestyle. Regarding the Risk's heavy schedule of dinners, sometimes as often as four evenings in a row, Caroline said, "Kirby thought anything was possible."

Laura also helped emcee a dance performance by Sherry and Mary Jo when they were about twelve. Sherry said:

> Mary Jo and I did dance recitals in the backyard. We had a PA system in the house. Laura was our announcer. We sold tickets to the show. We had a black suit and black hat, and we memorized the song to "Rutza, Rutza" at Mary Jo's house. We played the vinyl record so much it warped, and we had to buy a new one. We had three or four acts, and we changed in the basement. Laura would get on the PA system and introduce the act, and the speaker was hanging on the corner of the garage. I think we served cookies and soft drinks.

Mary Jo said, "That's probably the only way we could get people there."

A formal photograph of the Risk family, taken around 1954.

Sherry continued, "We had chairs set up with probably eight to twelve neighbors watching. We had a hose taped to the birdbath to make a fountain. We ran around the thing singing, 'Hurry, hurry, hurry. Rutza, rutza.' I'm sure it was lovely."

"Rutza, Rutza (Hurry, Hurry)" was recorded by the Bell Sisters in 1952. Heavy on tambourine, trombone, and tympani, the song has a bit of a Russian or "gypsy" sound. "Rutza" is Hebrew, and the root of the word means "to run."

Sherry was the family performer. In high school, she was on the speech team. Caroline's complimentary Hilton calendars from 1957 to 1959 are filled with jottings about speech team competition reminders:

> January 12, 1957: "Sherry, second poetry state speech."
> October 9, 1957: "Sherry on radio."
> February 1, 1958: "Speech contest, Sherry third and fourth
> February 8, 1958: "Sherry at Terra Haute speech, first."
> April 1, 1958: "Sherry selected outstanding senior girl in speech."

Three days after Sherry was selected "outstanding girl in speech," Caroline recorded that her daughter, age eighteen, had the mumps. Dr. Van made a house call. By April 18, Sherry was well and took home a first in "radio" at a speech competition in Monticello, Indiana. In the fall of 1958, Sherry started at Northwestern University as a speech major. On November 17, Caroline wrote, "Sherry called. A in speech!!!"

"Mother and Daddy were very supportive of my speech and my theater," Sherry said. "I was in a number of productions, and they always came up to see them. To commemorate some of those, Mother gave me some beautiful jewelry that Daddy had given her. Walt Disney came to one of my plays. He offered my boyfriend a role in a movie, but he didn't offer me anything. It was pretty heady stuff."

KITCHEN TABLE

The 1950s were before the era of fast food restaurants, and people did not dine out with the frequency that they do today. Kirby and Glenn Safford often ate lunch at the Risk's kitchen table while they talked business. Of course, with Kirby's "night owl" lifestyle, lunch was sometimes his first meal of the day. Caroline wrote many Kirby and Glenn menus on her calendars, "JKR and Glenn for lunch. Brats and Kraut, applesauce, coffee."

At Christmastime, the Risk family gathered to send greetings. Carol said, "We would all sit around the dining room table and stamp and seal the Christmas cards and letters that went to our customers. The letters announced that in their honor there were scholarships at Purdue. We would do it like an assembly line. Dad really engaged us in the business and made us feel very much a part of it."

Kirby also gave stock in the company as Christmas gifts to his children when they were young. Carol said, "Mother was afraid we would be disappointed that it wasn't a toy, so she'd want us to know how significant and important it was. And then many years later, we became members of the board. We'd have board meetings, and Mother was secretary."

Kirby often took Safford to lunch at the Lafayette Country Club. Sometimes, Caroline joined Kirby for lunch there. She wrote on her calendar, "JKR and CRR at LCC." Kirby also brought home the homeless.

Caroline wrote a memory on Kirby Risk Supply Company notepaper years later:

> One noon, Kirby came for lunch with two street "waifs" who he reported were hungry. It was no secret they also needed a bath. It was my assignment to accomplish that—for both boy and girl—with a haircut tossed in. They ate heartily in their new haircuts and clean skins, and then we proceeded to J. C. Penney's to replace some of the worn out clothes.

At that time, J. C. Penney was located on the Courthouse Square in downtown Lafayette at the corner of Third and Columbia Streets.

Mr. McDowell, the manager of J. C. Penney in Lafayette at one time, lived next door to the Risk family. Caroline recalled seeing James Cash Penney himself pull up in front of the McDowell home to visit the manager of his local store.

It was common for Kirby to care for people others overlooked or even looked down upon. Caroline wrote:

> Leon, a young man who was a ward of the court, was turned over to Kirby's care. He got a job with the construction company building the new Eli Lilly plant [near Lafayette]. Leon had a pregnant wife.

Neither was over 17 years old. Lilly's gave the weekly check to Kirby to distribute to Leon as Kirby saw fit. The new baby arrived and with the help of our friends, they were outfitted in their new home. Leon, with his history of taking what wasn't his, served with Kirby's consent as the driver of the car to deliver Risk kids to their various lessons, etc. Nothing bad came of this but not much good, either!

Carol remembered Leon. "Leon had been in jail," she said. "He was on probation, and Dad had stood up for him. And he had him drive us around. I think he got him a room at the Lahr Hotel. He got him a job."

Daughter Sherry said, "One of my memories is that many weekends Dad would go down to the Greyhound bus station on Sunday nights and drive kids back to Purdue. Take them to campus. Sometimes he'd bring them home."

Kirby also picked up hitchhikers. He was fearless in his mission to make mankind his business. Mary Jo said:

> He would pick up people in need and bring them home. Caroline had to have these strays in the house feeding them. She would always put a meal on the table out of the refrigerator. Then a lot of times, Kirby would go lie down on the couch and take a nap, and she'd be left to entertain the new acquaintance. Many of them ended up being really good friends of Kirby's later in life.

Unpleasant Surprise

Four months after the National Homes plane accident that killed Dr. Thomas Graham and injured the Price brothers and five months before Julie's birth, Arnold M. "Chuck" Smith, the vice president of Kirby Risk Supply Company, who shared the position with Glenn Safford, was killed in an auto accident. Chuck and his wife, Arlene, were attending a housewarming party at the new home of Dale Goslee, a former inside salesman for Kirby Risk Supply. The Lafayette *Journal and Courier* story from February 3, 1952 reads: "Smith was backing from a private driveway two miles southwest of the city onto State Road 25 during the heavy fog that blanketed this community

Saturday night and Sunday morning. When Mrs. Smith saw a car approaching through the fog, she jumped from the Smith auto a split-second before the collision."

This photo was taken in 1947 at the Blackhawk Restaurant in Chicago. Chuck Smith (far right) shared the vice president position of Kirby Risk Electric Supply with Glenn Safford. In 1952, Smith was killed in an automobile accident and his wife, Arlene, jumped to safety. Left to right: Arlene Smith, Kirby Risk, Ruth Safford, Glenn Safford, Dora Smith (Kirby's cousin with whom he was raised), and Chuck Smith (no relation to Dora).

Smith was an electrical engineer who started to work for Kirby after his graduation from Purdue University in 1938. Smith was originally from Caroline's hometown of Boswell. Kirby received letters of condolence from his friends at National Electric Products Corporation, Allen-Bradley Company, and Hunter Fan and Ventilating Company. On February 11, Parker T. Finch of Hunter wrote a note on letterhead with the byline, "Manufacturers of ventilating, desk and ceiling fans since 1886":

Dear Kirby,

There is very little that anyone can say when a sudden tragedy like this occurs; however, I know how you must feel and what a loss it will be to you personally and to your organization.

I just want you to know that you have my deepest sympathy and how sorry all of us here at Hunter were when we learned of the accident.

Kirby responded on April 10, 1952, with a thank-you and a sales lead with National Homes, before the days of central air-conditioning:

Dear Parker:

It was nice of you to write me at the time of Chuck Smith's death. His untimely passing left a gap in our organization.

Glenn Safford is now staying in the office practically all of the time and we are extremely thankful that we have Charlie Sweeny to take care of most of Glenn's outside work.

I had noticed in the paper the other day that our weather prophet from Rushville, Indiana, has predicted another cool summer for Indiana. I hope Jim Price did not read the report as he swears by Purcell's reports.

National Homes is again erecting one of their 1952 styles for this year's Home Show and will incorporate a Hunter Fan in the house. I feel sure that if we could start the season out with a good hot spell, we could then sell Jim on incorporating a Hunter Fan in each of his houses.

Should you be passing our way, be sure and stop off for a visit.

Sincerely,
Kirby Risk Supply co., Inc.
By James K. Risk.

Nearly sixty years later, Kirby's son, Jim, said, "Our biggest product line used to be Hunter fans—window, attic, pedestal, and ceiling fans. That was before central air-conditioning."

Before air conditioning was available, Hunter Fans was one of Kirby Risk Supply's largest product lines. Here, Hunter Fans are displayed at a trade show in the 1940s.

On March 29, 1952, Kirby wrote a thank-you letter to his pastor at Central Presbyterian Church, Reverend J. Dayton McCormick. He also enclosed a token of his appreciation:

Dear Dayton,

I question whether you ever stopped to consider how helpful you are when people are faced with almost insurmountable situations. At the time of Chuck's death, you were of great assistance to Arlene and to Carolyn and to me.

Your words at the funeral service were most comforting to all of us who knew Chuck and had lived in such close contact with him.

Will you please use the enclosed piece of paper to acquire some small item that you or your family might like but which you would normally not purchase.

The Risk Family is most happy that the J. Dayton McCormicks decided to move to Lafayette.

Sincerely,
James K. Risk

Throughout their lives, Kirby and Caroline befriended the pastors of Central Presbyterian Church. Patti Peyton Truitt grew up attending Central Presbyterian and was good friends with the Risks. "Caroline and Kirby would reach out to whomever was Central's minister," Patti said. "They had a sense of inclusiveness."

CHAPTER 11

GOD IN US

Patti Peyton Truitt was a member of the vibrant high school youth group that the Risks helped create at Lafayette's Central Presbyterian Church in the mid-1950s. Patti said, "Caroline and Kirby and some of the adults got together and said, 'Why is it that our high-school-age kids aren't going to Sunday school? What can we do? Let's not call it Sunday school. Let's call it something Greek, because that seems to appeal to high school kids right now.' So they came up with the name Epsilon Theta, which stands for 'God in us.'"

One of the other adults who founded Epsilon Theta was Martha Graham, the wife of Dr. Thomas Graham, who died in the 1951 National Homes plane crash. Gene and Lee Bingham were also active in leading the group. The Risks asked Lee to be the Epsilon Theta choir director. Today, Lee and Caroline are still good friends. The Risks helped found Epsilon Theta when Carol, Sherry, and Jim were teenagers. The Price children and Jane Hovde were also members of the group.

"They said it shouldn't be boring; it should be exciting," Patti continued. "So we would have our own little worship service that we would plan ourselves and a lot of fundraisers and banquets. We did plays. In its heyday, when I was in high school, there might have been two hundred kids."

This was 1950s America when the world shut down on Sunday so families could attend church and spend time together. Women wore their best dresses, heels, hats, and gloves to church. Men and little boys wore suits, and even without air-conditioning, in the blaze of summer, they kept their coats on during the service. Available at every pew was a cardboard fan on a stick, often featuring an ad for a funeral home printed on one side and an image of a church on the other. Parishioners sat in the Indiana August heat waving an ad for Hippensteel Funeral Home in front of their faces. Most stores, restaurants, and businesses were closed. No sporting events took place. After church, families visited friends and relatives or took a country drive. It was a day of worship and rest. It was Sunday.

"I was involved in the steering committee, and we'd go over to Risk house and Caroline and Kirby would have cookouts in the backyard," said Patti. She continued:

> Everything was planned to be really fun. They were fun loving, and so they could make any situation fun through their hospitality. And their hospitality wasn't concentrated on adults. It was really concentrated on their children and their children's friends and outreach. So whenever we would have a planning, steering committee meeting or whatever, they'd always say, "Come early, come for hamburgers," and just sort of open up their yard and their home to us.

Once a month the members of Epsilon Theta were responsible for the entire worship service at Central Presbyterian, giving a Bible reading, sermonette, and more. The Epsilon Theta Choir practiced once a week and sang at the monthly service led by the group.

Caroline and Lee Bingham worked with the kids who were participating in the Sunday service. During the week, Caroline and Lee met with the young person in charge of the sermon to review and help with delivery. "Caroline was amazing, gracious," said Patti. "She just kind of cut to the heart of things, and that's why with teenagers she was so good. She wasn't trying to be palsy-walsy. She was always the responsible adult who was understanding."

Caroline and Kirby's soft spot for children played a great part in their relationship with Patti and her circumstances at the time. Patti's father was Dr. Frank Peyton, who was the "new doctor" in Lafayette. He had delivered the Risk's "late-in-life" Julie.

"My parents were divorced when I was in seventh grade," Patti explained. "My stepmom was my mother's sister who my dad married. But she was like my best friend. She was wonderful. And so it really wasn't as bad as it might have appeared to other people. I didn't consider it a hard time, and in retrospect, I think there were positive things that came out. Maybe Caroline and Kirby said, 'Well, we're going to step in and show Patti extra love.'"

The fact that Kirby and Caroline wanted to make Epsilon Theta engaging and different is evident in a one-page report found in a file Caroline kept from her Epsilon Theta days. The Risks and other leaders of the high school group didn't institute "religious literature" traditionally used in the Sunday schools at Central Presbyterian. The report states:

> From this review it was apparent that the Epsilon Theta group is the only department which does not use the regular curriculum material. It is the opinion of the committee that no attempt should be made to force the regular curriculum material upon Epsilon Theta. By arranging and conducting their own programs, the members obtain much good training and experience.

Epsilon Theta programs included a class with Bible discussion, movies, guest speakers, a monthly sanctuary service and breakfast, the Epsilon Theta choir, election and induction of officers, steering committee meetings, picnics at the farm of Central Presbyterian member and Assistant Dean of the Purdue School of Agriculture David Pfendler, Christmas caroling, chili suppers, talent shows, and the Easter Sunday sunrise service at Lafayette's Columbian Park.

The Easter sunrise service conducted by Epsilon Theta was held at the amphitheater on Memorial Island in Columbian Park at 6:30 a.m. Group members learned of upcoming activities when they received the "Teen-O-Gram," Epsilon Theta's handwritten newsletter, which looks like it was copied on a mimeograph or "ditto machine". A ditto machine is a "spirit duplicator," a low-volume printing method used mainly by schools and churches because no electricity was needed to make quick, smelly copies. The term "spirit duplicator" refers to the alcohols, which were a major component of the solvents used as "inks" in these machines. Nothing smells quite like a fresh, slightly wet ditto copy.

The "Teen-O-Gram" dated April 10, 1955, preserved in Caroline's file, states that the members of Epsilon Theta were to be at the sunrise service at 6:00 a.m., with the choir reporting at 5:15. Carol Risk's best friend Anne Price, daughter of Jim Price, is listed as the teen to deliver prayers and scriptures.

Patti recalled:

> Epsilon Theta did a community sunrise service at Columbian Park's Memorial Island. It was fairly new then because it was a memorial to everybody who lost his or her life in World War II. I had the fun of doing the sermon my senior year. That would have been spring of 1957. I remember being out there with Caroline the day before, testing voice and microphone. I remember hearing, "He is risen!" And it bounced back. "He is risen! He is risen! He is risen!"

Caroline saved the printed program from the 1957 Easter sunrise service. Patti's sermon was entitled "The Glory of the Risen Christ." Jane Hovde and Jim and Sherry Risk were among the one hundred teenagers wearing robes, holding hymnbooks, and singing in the Epsilon Theta Choir. They stood on the amphitheater stage of Memorial Island—actually, a peninsula jutting into the park lagoon where ducks, geese, and swans paddle by.

At the entrance to Memorial Island is the Tippecanoe County War Memorial created by Park Superintendent Curtis Cointerman and Bert E. Loeb. During 1944, citizens contributed funds to build the

Memorial. However, it could not be built until 1948 because building a structure nonessential to the war effort was prohibited until that year. During the four-year wait, material and labor costs increased, and a fountain that was part of the original plan was omitted for lack of funds.

Loeb and his wife, June, donated money to build many significant structures in Greater Lafayette. In 1940, they donated $50,000 to honor Solomon Loeb, Bert's father, who owned Loeb's Department Store in Lafayette, with the construction of a baseball stadium at Columbian Park. The field was originally called the Columbian Park Recreational Center. In 1971, it was officially renamed Loeb Stadium.

Bert and June Loeb contributed more than $1 million in 1958 toward the construction of Loeb Playhouse in Stewart Center at Purdue University. The next year, they contributed monies for the building of Loeb Fountain, originally located on the Purdue Mall in front of Hovde Hall. In 1989, it was relocated to Founders Park near Beering Hall.

In 1971, Bert Loeb donated funds in loving memory of his wife of forty-nine years for the building of the June A. Loeb Memorial Fountain near the Tippecanoe County War Memorial in Columbian Park. After a near thirty-year wait, Memorial Island finally beheld the water feature that was part of its original design. Today, the limestone fountain that once flowed with water sprinkled with make-a-wish pennies tossed in by park visitors is filled with soil and florae; no water flows.

The entire community was invited to the Epsilon Theta Easter sunrise service, and a three-quarter-page ad was placed in the Lafayette *Journal and Courier* to encourage citizens to attend. Approximately seven hundred people arrived.

As the audience members sat in the metal seats of the amphitheater in their Easter bonnets and felt fedoras, the Epsilon Theta Choir paraded onto Memorial Island. They had gathered at the break of dawn, near a little white building that in the summertime was the "snow ball" stand or what today we call "shaved ice." The group marched two-by-two past the War Memorial's bronze plaque, affixed

The Central Presbyterian Church youth group, Epsilon Theta, conducted the Easter sunrise service on Memorial Island at Columbian Park, Lafayette, Indiana, in 1955.

into cement on a limestone base and flanked by cement eagles. The plaque lists those from Tippecanoe County who lost their lives in the Civil War, Spanish-American War, Mexican War, World War I, and World War II. (In the years to come, plaques would be added listing Tippecanoe County citizens who lost their lives in subsequent wars.)

The fresh-faced teens, prepped and propelled by Caroline and directed by Lee Bingham, filed onto the amphitheater stage as the processional hymn "Crown Him with Many Crowns" was played on the borrowed electric organ. A permanent sign rose above the proscenium that read, "A Living Memorial."

The Monday after Easter 1955, Reverend Dayton McCormick penned a letter of gratitude to Kirby and Caroline. It read in part:

Caroline Risk helped direct the Epsilon Theta youth group community Easter sunrise service in the late 1950s. Approximately seven hundred people attended the service at Columbian Park, Lafayette, Indiana.

Yesterday was a tremendous demonstration of the strong foundation you have succeeded in building under Epsilon Theta. The "Spirit" was so evident. There was a "lift" in their faces, their voices. It was obvious they knew they were on a winning team again. To Coaches Risk, I do off my hat! Your TWA dinner, your home hospitality your securing Lee as choir director . . . it adds up to as significant a contribution—if not THE—as has been made to Central's entire work all year.

May God continue to bless your entire family.
Dayton

A week later on April 11, 1955, Albert P. Stewart, the renowned director of the Purdue Musical Organizations who often sported an effervescent, toothy grin, wrote a letter to Caroline and Kirby on Purdue's Hall of Music stationery. Five years before, Kirby had helped with fundraising for the Purdue Varsity Glee Club's first European tour. Stewart's daughter, Sonya, was a member of Epsilon Theta. The letter reads:

> This is a note of *THANKS*. Thanks, first—as a parent most appreciative of your help and inspiration to our daughter. Thanks, second—as a citizen who has a deep and sincere appreciation of unselfish people. Thanks, thirdly—as a member of Central Church who recognizes service far over and above the call of duty. You are truly doing a wonderful thing. May God bless both of you, and yours.
>
> Most cordially,
> Al

The TWA dinner, to which Reverend McCormick referred in his note, occurred just a few weeks before the Easter sunrise service. It was a musical/fundraiser with a TWA (Trans World Airlines) theme. Caroline still has the blue program from the evening. The cover has a drawing of a twin-propeller plane and the words, "Flying High—Beyond the Blue Horizons." The performance was billed as "Flight #1955—Non Stop." Anne Price, Patti Peyton, Carol Risk, and Al Stewart's daughter, Sonya, were among the "stewardesses" performing. David Price was one of the many "stewards."

It seems like a monumental undertaking to plan a musical with nearly one hundred teenagers, who performed on March 3 and again on March 28, and pull off a community sunrise service with that same team of youth. Yet it may have been part of the Kirby and Caroline design to keep their own teenagers occupied so they not veer off the path of right living.

Anne Price recalled:

> Our parents worked together to keep us busy. Life was so simple then. Kirby was so interested in young people. He was so smart.

I was fortunate that our families got to do those things. I learned how important your family time is. You're an adult, so you can help make it easier for your kids if you want to invest the time to try to do it. I was very active in Epsilon Theta. I think Kirby and Caroline both had servant hearts.

In the summer of 1956, Epsilon Theta created their own space at Central Presbyterian called the "Upper Room." Jim and Roberta Price donated furniture for the new haven. A letter sent to Epsilon Theta by President Susie Harshbarger states, "The latest and best news yet is that Dave's parents, the James Prices are furnishing the Upper Room . . . This includes book cases, table, chairs, typewriter and lamps. How can we ever say, 'Thank you' enough! This means a room furnished so as to give a worshipful atmosphere for us as we get together for committee meetings and to prepare our morning devotionals and sermonettes."

It would be fair to speculate that Kirby asked Jim and Roberta if they would donate the furniture. Their daughter, Anne, said, "If Kirby saw something that he thought needed to be done, he would go to my Dad and say, 'There's a need. Jim, help me do that.' And then my Dad would do it."

As the years progressed and the original teenagers of Epsilon Theta graduated high school and left Lafayette for college, the group invited alums to return and sing on Easter Sunday or visit during other holidays. By 1959, Kirby and Caroline decided to step down as organizers. In May, a handwritten letter was drafted to parents at Central and signed "Your loving Teenager." It says:

Dear Folks,

No—I don't need money, but I sure do need your help. You know how much I've enjoyed Epsilon Theta . . . Well, they told us today, Mr. and Mrs. Kirby Risk are going inactive and will no longer be our sponsors. What a low blow! They're the greatest, and we'll sure miss 'em. Gosh—they've been with us since I've been a member. But after 5 years, I guess it is someone else's turn to help. . . .

Could you help just a little bit somehow, sometime?? All sorts of interesting things are available 'cause they've divided the Risk's responsibilities into a dozen or more small jobs.

The note is telling as to how much time and energy Kirby and Caroline gave to Epsilon Theta. Their tasks were divided "into a dozen or more small jobs" for many parents to share.

In Caroline's "Personal Record and Reference Book for 1959," which she obtained from Hilton Hotels, she wrote on Sunday, May 31, "EΘ last time. Reception for JKR and me. He ill. Couldn't stay. Anne and Duff graduate." (Duff McKenzie would become Anne Price's first husband.) Epsilon Theta had a yearly senior breakfast as their graduating class left the high school fold. This was the year Jim Risk graduated from high school and left Lafayette to attend Duke University. Julie, the Risk's youngest, would not be in high school for another few years, so Caroline and Kirby were stepping down from Epsilon Theta as the last of their three oldest children left the group.

On December 27, 1960, Epsilon Theta hosted a coffee gathering for alums returning to town on Christmas break. The typed flyer advertising the event to returning college students was written in the vernacular of the popular beatniks of the time who read poetry in coffeehouses. The entire note is written in lowercase type:

salutations!

here's your chance, man! motivate down to the educational building of the central pres pad this tuesday, december 27, 1960, from 7:00 to 9:00. like it's going to be a way out party . . . so beat that a pair of bongos would be put to shame! to the accompaniment of expresso [sic] (café coppacino [sic]), dim lights, greetings from other epsilon theta alums, and way-out conversations, you are invited to air your philosophies, read poetry, sing folk songs, and like that.

uncurl your locks, kick off your shoes, grab your existentialist friends and arrive.

like that's an order!!!

The 1950s were over; the Risks had moved on, and Epsilon Theta also shifted forward, changing with the beat of the new decade.

CHAPTER 12

OPEN-DOOR POLICY

Kirby and Caroline moved on to devote their caring ways to help Cuban refugees who arrived in Lafayette with the help of the Presbyterian church. The arrival of Cuban immigrants to America began with the rumblings in Cuba in the 1950s and Fidel Castro. After his successful guerrilla campaign to take down dictator Fulgencio Batista's regime in 1959, Castro served as the country's prime minister, first secretary of the Communist party, president, and commander in chief. He stepped down in 2008. He was a controversial ruler, both revered and despised.

Cubans began to flee their homeland from 1959 through 1962 following the rise of Castro. His regime alienated the upper and middle classes and confiscated hundreds of millions of dollars in private property, nationalized industry, health care, and education. Subsequently, the initial exodus of Cubans consisted primarily of upper and upper middle class families in professional and managerial occupations. Then the historic Bay of Pigs fiasco occurred.

The Bay of Pigs is the name Americans gave to the CIA-sponsored invasion of Cuba. Cubans refer to the Bay of Pigs Invasion as "Playa

Girón," which is a beach on the bay that bears the name "Bahía de Cochinos." In this instance, the translation of "Cochinos" is not "pigs," although pigs are also called cochinos. Cochinos is the name of a fish, thus the "Bay of the Fish, Cochinos."

In 1960, the CIA set up special training camps in Florida, Alabama, and Louisiana for recruitment of Cuban exiles to form Assault Brigade 2506. The Brigade's mission was to land in Cuba and attempt a military overthrow of the government. When these American-trained Cuban exiles left the coast of Florida on the night of April 16, 1961, they thought they were sailing to take back their homeland from Castro's grips. Instead, they sailed into one of the most misunderstood and disparaged chapters of America's Cold War.

On April 17, 1961, these 1,400 people landed in the mosquito-infested inlet off of Cuba's southern coast and were ambushed. Due to leaks within the U.S. Department of State, the Cuban government had prior knowledge of the invasion and sent their troops to await the unsuspecting, American-trained exiles. The week before, the CIA had become aware of the leak, yet proceeded with the ill-fated plan to invade.

Initially, the battle looked promising. American planes struck at Cuban air force bases and destroyed Cuban planes on the ground. But the tide quickly turned on the rebels. Some historians say President Kennedy was anxious to cover up America's role and inexplicably called off all American air support, leaving the exiles stranded on the beach. In *Jacqueline Kennedy, Historic Conversations on Life with John F. Kennedy*, published in 2011, the president's wife writes of the moment her husband received word that air support should cease. The Kennedys were in their bedroom when there was a phone call from Secretary of State Dean Rusk. Rusk advised the president to cancel the air strike. Jacqueline Kennedy continues, "Jack just sat there on his bed, and then he shook his head and just wandered around that room, really looking in pain almost, and went downstairs, and you just knew he knew what had happened was wrong."

Over a course of two days, the men of Assault Brigade 2506 were either killed or captured by pro-Castro forces. In the end, 114 died and nearly 1,200 languished in Cuban prisons for almost two years until the Kennedy administration paid more than $50 million in food, medicine, and cash for their release. A number of American pilots died in action because they refused to abandon the exiles.

Just five days before the slapdash invasion, President Kennedy had emphatically told the media that the United States would not make any sort of intervention in Cuba under any conditions. The debacle caused Kennedy to lose faith in the CIA. Jacqueline Kennedy said:

> when it happened, . . . it was in the morning—and he came back over to the White House to his bedroom and he started to cry, just with me. . . . —just put his head in his hands and sort of wept. And I've only seen him cry about three times. . . . And he cared so much. . . . all those poor men who you'd sent off with all their hopes high and promises that we'd back them and there they were, shot down like dogs or going to die in jail. He cared so much about them.

Afterward, Castro publicly branded the United States as an enemy of Cuba. Yet Cuban immigrants continued to take refuge in America, including Lafayette, Indiana.

Pedro Granadillo Jr. was fourteen when he and his parents, Pedro Sr. and Zoraida, arrived at the Purdue University Airport via Lake Central Airlines. They soon became acquainted with the Risk family. Pedro Sr. was a Presbyterian national missionary who had taught mathematics and accounting for twenty-five years at La Progresiva, Cárdenas, Cuba, the Presbyterian National Missions School.

Fifty years later, Pedro Jr., age sixty-four, explained:

> It was well-known that Dad was not supporting the Castro regime. He wasn't doing anything wrong; he just didn't support it. During the Bay of Pigs in April 1961, Dad went into hiding. Then, when it was clear that the invasion was not going to work out, he came out of hiding. He was arrested and taken to a camp out in farmland surrounded by wire fences where they put males who were against the government. Dad was lucky enough that he was released five days afterwards. Then Mom and Dad decided it was time to leave Cuba.

The Granadillos obtained visas to go to Jamaica, part of the British Commonwealth. They couldn't come to the United States because Cuba had no relations with America. Even though the family had secured visas, the problem was finding seats on an airplane out of Cuba.

Pedro Jr. said, "One of the ministers at the Presbyterian Church in Cuba happened to know somebody. We didn't know who this person was. Turned out, my parents learned years later that it was the person running the airport in Havana. We were told to show up at seven in the morning and see if there would be seats for us."

Pedro's parents were instructed to give a priority list as to who in their family of three would get the first available seat, second available, third available. Pedro Jr. recalled, "I'm not really sure of the order. At one time, I thought it was me, my Dad, and my Mom, but later I got the sense from my Mom that it was really going to be my Dad if only one person could go. Because my father had been taken away, my Mom and Dad were worried about it."

The first day the Granadillo trio arrived at the Havana airport, there were no available seats on the airplane. The second time they showed up, all three obtained seats to Kingston, Jamaica, the first stop on the way to their new lives in North America, which they thought would be a temporary place to live until they could return to their homeland after the Castro regime was over.

The Granadillos were in Jamaica for about two weeks, living in a house provided by someone in the Presbyterian church to be used for the Cubans who were fleeing. They took a bus to the US Embassy there and obtained visas to the United States, landing in Miami, Florida, at the end of June 1961.

Pedro Jr. said, "One of the YMCA facilities in Miami was helping to relocate Cubans who did not want to stay in Miami. Depending upon your religion, you went to a booth. So we went to the Presbyterian booth, and we were matched with Central Presbyterian Church in Lafayette."

The July 20, 1961, edition of Central Presbyterian's newsletter, "The Chimes" (named after the clarion bells that ring from the church's stone tower), includes a story entitled, "Our New Presbyterian Friends from Cuba." The story reads:

Pedro, Zoraida and Pedro Jr. Granadillo arrived in Lafayette Thursday, July 6 and were introduced to the congregation Sunday, July 9. They stayed with the Thomas McCaw family the first week; now are in an apartment in the Kirby Risk home; and by the time this issue is delivered might be living in their own two-bedroom home, for which the Resettlement Committee, Mrs. Kirby Risk, Chairman, is asking the congregation for its help in furnishing.

Pedro Granadillo Jr., age fourteen, arrives with his parents, Pedro and Zoraida, at the Purdue Airport, West Lafayette, Indiana, on July 6, 1961. The Granadillos were Cuban refugees who lived in the Risk family's basement apartment when they first came to America.

Pedro Jr. remembered, "The first Sunday that we went to church, I just about cried through the whole service. It was a big shock, because the customs and the surroundings, the buildings, everything was different. And I didn't understand English. The only one of us who spoke English was my Dad because he had studied in New York. You miss your friends and the family you left behind. You're in a foreign country. Everything is different, and you don't understand what people are saying to you."

Central Presbyterian member Patti Peyton Truitt recalled of her family's experience, "I can tell it from my father's perspective. The Cuban refugees came into the Purdue Airport. The members of the congregation that were going to adopt the families were at the airport. My father saw a young couple come walking off the plane, and he said, 'They look energetic. I'm going to adopt them.' It was Nancy and Alfredo Lopez. They are in Florida. They still call me every Christmas, now that my folks are gone."

Patti's father, Frank Peyton, was an obstetrician in Lafayette (he had delivered the Risk's youngest, Julie). Patti said, "My Dad had them live in the basement of the Woman's Clinic. Made a little apartment for them down there. We worked to get jobs for them at the Woman's Clinic."

After Caroline retired from leading Epsilon Theta, she took up the cause of the Cuban Refugee Resettlement Committee and opened up her home for the Granadillo family to live in her basement apartment. Pedro Sr. began working in a local accountant's office. His wife, Zoraida, and Pedro Jr., who was in ninth grade, took English lessons.

Kirby's son, Jim, and Mary Jo Mohlman Risk were sophomores in college and dating the summer the Granadillos arrived in Lafayette. They took Pedro Jr. under their wing. Pedro recalled, "The people in Lafayette were incredibly friendly to our family and helpful. I can't say enough about the Risks. We felt like we were part of their family. Jim and Mary Jo took me out just about every night for a little while. Caroline had a 1959 convertible, and they used to take me to the Frozen Custard. It was kind of Jim and Mary Jo to take a fourteen-year-old out who doesn't speak the language."

Mary Jo remembered the car. "Caroline had a beautiful convertible Packard that was cream and blue," she said. "It had a beautiful leather interior. Just gorgeous and huge. Cars were bigger then—tanks. Many times a bunch of us would get in the car and Jim would drive us somewhere. Jim and I used to take Pedro out and do things with him; we took him bowling."

The Granadillos had landed on Lafayette soil in July 1961, and they had settled into the Risk's basement apartment when just a few weeks later, Pedro Sr. was contacted by a Presbyterian mission school in Utah, asking if he would like to teach there.

Pedro Jr. said, "You have to understand that most Cubans who left at that time thought they'd be in the US for two or three years and eventually go back. You don't think you are here permanently."

So the Granadillos, after being in Lafayette for a short time, moved to Utah and lived there for two years. Pedro Jr. explained, "Mom and Dad felt that Utah was a tough place to live. We were in the middle of the Wasatch Mountains. The town had 1,200 people. It was like you were in the middle of nowhere."

Even though the Granadillos had lived with Kirby and Caroline for just six weeks, the Risks kept in close touch with the family when they were in Utah, traveling there for a visit, calling, and writing letters. Pedro Jr. continued, "I think that there is a theme in here about deep care. Think about it. I would say that most families, if they have people stay with them for six weeks, and those people move out to Utah, most people would follow up a little bit—a Christmas card—but not this family. Kirby and Caroline cared about my Mom and Dad. They were worried about them."

When the Granadillos considered a move from Utah to Puerto Rico, Kirby and Caroline talked them out of the idea and persuaded them to move back to Lafayette. In a scrapbook/photo album Caroline compiled years later, which she titled "Treasured Memories and Foreign Friends," she wrote:

> Pedro [Sr.] felt guilty not working for the church, so they left to go to Presbyterian School, Wasatch Academy in Utah. Kirby and I visited them there—maybe twice. They didn't complain, but it was frigid cold—they didn't even have a furnace, and it was a second-class school. Pedro felt the language was a burden for Zora [his wife] and called us to say he'd like to go to Puerto Rico. Kirby had a fit!!

Pedro Jr. said:

> I remember Kirby advising my Mom and Dad not to go to Puerto
> Rico. Which, quite frankly, was probably one of the best pieces of
> advice my parents ever got. I think that would have been a huge
> disappointment for them and for me. Puerto Rico has a lot of is-
> sues—crime and drugs. I'm not sure what kind of education I would
> have gotten. I certainly would not have been able to go to Purdue.
> My Mom and Dad didn't have any money. I paid my way through
> school working at Kirby Risk.

When the Granadillos returned to Lafayette in the summer of 1963,
they once again lived in the Risk's basement. Pedro Sr. taught at what
is today Frontier School in Brookston, north of Lafayette. Pedro's
mother was a seamstress at J.C. Penney downtown on the square. Pedro was a junior at Jefferson High School on North Ninth Street.
After school, he walked to Ferry and Third Streets to work at Kirby
Risk Electric in shipping and receiving. The following January, Pedro
met his wife, Barbara, a local girl who was also a junior at Jefferson
High School. Barbara's parents owned Sites Grocery Store in Lafayette. They both attended Purdue. In 1970, Pedro Jr. graduated with a
degree in industrial engineering. Barbara earned a bachelor's degree
in speech, pathology, and audiology as well as a master's degree in
audiology and speech sciences.

Kirby's genuine interest in others and his ability to see other's
needs, pain, and attributes made him a wonderful advisor on life and
business.

Pedro Jr. remembered:

> When I was in my senior year at Purdue, I interviewed at a number
> of companies, and I had narrowed it down to Proctor and Gamble
> and Lilly. I remember going to talk to Kirby about what he thought.
> What advice could he give me? I had already looked at apartments
> in Cincinnati. I liked Cincinnati. I liked the Cincinnati Reds. I was
> really quite intrigued with what Proctor and Gamble had shown me.
> But Kirby talked about the Lilly family and their values and what
> they stood for, what they do for communities. I got attached to all

of that, and I ended up going to Lilly in Indianapolis. Kirby had more influence on me to go with Lilly than anyone else, which, of course, I have zero regret. It is a wonderful company, and I felt very privileged to serve them in many different capacities.

Pedro Jr. joined Eli Lilly and Company, rising to become one of their top officers, serving as a senior vice president of global manufacturing and human resources and retiring at a rather young age. Pedro Jr. and Barbara live in Naples, Florida. Jim and Mary Jo Risk have a vacation home near their residence. The two couples stay in contact and vacation together. In 2005, Pedro Jr. and Barbara gave funds to establish Purdue University's Pedro Granadillo Professor of Industrial Engineering.

Pedro Jr. said, "The first American money I ever earned was mowing the Risk's lawn. It was a silver dollar. My mom kept it and had it embedded into a Plexiglas cube. I still have it."

Mary Jo recalled:

> The Cuban refugees were professional people who came here with no worldly possessions. What a horrible thing. They got out with the clothes on their backs. Most of them didn't speak English, or if they did, it was a very small amount. You'd go to dinner and you'd have a little bit of push and pull to try to figure out what everybody was saying. These were really classy, honest, good people—hard workers who would end up being your best friend. They really did. The women were very close to Caroline.

Pedro Jr. said, "My Mom and Dad thought of Kirby and Caroline as their best friends or parents. The love was pretty deep."

The Risks helped several Cuban families throughout the 1960s. Pedro Jr.'s Uncle Gaspar and Aunt Mirian Bejarano came to Lafayette in 1967. Both worked for Kirby Risk Corporation. Jim said, "Gaspar was our CFO until he took medical retirement and passed away a few years after. We were probably the closest to them, because I worked with Gaspar and Mirian for years. They watched everything unfold. Mirian is almost closer than a son or daughter in feelings toward my mother."

Caroline became close, lifelong friends with the Cuban refugee women and their families who lived in the Risk family's basement apartment when they arrived in the United States in the 1960s. Caroline, Zoraida Granadillo, Lens Hernandez, and Carol Risk are shown here on Easter Sunday, 1967.

Another Cuban couple was Angel and Lens Hernandez. Pedro Jr. said, "Mom and Dad and Angel and Lens were the best of friends in Cuba. My parents were their son Diego's godparents. When we went to Utah, my parents recommended Angel and Lens to the church because they knew they were in Miami. Then Caroline and Kirby did exactly the same thing they did with us. Angel was an accountant and he took the job that my Dad had originally." The first job in the United States that both Pedro Sr. and Angel held was with the CPA office of C. D. D'Aust in Lafayette.

Like the Granadillos, the Hernandez family began their stay in Lafayette living in the Risk's basement apartment. Before immigrating, Angel, who had a gregarious smile and great sense of humor, had been business manager of all Presbyterian schools in Cuba, which was sponsored by the Board of National Missions of the United Presbyterian

Church in the United States. Eventually, Angel worked as assistant treasurer and manager of investment accounting at National Homes Acceptance Corporation. Then he became an executive vice president at Lafayette Savings Bank and later, vice president of Soller-Baker Funeral Homes. Angel gave time to Central Presbyterian Church and many Lafayette community needs. He received the Americanism Medal from the Daughters of the American Revolution, the highest and most prestigious award bestowed by the DAR upon a naturalized American citizen. He passed away in 2011.

Jim said:

> Angel was a gregarious, fun guy. Just wonderful. The common theme with all of these people was their integrity, their honesty, their commitment to doing what was right. Hard work. Pedro's father was one of the most respected people in the Cuban community, and that followed here. Not because of money, but just because of his honesty and integrity. It just exuded from him. He was handicapped because of the language, but wow. He had a positive impression on me and on his son.

Kirby and Caroline also invited international students from Purdue to their house for dinners. Mary Jo recalled, "They would be there for holidays. I remember the first one was Mani Subramanian from Madras, India. The first meal he ate with us was on Thanksgiving. Well, he didn't eat any meat or eggs. It was difficult. Caroline was trying to fix some rice for him. We still keep in contact with Mani. He ended up marrying an American girl and eating meat, rare. Things change."

When Mani, short for Mahadevan, wanted to marry his wife, Ruth, an American, his brothers and parents were uncertain of the union. His family visited the United States, and the wrinkles formed by the "mixed" relationship were smoothed out with the help of Kirby. Jim said, "A family like Mani Subramanian's comes from India to inspect what is going on, never having been to the States. Dad took them for a four-day visit to New York City—just to show them a slice of America. Dad got the marriage 'blessed.' So Mani married Ruth, and they've had a great family."

In the late 1970s, Mani was a professor of electrical engineering at Purdue University where his research was instrumental to the creation of the promising, small, portable "ruby laser."

There is a long list of international students whom Kirby brought home and Caroline entertained, sometimes with the help of Jim. Jim said, "There were many students. I developed close relationships with most. I'd take Mani out to shop and come back and cook curry at two in the morning. Mom would entertain them. Dad would initiate it. Mom would execute it."

As when Kirby picked up the homeless and brought them to Owen Street for Caroline to feed, bathe, and clothe, he brought home international students and left much of the hosting to Caroline and their children.

A Hawaiian boy, Kimo Kaholakula, was discovered during a Purdue Varsity Glee Club tour accompanied by Kirby and Caroline. The Risks were major benefactors of the choral group, making some of their trips possible. Al Stewart, director of the Varsity Glee Club, said years later, "We were in Hawaii and we were on a boat. There was a boy entertaining, and as I left the boat I said, 'You're pretty good. Are you going to go to college? Why don't you come to Purdue? We have a good school.' I walked off the boat. Kirby stayed back."

Two weeks later, Kirby told Al that he had made arrangements for Kimo to live with the Risks and attend Purdue. Jim explained, "He was here in 1969. And he ended up being a favorite performer in the Glee Club. He went back to Hawaii because he was homesick and didn't like the cold weather here."

In Caroline's "Treasured Memories and Foreign Friends" scrapbook, she crafted a list of those from overseas whom she and Kirby loved and helped. There are seventeen names on the list, with the Granadillos being the first to arrive in 1961. Others who became like family were from Hawaii, India, China, Korea, Africa, Mexico, Kuwait, and Greece. The scrapbook is filled with letters from international Purdue students, their parents, and grandparents. Some letters from students begin, "Dear Mama and Papa Risk," or "Happy birthday, Papa Kirby." There are numerous photos of special moments experienced by the Risk's extended global family. Snapshots of weddings, babies, and graduations pepper the memory book. Birthday and Christmas cards from across the world are filled with notes of gratitude and genuine adoration for Kirby and Caroline. On September 9, 1969, the grandmother of Kimo Kaholakula wrote:

> Let me introduce myself. I am Kimo's grandmother, Mary Kaholakula living on the Island of Maui. First of all, I want to thank you both from the bottom of my heart for what you are doing for my grandson. . . . My heart is so full of gratitude knowing that some one wonderful as you two are taking such good care of my grandson, Kimo. His many friends and former teachers will be happy to know that he is going to Purdue.

A photo accompanies the letter. Mary and her dog "Sparky" stand outside in front of a shiny dark blue Buick, with a backdrop of palm trees and blue skies. Mary wears a pink checked housedress, her grey hair is pulled back, and her dark skin and wide features speak of her Hawaiian ancestry.

In 1974, the Risk's youngest child, Julie, was one of just a few female graduates from Purdue's Krannert School of Management. After she graduated and was in the workforce, she understood that her upbringing was not the norm. Julie recalled:

> I didn't realize how lucky we were growing up until I worked at General Motors. Diversity was such huge issue in the 1970s and 1980s. I can remember being sent to some conferences that were on diversity. It was like, "I don't get this." Because growing up we had Cubans living in our house; we had people from India living in our house; we had Hawaiians living in our house. We had black people who were great friends. I had a true appreciation of being taught to be genuine to all. I was never aware that it was out of the ordinary until I was probably thirty. I was sitting in these conferences, and they'd go around the room and ask if anyone had any diverse experiences. And many didn't, or if they did they were all negative. I told my story, and their jaws dropped. I had the real

"a-ha" moment when I was at that diversity seminar. I almost felt
like I was bragging, because they could hardly believe it.

The Cuban immigrants and international students the Risks helped
became lifelong friends. Once the refugees moved into their own
homes, they continued to drop by the Risk home for visits, often
bringing Kirby one of his favorite things—dessert. As time marched on
and the international students married, Kirby and Caroline attended
all of their weddings.

Kirby's favorite song was "Mankind Should Be My Business." He
loved hearing the tuxedo-clad young men of the Purdue Varsity Glee
Club sing the melody that harkens from Charles Dickens' *A Christmas
Carol.* In Dickens' story of the trials, failures, and triumphs that occur
in daily living, Marley's Ghost despairs over "life's opportunities mis-
used," and reveals that the most important force in life is compassion-
ate understanding of our fellow human beings.

Pedro Jr. said, "I don't ever remember Kirby talking about himself.
He never said, 'I accomplished this; and I did this or that.' He asked
a lot of questions. He was more interested in what you were doing,
than for him to tell you what he was doing. Which to me is an incredible characteristic of a leader, which is called humility. I don't ever
remember Kirby expounding about the business. Jim is the same way."

Pedro Jr. saw how Kirby and Caroline used their time to benefit
the Cuban community. He said, "What is really important in my view
with Kirby and Caroline is that they had a willingness to spend time
with this group and help them in many different dimensions. Without saying it, their way of helping you was to open the door a little bit.
It was, 'I'm not going to give you fish, I'm going to teach you how to
fish.' That is really important because that is what the US is all about.
They provided opportunity."

Patti Peyton Truitt echoed these sentiments: "Kirby and Caroline
had such a gift for hospitality and reaching beyond themselves to
whomever God put in their basket at the time. Just unselfishness.
They shared their resources and their time. As I get older, I realize

what a special resource time is, and how you spend it is what's important. Kirby and Caroline always had that sense."

Kirby and Caroline's open hearts and open doors continue to give exponentially as Pedro Jr. sits on the boards of several pharmaceutical industries while nurturing a fine retirement life in Florida, making colorful paella, and eating his wife's empanadas and black beans and rice, Kirby's favorite recipe, handed down by Zoraida, Pedro Jr.'s mother.

He recalled, "Until Mom died in 2010, a picture of Caroline and Kirby was on her nightstand."

CHAPTER 13

JUST DESSERTS

I ce cream, frozen custard, homemade pie, glazed donuts, and cream horns—confections sweetened Kirby's life and the lives about which he cared. Like everything in his over-the-top life, desserts were done on a scale that tipped overboard and spilled out into the world to leave a sugary trail of happiness.

Pedro Granadillo Jr., who lived with his family in the Risk basement apartment when he was fourteen, remembered Kirby's treasure chest of churned goodness. He said, "To get to the stairs that went up from the apartment into the Risk's kitchen, we walked through an unfinished section of their old-fashioned basement. In there, they had a deep freeze, and it was filled with ice cream."

Kirby's son, Jim, recalled:

> At that time in the summer of 1961, Baskin-Robbins had a store in Evanston, Illinois, and none in Indiana. I would be up there with Dad, and we would stop into Baskin-Robbins across from the Or-rington Hotel. He'd start ordering Jamoca Almond Fudge, Choc-olate Almond, Pink Grapefruit, Lemon, Chocolate, Vanilla Bean, and Peppermint Stick. I can still remember the specific flavors. We'd

end up getting twelve flavors. We'd get three or four gallons of the more popular ones. The sales clerks would run a knife around the cardboard containers and then take a wire and cut through the ice cream. The staff would get so tired; I'd get behind the counter and help them. They would pack our order in dry ice. We would bring back twenty-four gallons of ice cream.

Kirby and Caroline served ice cream and frozen custard at many church and community get-togethers in their home, when family and friends came to visit, and when Purdue fans gathered for football games.

It's easy to understand why Kirby liked Baskin-Robbins. It was a company founded on the principals Kirby lived by, and it created his favorite food. Two brothers-in-law established what would become Baskin-Robbins in California in 1945, with the dream to build an innovative ice cream store that was a neighborhood gathering place for families. They desired to offer a variety of flavors made with the best ingredients, and they pioneered the concept of franchising in the ice cream industry. Irv Robbins said, "We sell fun, not just ice cream." With thirty-one flavors offered for each day of the month, Baskin-Robbins won Kirby's heart and taste buds.

By the mid-1960s, Baskin-Robbins was an ice cream empire with more than four hundred stores throughout the United States, eventually opening a shop in Lafayette, Indiana. In the 1970s, the chain went international, opening stores in Japan, Saudi Arabia, Korea, and Australia.

Nearly any time Kirby had someone in the car in the spring and summer, he drove past the Frozen Custard stand owned by his friends Charles and Florence Kirkhoff on Wallace Avenue near Columbian Park. Across from Loeb Stadium, the Frozen Custard still churns out ribbons of frozen velvet. Rooftop neon signs shaped like an ice cream cone, sundae, and soda beckon passersby, as locusts drone in the surrounding trees on humid August evenings.

The Frozen Custard was only open during Indiana's warm weather months, so Kirby stocked Baskin-Robbins in his home freezer as fall-back stash in the off months. When the Frozen Custard opened for

Kirby loved ice cream. One of his favorite haunts was the Frozen Custard stand in Lafayette, Indiana. He treated his children and their friends, his staff, business associates, and the numerous people who visited his and Caroline's home with mounds of ice cream.

the season, it was a sign of spring like the first robin or blooming dandelion. Caroline wrote in her 1957 Hilton calendar on March 30, "Frozen Custard opens." The next year, on Tuesday, April 29, she wrote, "Open house at Market Square. Served three quarts of Frozen Custard, cake and cookies."

Market Square is an outdoor shopping mall built by National Homes Corporation. For years it boasted a 3-D sign resembling stacked children's alphabet blocks that rose into the air spelling out—M-A-R-K-E-T-S-Q-U-A-R-E. The primary colored "blocks" called 1950s shoppers to a new era of consumerism. Caroline helped the Prices with the open house for the novel merchandise mecca. When it opened in 1958, Market Square was the latest in prefab shopping centers near neighborhoods created by National Homes and beholding fine stores like L. S. Ayres. For Lafayette, Market Square was one of the first pulls of commerce to the suburbs and away from downtown.

Jim's wife, Mary Jo, said of her father-in-law, "Kirby was one of a kind. There's no way you can pigeonhole him. But he did like to have a good time. Caroline always said, 'I don't know what I'd do if he drank, because he's wild enough without drinking. If he drank, he would be off the wall.' She said at least she knew that when he got in a car and drove somewhere, if he was high, it was on ice cream. It was a sugar high."

Kirby loved kids as much as he did ice cream, and often, he combined the two in his eye-popping Packard. Family friend Anne Price McKenzie Goodnight said, "We called Kirby's car 'the hearse' because it was black and it had jump seats. Lots of us kids could get in it. In Lafayette it was really a fancy deal, because it was big, like a limousine. We didn't have vans back then. Kirby would pile everyone in and drive us around. If we had a crush on a boy, he would drive in front of his house, and we'd all get down on the floor. He loved doing that stuff. He made it so fun."

This was the late 1950s and early 1960s when air-conditioning was nearly unheard of in homes and most certainly not available in automobiles. But Kirby's ice cream fetching, kid-toting "hearse" was equipped with AC. Pedro Jr. said, "It was the first car I ever saw with air-conditioning."

Jim explained, "It had clear cylinders in the back window that threw the cooling out from the air-conditioning unit in the trunk."

Pedro continued, "Going with Kirby to the Frozen Custard was an experience. He would always go to the window where Elinor was. He'd order for everybody. If you ordered one dip, he'd give you two. Chocolate nut sundae was what I used to love to get."

Elinor Stingly was the crusty custard captain at the "cone window." She would have been in her early fifties when Kirby's kids were in high school and he was chauffeuring them to belly up to Elinor's window. She was known as the "cone lady." There were window rules at the Frozen Custard, and Elinor, with her stone-faced scowl and gruff rebuffs, was the enforcer. Many feared the slight woman in the blue and white paper ice cream hat and matching smock.

Anne Price said, "One time Kirby got mad at the Frozen Custard because he wanted something done differently. So, he would have his kids go up to the window. He would be out in the car, but he wouldn't go up. Something upset him. He wouldn't go up because it was just the principle of the thing."

Jim explained, "They have a policy not allowing mixed flavors. A customer cannot order a scoop of chocolate on top of a scoop of vanilla. Dad just wouldn't accept it. In our business culture, you exceed customers' expectations, and 'can't' isn't a word."

Today, the Frozen Custard enforces many of the same rules (and then some) that it dispatched back when Kirby was pulling up in his Packard. Signs are still posted on windows and walls instructing patrons of each ordering window's purpose. The windows are a mere two feet apart, and the Frozen Custard staff behind the windows stand just an arm's length away from one another. Yet Elinor's cone window was for *cones only*. A patron could not order a soda or sundae at the cone window. If an unsuspecting new customer failed to read the signs, waited in line, approached the cone window, and ordered a chocolate soda back when Elinor was still the cone window warlord, she would bark, "Window over is for drinks! NEXT!" Elinor kept her line moving, and she had no patience for those who couldn't read the notices and abide by the Frozen Custard Magna Carta.

Another sign reads, "We do not mix flavors." In other words, you cannot have one scoop of chocolate and one scoop of strawberry cohabitating, touching like a pink and brown intermarriage, on a singular cake cone. This was the rule set down by Elinor's employers, the Kirkhoffs, which sent Kirby packing to his Packard. But eventually, Kirby and Caroline won over Elinor.

Jim said, "Dad bantered with her. We'd tip her regularly, and we were just dear friends. Mom sent her turkeys at Christmas. Elinor's husband sold popcorn at the Frozen Custard. Their son was my trainer in high school. They just became part of our extended family."

Popcorn was another Kirby weakness, but he didn't eat it in traditional ways. Jim said, "Dad liked to get a cone and popcorn and dip his cone in the popcorn and eat it.' At home, Kirby ate it like cereal. Anne Price recalled, "I can remember being around their kitchen table. Kirby would take popcorn and put milk on it. I watched him eat it, thinking, *oh my gosh*."

With Kirby's finesse for seeing the emotional needs in a person, the buttons to push to answer those needs and make the person glow with acknowledgment, he befriended Elinor. Jim said, "Elinor would stop the whole line and make sodas for us. She kept a picture of Dad and me at the window until she passed."

Jim's sister, Julie, remembered, "I'd come up and say, 'I'm Kirby's daughter,' and she'd pull out the picture."

Elinor passed away in 2009 at the age of 101, having retired from the Frozen Custard when she was 96. She stood sentry over the cone line for fifty-one years.

Throughout his life, Kirby indulged his children, their friends, his grandchildren, and other kids with the joy of dessert. Patti Peyton Truitt tells a story about her boys, Randy and Teddy. "In the mid-1970s, we had gone up to the Purdue/Wisconsin game with a whole bus full of people Kirby and Caroline hosted," she said. "Kirby was talking to Randy and Teddy who were not more than nine and ten. They were in the flag football program, and they were telling Kirby who listened so intently. Kirby said, 'Oh, I'd love to come to one of your games.'"

Kirby attended the Truitt boys' flag football game the following Tuesday night. After the game, he gathered the entire team around him and said, "How would you all like to go to Dunkin' Donuts?" Kirby took the team and many of their parents for donuts, his treat. Patti continued, "Everyone ate their donuts, and we were about to leave, when Kirby said, 'Oh, wait. We're not done. We're going across the street to Baskin-Robbins.' So he took the whole team and bought them ice cream on top of their donuts. He was better than Santa Claus to those little kids. He had time for people of all ages and all positions in life."

With Kirby's whirlwind vivacity, night owl hours, spur of the moment impulses, constant seeking of new ways of commerce, new manners of making mankind his business, new committees to form, execute, and conquer, and dependency on others to clean up the loose ends, one may wonder if today he would have been diagnosed with attention deficit disorder (ADD). It seems Kirby could never put his mind in neutral.

Studies have shown that those with ADD find that eating sugar helps them stay alert, calm, and focused. Or perhaps Kirby liked sweets because of the "serotonin connection." Serotonin is known as the "happy hormone" because the level influences our moods and sense of well-being. One way to temporarily increase serotonin levels is to eat foods that are high in sugar and carbohydrates.

Kirby's unconventional sleeping schedule speaks volumes as well. Researchers have found that many people diagnosed with ADD report that they have trouble sleeping at night, and when they do finally sleep, they have difficult waking. Kirby's high-energy, full-steam ahead, project-oriented life also goes hand-in-hand with what researchers know about ADD. As long as these persons are interested in or challenged by what they were doing, they are engaged. When the person loses interest in an activity, he or she disengages, in search of something more interesting. Sometimes this disengagement is so abrupt that it induces sudden, extreme drowsiness, even to the point of falling asleep.

Roger Swindle, who worked for Kirby beginning in 1954, said:

> Kirby and Glenn Safford's offices were right next to each other at the old place [Third and Ferry Streets]. For years, I went to the post office early each morning, picked up the mail and came in to sort it. Glenn had a huge desk. I would arrive in the morning, and Kirby would be there laying on the desk taking a nap. He had been working there all night. He curled up there and took a little nap. I found him a couple of times like that. He used to have a lady who worked for him as a housekeeper, and she told me that he would sometimes come to the house and say, "Laura, wake me up in ten minutes." He would plop down on the bed for ten minutes and then go do something else.

Today, doctors may be inclined to "diagnose" Kirby, but the bottom line is Kirby managed his life in a way that worked well for him. He accomplished so much in a creative way and bettered the world in the process. He should be commended for fashioning his lifestyle to suit his unusual chemistry and ideals . . . and for marrying the right woman.

Mary Jo recalled:

> He was a very kind man. He kept weird hours, so you never knew when he was going to come over. It was usually late at night when you were sleepy. His hours just weren't the same. Caroline was a saint. Even when Jim and I were dating, Kirby would sleep in until noon sometimes. So you're kind of tiptoeing around. Caroline would wait to see when he got up if he needed something. Her whole life revolved around that. She had to be up at the crack of dawn with kids. I don't know when she really got much sleep. I remember one time, they came over and she said to Jim, "I'm really tired. Dad wanted to go out and get a donut at two in the morning." And she'd been up since six. Jim said to her, "Mom, why didn't you tell him you are too tired?" And Caroline said, "Well, your Dad wanted company."

Caroline was loyal to Kirby and his ways. She never wavered. Perhaps it was because Kirby was eleven years her senior, but it was more likely because she loved and respected him for his compassion, fun, and lavish ways during a time when a woman's place was in the home and the husband was the head of the house. She followed his lead. Mary Jo said, "The thought of saying 'No' or 'I'm too tired' or 'I don't feel well' wasn't the way their life went. Kirby made all of the decisions, and Caroline just had to be ready to go at a moment's notice. He might come home and in five minutes want to go to Chicago. She was expected to be ready. It wasn't a peaceful or simple life, let's put it that way."

From the local Frozen Custard stand, to famous New York eateries, Kirby became friendly with the wait staff wherever he ventured. When in New York City, the Risks frequented Hicks Ice Cream Parlor. Gael Greene wrote about Hicks in "Everything You Always Wanted To Know About Ice Cream But Were Too Fat to Ask," published in the August 3, 1970 issue of *New York Magazine*. Greene describes Hicks as "the venerable fruiterer at 16 East 49th Street," and tells readers that, "Hicks fruit-laced flaming and hot fudge extravaganzas are a special joy." Greene also describes the gentleman behind the counter for twenty-six years as a "manic prankster soda chef" and "a self-styled, loveable tyrant." It sounds as if the fellow emitted shades of Elinor.

Jim recalled:

> Lou Jennings was the famous soda jerk written up in many publications. He wore a red and white striped shirt with garters around the arm. Dad had befriended him to the extent that he recognized me as Kirby's son. He knew what I liked. An unsuspecting customer would order a sundae. Then Lou Jennings would begin creating the order and just keep heaping more ice cream on, and the customer would say, "I don't want all of that." And Lou would place it in front of the customer who continued to complain, and then slide it down in front of me. He could slide a sundae twenty feet down the counter, and it would stop in front of someone. He was sarcastic, too, but funny. It was an experience.

Jim's younger sister, Julie, remembered Hicks for its special salute to her. "We always went to Hicks," she said. "We'd walk in and Lou would shout, 'Julie Julep.' It was a sundae he made for me."

In his article, Greene quotes Jennings: "First God created heaven and earth. Then he created soda fountains. And that is how it should be. Don't let the devil fill your mind with thoughts of calories . . ."

CHAPTER 14

WEDDED BLISS

On January 1 of her 1957 calendar, Caroline wrote of her daughter and her daughter's fiancé who would become another "Jim" in the family. Caroline penned, "Carol and Jim [Lankton] return from Peoria. Carol with *ring*." The following day Caroline jotted, "Julie starts nursery school." As Kirby and Caroline's eldest child was about to marry, their youngest, age four, began preschool.

Kirby knew Jim Lankton through Beta Theta Pi Fraternity at Purdue. Kirby served as director of the house association for eleven years. He organized their fiftieth anniversary celebration in 1953. Kirby invited this bright young man home for dinner, and Jim ended up becoming his son-in-law.

For Caroline, 1957 was sprinkled with wedding plans as she went along with her busy day-to-day life of managing her family of six, working in her front porch-turned-office on Kirby Risk Electric payroll and taxes, traveling in the National Homes plane with the Price family to New York and Chicago, hosting dinners, large and small, leading Epsilon Theta at Central Presbyterian Church, and keeping up with Kirby's helter-skelter schedule.

As little Julie took piano and dance lessons, Sherry attended slumber parties and excelled at Jefferson High School speech meets, Jim played on Jefferson High School's football, basketball, and golf teams, Caroline shopped with Carol for a wedding dress at L. S. Ayres, a department store that was in the new Market Square shopping center built by National Homes Corporation. Sherry went along at the suggestion that she might want to wear the same dress when her wedding "turn" came. Carol and Jim Lankton's nuptials were scheduled for August 25. In April, Caroline began sprucing up the Risk home on Owen, inside and out, for the reception would be in the backyard. Emmett Koehler and his crew from Koehler Brothers Nursery in Lafayette planted and primped the Risk's landscape. In June, Kirby installed air-conditioning in the kitchen. August in Indiana is a very hot month for a wedding. Few homes had air-conditioning in 1957.

Sherry said, "Carol and I both had summer weddings and receptions in the backyard. In both cases, once the decision was made about the wedding, my father started some project on the house. Mother nearly had a nervous breakdown before both weddings because there was something major that had to get done."

Kirby also planned a three-week trip out east in June for Carol to take with her best friend and maid-of-honor, Anne Price. Kirby loved to plan excursions for his children, pulling out maps on the kitchen table, charting itineraries, and booking air flights and tours. Anne said, "Carol was getting married that summer. I don't know how she went on vacation and planned the wedding at the same time. We went in June. It was a wonderful trip."

Carol had been attending DePauw University, but she stopped when she married Jim Lankton. Perhaps Kirby thought she deserved a "last hurrah" before she settled down.

Caroline, who turned forty-five that year, wrote on July 27, "Stayed home all day." It was a novelty for Caroline to be home for an entire day without a volunteer commitment, an appointment for herself or her children, a sporting event, or a meeting—so novel, she recorded the event, which was actually a *nonevent*.

Laura Wolf, who lived in the Risk's basement apartment, helped Caroline prepare the house for the hundreds of guests that would attend Carol's wedding reception. Caroline wrote in her calendar on August 1, "Laura wash and starch Sherry's curtains." On August 14, she wrote, "Polish tops of furniture. Wash living room windows and take curtains down."

The next day, Corrine Clark visited the Risk home to talk about flowers for the wedding. Corrine owned Clark's Flowerland, which was located near Market Square shopping center on Elmwood Avenue. Many Lafayette shopkeepers who were also friends were called into action for the Risk nuptials. As August 25 approached, Caroline's calendar was filled with wedding to-dos. There was an appointment for Carol's photograph in her wedding gown and a party for Carol given by a friend. The rehearsal was August 23 with a dinner afterward at the home of Jim and Roberta Price. The next day there was a tea for the bridesmaids. On August 25, Caroline drew a heart on her calendar encircling the names "Carol and Jim." An arrow pierced the heart and pointed to "4:00," the hour of the wedding at Central Presbyterian Church.

Anne Price said, "Carol's wedding was the most beautiful I'd ever seen. I'd never seen a wedding like that before. They had the reception at home—the whole backyard. It was just so beautiful."

One of the special wedding gifts that day was from artist Marques Reitzel, Kirby's longtime friend whom James Kirby Sr. had helped to attend art school. At that time, Marques, age sixty-one, was living and teaching in Pescadero, California. He gave Carol and Jim Lankton a painting entitled "Blossoms." It depicts a group of rough-hewn barns and shanties in front of a towering metal water tank on a spring day. In the foreground is a tree in bloom, perhaps a dogwood. The sadness of the dilapidated brown buildings contrasts with the tree's lustrous blossoms. Marques passed away in 1963.

The summer after Carol's nuptials, Kirby and Caroline celebrated their twenty-fifth wedding anniversary with a family trip to Hawaii. Just a few months before, in March 1958, the movie musical *South*

Pacific had been released and was a box office success. The movie, filmed in Hawaii, stared Mitzi Gaynor and Rossano Brazzi and was set during World War II. Hawaii would not become a state until the next year when the Hawaii Admission Act was passed and signed by President Eisenhower. On June 27, 1959, Hawaiians voted to join the Union as the fiftieth state. To Americans at the time, Hawaii was paradise on the big screen, sugar planta-

The Risks celebrated their twenty-fifth wedding anniversary the summer of 1958 with a family trip to Hawaii aboard the Lurline. *Pictured here are Kirby, Jim, Julie, Carol, and Caroline.*

tions, luaus, and hula dancers about to become a star on the American Flag.

The Risk's youngest, Julie, said, "I was five when we flew direct to California and got on a ship [the *Lurline*] and sailed to Hawaii. I swam with the Nixon girls. Learned to hula on the ship on the way over." Richard Nixon was the vice president of the United States at the time, and he happened to be in Hawaii with his family at the same hotel as the Risks.

Sherry, the self-described "wild child" of the Risk family ("wild" in the 1950s sensibility) has fond memories of the trip. She said:

> Before the trip, I stayed out later than I was supposed to several times with my drag-racing boyfriend, Ted. I remember my father taking me on the side porch and having one of his serious talks with me. He said that perhaps I would not be able to go with them on the trip. And I said, "Well, that would be fine because I would be at home with Ted." That didn't work. It ended up, I did go with them and had a blast.

The family left Lafayette on June 4 and returned on July 15, but Sherry stayed longer to take a summer session at the University of Hawaii before she would enter Northwestern University as a freshman that fall. Sherry said:

> I signed up for two classes, which to the end of my father's life he loved to tease me about, and that always ticked me off. Because they were serious classes. One class was "art" and the other was "Dances of Hawaii," which was taught by a woman who rarely gave high grades, and I got an "A." I was really proud of that. But my father always loved to tease, "Oh, yeah, Sherry was in Hawaii taking underwater basket weaving." And I'd say, "But it was hard work, and I got an 'A', and nobody else did!" We learned the lovely hula hands and had a long piece of bamboo we used. It was a rhythmic thing. I thoroughly enjoyed it. I gained twenty pounds that summer because I would walk to a little store and have powdered sugar donuts and fresh pineapple every day before I caught the bus to campus or down to the beach. I wore loose-fitting muumuus. I just had a wonderful time.

Sherry was different from her sister, Carol. Sherry recalled:

> Carol was a good student and didn't really date. I don't think she gave our parents much grief. I was dating from the beginning and going steady, which mother couldn't stand. I came in wearing the class ring and the letter sweater, and she said, "Why do you have to have all that stuff?" I got a kick out of dating a guy who had looked like the guy from *Grease*. He had black hair that was swept back, and he wore a leather jacket. He liked to drag race, and I'm sure that gave my parents pause. My father and I had a number of different run-ins and talks of grounding me because I rebelled a bit. So it was a totally different time for them.

Could Kirby see himself in his daughter? In high school, Kirby had rebelled, acted out, and his parents had sent him to Porter Military Academy. His father sent him letters of instruction on how to be a "nice, clean boy" and not cause his mother and grandmother any worry. Kirby liked fast cars. Sherry liked men who owned fast cars.

Kirby was all about fun, traveling, and seeing the world. Sherry stands ready for the next adventure. She is artistic, an actress, a performer. Kirby and his daughter were somewhat alike. The difference is, Sherry was a young woman in 1950 through 1960, and society's post-World War II expectations of women were to get married, have children, and make the perfect home while the husband drove off to work and out into the world. Yet Kirby, even in that era, believed his daughters could do and be anything.

Sherry said:

> My father was hugely liberated about men and women. And my mother was classically traditionally focused. You know the wife takes care of the husband, and make sure you're dressed right for dinner. The man makes the decisions and all that. My father, on the other hand, gave me a totally different message. He said to me, "You can do anything you want. You can be anyone you want." He talked about the possibility of my running the company at some point—that I would have the capability to do that. I always felt encouragement and wonderful support from him. That was liberating and wonderful. But there were cross-current messages.

Sherry recognizes that her father liked control, and that Kirby and Caroline were perfectly matched. While Kirby controlled their life together, he lavished Caroline with gifts, trips to nice places, and the best hotels and restaurants. Caroline, the country girl from Boswell, would say, "Kirby, you shouldn't have. It's too much. It's too extravagant."

Sherry said, "I think that fed him, too. So their marriage relationship was solid and strong and wonderful, but I grew up with a lot of my father in me. I watched some of that, and some of it drove me crazy. I can remember saying to Mother, 'I hate him.' I was rebellious and pushed against him. And she'd say, 'Oh, Sherry, you can't say that. You will never find anybody like him. You would be so lucky if you could. There is nobody else in the world like him.'"

PRANKS

Anne Price married Duff McKenzie in 1958. It was the marriage that began an onslaught of wedding pranks. Kirby and Roger Branigin, who would become Indiana's governor, instigated the first trick at Anne's nuptials, setting off a practical joke snowball effect that rolled through several years of weddings in the Risk and Price circles. Kirby, Jim Price, and Roger Branigin tried to "out prank" each other, often to the chagrin of their wives, children, and future in-laws. Wedding guests were treated to laughs, shock, and in a couple of instances, noxious odors.

Anne said, "Kirby and his cohorts iced down every bathtub in my parent's house. They had watermelons and champagne in them, except for in my bathroom. Because I was the bride, they didn't do it in mine. We were having the reception at home, so my mother was about ready to die. This was on Cypress Lane in Vinton Woods. We had moved there in 1956. So it was still a new house."

Carol and Sherry Risk were matron of honor and bridesmaid, respectively, in Anne's wedding. Caroline helped Anne dress for the wedding, which was a special gesture for Anne. She said, "She was the one I picked. Or my mother picked, because mothers have a lot to do at weddings."

Anne's brother, David, married Jane Hovde, daughter of Purdue President Frederick Hovde, on August 19, 1961. The reception was in the back garden on the grounds of the president's home at 515 South Seventh Street. Jane recalled:

> At my wedding, Kirby hired an organ grinder with a real live monkey to walk the reception line (asking for donations to the Purdue Grant-in-Aid program). Then he hired a little boy from the [Lafayette] Country Club, Ernie Schilling. He dressed him in a dirty T-shirt, put dirt all over his face. He was just a mess, and he was selling popcorn and peanuts in those little sacks like you get at the circus, ten cents a bag.

The Hovde/Price wedding was also held at Central Presbyterian Church, which was not air-conditioned at the time. Frederick Hovde had large air-conditioning units from Purdue University delivered to the church for use that day. Jane said, "A half hour before we went down to the church, someone called from there and said, 'Dr. Hovde, there's smoke coming from the air conditioners.' Daddy runs down to the church, and of course there's nothing. Kirby or somebody called to scare him."

One can see the affable Frederick Hovde, tuxedo coattails flying, as he zoomed six blocks down the hill from his home to check out the "smoldering" air conditioners he had borrowed from his employer.

Sherry Risk, wearing the same dress her sister Carol had worn, added yet another "Jim" to the mix when she wed Jim Stark on July 4, 1963. Jane Hovde was a bridesmaid in Sherry's wedding. The Risk, Price, and Hovde friends switched roles as bride, groom, bridesmaid, and groomsman in a swinging door of matrimony beginning with Carol Risk's wedding in 1957 through Jim Risk's wedding in 1966.

Sherry's blessed event came to be known as the "manure wedding." Jim Price and Roger Branigin had a truckload of manure delivered to 719 Owen Street with the plan to dump it on the front lawn. However, Kirby had hired security for the reception, and the truck was sent away. The

Sherry Risk and her father
on her wedding day, July 4, 1963.

*Owen Street in Lafayette, Indiana, was well-marked for the wedding
reception of Jim and Sherry Risk Stark on July 4, 1963.*

security man told the driver, "We're not accepting any gifts that aren't
wrapped."

Anne Price remembered, "Caroline about died with that manure.
Dad also brought this big ton air conditioner and had it delivered to
the Risk's driveway. It was really heavy. It was so hot, Kirby just rigged
it so it could air-condition the reception tent."

A banner was strung across Owen Street that beckoned passersby,
"Welcome Risk's Sherry Party. Free food and beer."

A manure aroma marked the spot.

ANOTHER CRASH

Four months after Sherry was married, there was another National
Homes airplane crash. George and Eleanor Price, along with Alen C.
Dibble, advertising director for National Homes, were flying in the

company twin-engine plane to a convention held at Greenbrier Hotel near White Sulphur Springs, West Virginia. According to an article in the *Evening Times* of Cumberland, Maryland, on November 5, 1962, the National Homes pilot overshot Greenbrier Airport while attempting to land and crashed into Greenbrier Mountain.

Eleanor Price was killed. The pilot and copilot also perished. George Price, age forty-six, walked for three hours through rugged mountain terrain, searching for help, knowing his wife was gone. A group of Boy Scouts found him. The newspaper story reported that George was in a nearby hospital in good condition and Dibble was there in serious condition.

George's niece, Anne Price, said, "Alen Dibble lived, but he was forever crippled. He was pinned underneath the plane, and gasoline was dripping on him. The plane was supposed to return to Lafayette later and pick up my father [Jim Price] to go on a hunting trip. I was at my parents' house at the time, and Fred Hovde came over and said the plane was missing. So Dad went down with Jack Bogan. He was with Mitchell Agency Insurance. Dad knew he would have to deal with bringing a body from another state."

This was George's third accident where he had been burned. Around 1950, he had been in a gas explosion on a boat, and he had since survived two National Homes airplane crashes. Dibble remained in the hospital for quite some time. Jim Price dispatched a nurse from Lafayette to stay with him around the clock. It was a flashback to his own recovery and loss after the 1951 crash. Dibble knew Frank Blair, who then was the anchor for NBC's *Today Show*. Blair had just produced a video about National Homes that Dibble had orchestrated.

Anne said of her aunt and uncle, "George and Eleanor had just gone to New York, and she had been Christmas shopping. So all these presents came that she had sent on to the house, and they tried to figure out whom they were to go to. My twin boys were really young. They had just been born in August. She had bought little bicycles, and there were two of them; so we knew who they were for."

In 1965, Price & Price, Inc. announced Vinton Highlands, "Indiana's first totally planned residential community." The Lafayette Dam and Reservoir with a 3,000 acre lake was in the works (the lake never came to pass), and National Homes planned three new neighborhoods near there in the "Wildcat Creek Valley." The sales packet reads, "Nearby, too, will be access to tomorrow's modern super highway—Interstate 65—that connects Lafayette with Chicago and Indianapolis."

The three new residential sections that were part of Vinton Highlands were Glen Acres, Ivy Hill, and Greenbriar. The Greenbriar name is spelled differently than that of the mountain range where Eleanor Price died, yet the sound of the word may ring with memories for some.

PRANK ON

Jim Risk married Mary Jo Mohlman on July 30, 1966. After the Risk/Price/Branigin track record of wedding hijinks, Mary Jo was worried. She said, "I kept saying to everybody, 'You know I haven't participated in any of this, and I don't deserve any of it.' Because between Jim Price and Kirby, you never knew what was going to happen."

Jane Hovde Price and David Price were in Jim and Mary Jo's wedding. Five years earlier, Jim and Mary Jo had been in Jane and David's wedding. It seems each character in the wedding cast simply switched places at each ceremony.

The rehearsal dinner was held in Kirby's and Caroline's home with a large table set up in their living room. David Price brought a special treat. Jane Hovde Price remembered her husband's antics. "David had a friend who had a pet skunk," she said. "He took it to Jim's rehearsal dinner party on Owen Street. But the skunk got loose. There are pictures of people's fannies under the shrubbery outside trying to get this prized pet skunk."

David's sister, Anne Price, remembered, too. "I don't think Caroline thought that was very funny. She stood bolt straight.

Jim and Mary Jo's reception was at the Lafayette Country Club on Ninth Street where David struck again. Jane said, "David snuck into the women's locker room and stole Mary Jo's going-away shoes. Nobody knew this. The wedding reception went on, and Mary Jo went back to change. Pretty soon, the word came out that Mary Jo wasn't coming out until somebody turned in her shoes. Well, duh. Who would have taken them but David?"

Mary Jo said, "I wasn't going to go away without my shoes. So, Roberta [David Price's mother] comes in, and says, 'Well, I'll get those shoes!' So she runs out and gets David by the nape of the neck, and says, 'You give me those shoes!'"

Anne Price said, "I can remember Jimmy [Risk] saying to Mary Jo, "It doesn't matter. We're going to miss the plane. We're going without the shoes. And Mary Jo said, 'Oh, no we're not.'"

David retrieved Mary Jo's going-away shoes, which he had hidden in the Lafayette Country Club's grand piano.

Anne Price said, "This was such a good prank, because Jimmy had planned this whole thing, and all of the sudden it wasn't going the way he wanted it. He was so frustrated."

The plight of the missing going-away shoes set the tone for Jim and Mary Jo's marriage. Mary Jo was not Caroline Risk. Mary Jo would say "no" when necessary for her own well-being. If Jim were to expect Mary Jo to go out for a donut at two o'clock in the morning, as Kirby did Caroline, it would not happen. Mary Jo said, "I'd just say, 'No.' Jim knows better than to even ask."

Perhaps, Mary Jo's self-assurance stems in part from her parents' early deaths and her subsequent role in raising her younger brothers. Mary Jo said, "My mother died at fifty-seven and my father at sixty-two. Mother died in 1964. My father died in 1967. So my mother was gone before we were married, and my father died when we were married less than a year. My mother died a year after I graduated from Purdue. I stayed home to help with my two brothers who were in grade school."

Later, Mary Jo moved to Chicago to work for a market research firm. She returned to Lafayette to marry Jim Risk.

Little sister Julie remembers her big brother's wedding. She recalled:

> Jimmy and I were very close, and I can remember sobbing when
> he and Mary Jo went on their honeymoon. I was fourteen. With
> Jim married and gone, I wondered who would rescue me from my
> Dad's Sunday drives. After church on Sundays, my Dad loved to
> go driving and check things out. He was really involved in New
> Directions, a facility for wayward people who needed help getting
> back into a "new direction." I remember driving to check out that
> facility. When Jim was with us on a Sunday after church, I'd say,
> "Rescue me. Take me home." Then Jim got married, and I thought,
> "Who will rescue me?"

One week after Jim and Mary Jo married, Jane Hovde's sister, Linda,
was married with the reception again on the grounds of the Purdue
president's home. So the circle of friends planned and attended two
weddings in a week's time. Jane, who was in both weddings, said, "Oh
my, it was a circus. It *was* a circus. Kirby had a calliope playing music
at the front walk. People loved it. It was very loud."

Today, walking along reticent South Seventh Street past 515, it is
difficult to imagine a gaudy calliope parked on the sidewalk, blasting
high-pitched, carnival strains into the quiet of the neighborhood. Unless one knew Kirby Risk.

Mary Jo was Catholic, and she had attended Catholic schools. She
and Jim, a Presbyterian, were married at the Cathedral of Saint Mary
of the Immaculate Conception with a Presbyterian minister participating. Mary Jo said, "When we got married, it was a big issue. We
were 'okayed' by the bishop, and our wedding was the first in town
like it. When both ministers [a Catholic priest and a Presbyterian
minister] stepped out into the church at St. Mary's for the ceremony,
it was quite the thing. Times were different. We were kind of different. We baptized our first child Catholic, and then I became a Presbyterian."

Fast-forward, and Julie Risk married Mark Pope on June 15, 1974.
Julie said:

I converted to Catholicism when I got married. I didn't tell my parents for a long time. I went to St. Thomas Catholic Church with Mark when I was at Purdue. I loved it. I don't think I ever loved Central Presbyterian. However, I was older, and I think it was more age than where I was going to church. But I was also going with my boyfriend. I had to get my birth certificate and my baptism certificate. I can remember we were sneaking around the house trying to find them. I'm not sure my parents and I ever discussed it. Now my boys are going to churches other than Catholic Churches. So I have to be fine with that.

Even though Julie's wedding occurred several years after those of her siblings and the Price and Hovde children, her big day didn't pass without a gag.

David's sister, Anne Price, remembered, "My dad died about three weeks after Julie got married. He did get to go to her wedding. He really wasn't well, but I do know he had chocolate-covered rabbit droppings at the reception. He just loved that. He loved Julie. He adored her when she was a baby."

Julie Risk and her father on her wedding day, June 15, 1974.

Even in his declining days, Jim Price, the entrepreneur behind National Homes Corporation who loved a good wedding prank, came through in his predictable style at his beloved Julie's wedding. He brought a large, lovely box to the wedding reception and placed it at the center of the food table. He claimed that inside the gift-wrapped box were chocolate-covered rabbit droppings. This time the Risks had to "accept" the delivery because the manure was gift-wrapped.

Jim Price and his son, David, laughed over Jim's wedding gift to Mark and Julie Risk Pope. Inside the white gift-wrapped box were chocolate-covered rabbit droppings. Glenn Safford is on the far left next do David Price. Jim Price is on the far right.

Many years later, Kirby took a stand regarding his first grandchild's wedding. Carol recalled:

When our son Steve was married in 1981, Dad was eighty. My daughter-in-law had always wanted a fall wedding. That was pretty bad because Dad never missed any Purdue home or away football games for years and years and years. I said it was going to be a problem because the wedding was in Pennsylvania. They decided to get married the same day as the Northwestern away game. But Dad was not going to miss the game! It was his first grandchild! We were all a little disappointed. Mother came with Jim. We were all out there. We had a lovely rehearsal dinner without Dad. Then Mother and I arrived at the church in the limousine, and there was Dad sitting on the steps. When Mother saw him, she started crying, and so did I. He had left at halftime of the Northwestern game, flew in on a charter flight to Pittsburgh, and had a cab waiting for him. He wasn't going to miss seeing Purdue play, and he wasn't going to miss his grandchild's wedding.

Anne Price and her husband were in on Kirby's plans. They took Kirby to the football game and helped him leave at halftime to catch the plane to make the wedding. Anne said, "Even if Kirby was there for just part of the game, that counted. That was important to him."

Daughter Julie agreed: "Dad was true to his conviction of not missing a Purdue football game. He wanted to honor that, but certainly not miss his grandson's wedding."

CHAPTER 15

JUNIOR ACHIEVEMENT

Kirby was the pied piper of the "free enterprise system." He wanted young people to get a jump-start on how to thrive in that system. In the fall of 1955, Kirby and Dr. William (Bill) Sholty founded Junior Achievement (JA) in Lafayette. Bill brought the idea to Kirby who ran with it. The two traveled to New York to set up the Lafayette chapter, which received its charter the next year. The Lafayette organization received start-up funding from the Greater Lafayette Chamber of Commerce and the Tippecanoe County Industrial Management Club—an organization made up of "factory foremen and supervisors." Horace Moses, a Springfield, Massachusetts, paper company executive, had started JA nationally in 1919. He saw that farm children had organizations such as 4-H to give them practical career training, so he formed JA to offer the same sort of preparation to city kids.

During Kirby's time, JA taught high school students how to run a company through a learn-by-doing formula. Teenagers created their own businesses, elected officers, sold stock, and made or sold a product. Each mini-company produced and marketed anything from aluminum coat hangers and cork trivets to toothbrush kits and Christmas wreaths and was run like a microcosm of the real work world.

On December 8, 1956, the Lafayette *Journal and Courier* ran a story entitled "Young Magnates Set Up Factories, Taste of Capitalism Spurs Production Efforts," written by Donald L. Reeder. Reeder's opening sentence speaks to the pop culture of the time. It reads: "The phrase 'profit and loss' has crowded out all thoughts of 'rock and roll' in the minds of 80 energetic Jefferson High School pupils. While their teenage companions concentrate on drag races and Elvis Presley, these youngsters are absorbed in such startling topics as production quotas and operation of power saws."

In a 1978 magazine interview, Kirby said, "Junior Achievement gets youngsters well-tuned to the importance of economic awareness. The practical experience gained is so much more effective than any classroom work available."

Each company of about twenty students had a corporate sponsor and advisors, businessmen (few businesswomen existed in Kirby's time) who gave the group insight about production, business, and sales. In Lafayette during the first year, there were four JA student-run companies sponsored by National Homes Corporation, Lafayette Life Insurance Company, Alcoa Manufacturing, and Kirby Risk Electric. The men who led the companies were Kirby's friends and business peers. There were about eighty student members at the time. The JA companies met for two hours one night a week in the basement of the YMCA building, which was downtown at Seventh and Columbia Streets. Later, the second home for JA in Lafayette was at Kirby Risk Electric Motors at First and Smith Streets.

The students named their companies, incorporating syllable fragments from the monikers of their sponsors. For instance, in 1957 there was FAIR-JAC, sponsored by Fairfield Manufacturing, and KIRBY-KO, backed by Kirby Risk Electric. Each company elected officers, created a budget, and produced an annual report. Bonuses were paid to the workers and dividends paid to the stockholders.

Kirby's youngest, Julie, said, "Even before I was old enough to be in JA, I remember all of the JA companies were down at the motor shop, which is now Kirby Risk Mechanical Solutions and Service down at First and Smith Streets. I'd go down and see all the high school kids making their products."

After the students produced their wares, they often sold the goods door-to-door or through friends and relatives. Aluminum hangers were a popular product sponsored by Alcoa. Julie said, "I still have the aluminum hangers all over my house. Of course, when I got to high school I was in JA all four years. You could be different officers of your company, and you decided on a product. You determined the cost of the raw materials, how long it would take for production, what the sale price should be. It was a perfect economics class."

The 1956 *Journal and Courier* article goes on to state:

> Although the adult advisers keep a sharp eye on proceedings and pass on a few sage words when a crisis arises, the JA youngsters bear full responsibility for whatever financial prosperity or disaster is heaped upon them. Surprisingly enough, the pint-sized industrial magnates usually manage to come out on top. Of course, there are unfortunate cases, like the pupils who found out too late that their shampoo turned hair an entrancing shade of green, but the national average is a handsome 10 percent profit for the more than 2000 JA companies.

In 1958, Jim Risk, age seventeen, was president of his company, KIR-LEC-KO, sponsored by Kirby Risk Electric. Jane Hovde, Purdue president Frederick Hovde's daughter who would marry David Price, was vice president. KIR-LEC-KO created something unusual compared to the many candles, trivets, and hangers that were produced over the years—a glass-enameled copper dish/ashtray. Their annual report reads, "We feel the product selected, a glass enameled ash tray, although more difficult than the average product to produce, compares with the ash trays found in the gift department of the better department stores and gift shops." In 1958, smoking was the norm and was still looked upon as a fashionable pastime. It was not until 1965 that

Congress required all cigarette packages distributed in the United States to carry a health warning.

The report written by the students goes on to state that the selection of the glass-enameled copper ashtray was nearly ideal. Stating, "They are somewhat different than the average product because not only was the production intricate, but also an art. Many were made according to customer specifications."

The wage for KIR-LEC-KO production workers and officers varied between twenty-five cents to thirty-one cents per hour. Fifteen percent sales commissions were paid. KIR-LEC-KO sold their ashtrays door-to-door, in department stores like Loeb's and J. C. Penney in downtown Lafayette and in the Market Square shopping center. The ashtrays sold for two to three dollars and were offered in various sizes, designs, and colors. Today, Caroline Risk still has the orange glass-enameled copper ashtray made by her son's JA company back in 1958.

HANDS ON

At the end of the school year in May, the Future Unlimited Banquet was held at the Purdue University Memorial Union ballroom to recognize the adult leaders and award the "achievers" and their companies. For many years, the Purdue Varsity Glee Club performed, directed by Kirby's good friend Al Stewart.

At the 1958 banquet, Kirby's daughter, Sherry, age eighteen, the award-winning high school speech team participant, presented the awards. In 1959, Brian Lamb presented the honors. At an early age, Brian and Jim Risk became lifelong friends. Brian was one of the managers of the basketball team for which Jim played at Jefferson High School. Brian's high school radio and TV teacher, Bill Fraser, taught him the basics of broadcasting and interviewing. Brian worked at WASK Radio in Lafayette, and in 1961, he coordinated the local television program *Dance Date*, similar to Dick Clark's, *American Bandstand*.

Today, Brian is founder and chief executive officer of C-SPAN, a television network dedicated to coverage of government proceedings and public affairs. In 2011, Brian's alma mater, Purdue University, created the Brian Lamb School of Communication. Brian is a recipient of the Presidential Medal of Freedom. When seventeen-year-old Brian presented awards to achievers at the 1959 Future Unlimited Banquet, his own unlimited road lie ahead.

Jan Griffin Koehler was hired as the Lafayette Junior Achievement director in 1977, and she held that position for more than thirty years. Jan participated in JA when she was in high school in Michigan. Kirby and son, Jim, first interviewed Jan at the National Junior Achievers Conference , which is held yearly at Indiana University in Bloomington, Indiana. They wanted her to come to Lafayette for a second interview and to meet the JA board. Kirby and Jim were going to be out of town, so they suggested that Jan stay with Caroline while they were away. Jan said, "Right away, they were welcoming me into their home. Kirby was very special about deciding that type of thing."

Jan was the third director in four years. She recalled:

> I think the first directors kind of bucked against how Kirby worked. Whereas me, being a woman and younger—I was twenty-three when I moved to Lafayette—it made the situation different. I met my husband two weeks after. It's a great town. I like it here, so I just made it work. Both Kirby and Caroline are amazing people. The more I "grow up," the more I realize how absolutely special they were and how lucky I was to have them in my life.

The way Kirby "worked" was very "hands-on." Jan said, "He had his finger in everything. Kirby signed all of our letters. Every year, he took the budget and divided it amongst the contributors, and that's how much they gave. He pretty much told them what they were to give."

Because Kirby felt that each business should give an equal amount to the organization, it became tricky when a company wanted to contribute more than the amount they were asked to give. Jan said, "In the early 1980s, Jack McDowell was at Green Giant, and he knew they could give more money, and he wanted to give more money. Kirby coaxed everyone else up to that level."

At one point, Kirby went to McDowell and said, "Don't give any more money because I have to make it even, and there are businesses that can't give that much." To which McDowell replied, "So, don't make them give that much, but let those who *can* give more—give more."

When Jan became director in 1977, businesses, large and small, were giving $700 a year. Jan said, "He was very determined that it was equal and that everyone had an equal say. Everyone who gave had a seat on the board, so I had a very large board. Kirby sent the contributors letters, and if they didn't send their money, he'd be calling them. But he did it in such a nice way, people wanted to do things his way. He did so much good."

As director of JA in Lafayette, Jan didn't have to pound the streets looking for dollars for her nonprofit organization. She had Kirby. Angel Hernandez, the Cuban friend who lived in the Risk's basement for a time, became manager of investment accounting at National Homes Acceptance Corporation, and later worked at Lafayette Savings Bank, was the treasurer for JA for many years and handled all of the "money side."

For the most part, Jan let Kirby, who was seventy-six when she was hired, run the show. It was his baby, and he knew how he wanted things to be done. She said, "I didn't get a lot of late phone calls, but a lot of people did, particularly if things weren't going as he wanted. That's when he got these brainstorms. He was a night person."

Beginning in 1969, Jan Lehnen was Kirby and Jim's secretary (a position termed "executive assistant" today) for a stint of thirty-nine years. She helped Kirby with his numerous charitable endeavors, including the Future Unlimited Banquets. Jan Lehnen said, "Caroline would make all of the name badges because she had beautiful handwriting. Kirby, Caroline, and I would also arrange the special seating."

Jan Koehler remembered:

Kirby was heavily involved in the seating of all eight-hundred people who came to our Future Unlimited Banquet. He decided where they were going to sit. It got to be difficult when Junior Achievement was growing. Everyone that was involved was invited—the companies, the board members. Kirby assigned the seats up to the very end. Kirby didn't use people, but he *knew* people. He knew who to put with whom. He knew who needed to talk with whom to do the next thing that needed to be done for the community.

Jan Lehnen was an integral part in helping Kirby achieve what he wanted with JA in Lafayette, typing many a letter that Kirby signed. She remembered:

> Kirby loved Junior Achievement. Well, he loved kids. For the first twenty years I worked there [Kirby Risk Corporation], every head honcho of every company in town was on that JA board. Their presidents always went to those board meetings. They would expect their JA fundraising letter every year, and they would include their contribution in their budget. I don't think they do that anymore. As time went on, things just changed. They delegated it to an underling.

In the early days of JA, Kirby and Caroline kicked off the year with a cookout with steaks on the grill at their home. As the group grew, the cookout was moved to The Trails, a restaurant and banquet hall. Jan Koehler said, "Kirby was very specific about what the menu was and did all of the arranging. He was very welcoming. That is one of the things that stands out about him. He welcomed everyone no matter who you were. When you talked to Kirby, you felt you were one of the most important people in the world. There were never any airs, and there could have been. He took his business and really grew it. Jim has taken it way beyond that."

Whenever there was a party or function that required invitations, Kirby insisted that the envelopes be hand addressed. Jan Koehler remembered, "Jan and I sat and addressed thousands of invitations, because you did things that way. No, you can't do labels. So that became ingrained in me. If you're going to do fundraising, get the names right. Kirby was a stickler about that."

The businesspeople who were advisors for the student-run companies volunteered their time on a grand scale. Jan Koehler said:

> When I first came here, it was a thirty-three-week program. You'd start in September and go until April—every Wednesday night. It was a huge commitment these people made. It became expected. It was part of the management development for all the companies. I had one of the top boards. The commitment diminished when the CEOs of companies stopped living in the community, which has totally changed Lafayette. These people lived, breathed Lafayette. They grew up here, their children grew up here, went to school here, whereas now, it's different. There's a change in the whole corporate structure.

Lafayette, Indiana, is not an anomaly. The city has kindred communities across America where the mom-and-pop store, the company headed by the fellow who made its first dollar, the local guy running the show are no more. These businesses have been replaced by the bigger box stores, the larger corporation, and the manufacturer overseas that can bail out a drowning entity by producing a widget at a lesser cost. And the gentlemen in fedoras who closed deals with just a handshake have vaporized.

Jan Koehler summed it up: "You don't find many Kirby Risks in companies now, which is how far we've come. But it is interesting, if you watch what economies are doing now. We're now getting more entrepreneurs. Trying to go back. Hopefully, local, state, and national governments will realize that it's those small businesses that really make it."

Who you know gets you where you want to go, still today, for the most part. But Jan Koehler recognized how today it is more difficult to know the heads of companies who don't live in the community. She said:

> Back then many of the businesses were locally owned. Fairfield was a local corporation. Rostone was a local corporation. Duncan Electric. That was the beauty of Lafayette. People like Kirby had

the foresight to make sure that, even though the University is here, Lafayette is also a real town. Not just a University town. They made sure we had white-collar jobs, blue-collar jobs, and they were taking care of everyone, not just the University people. But he was also very proud of the University and very involved in the University.

Jan Koehler knew how Kirby was loyal to Purdue and integral in raising funds for his alma mater through stories told by her mother-in-law, Alice Koehler, who was secretary for the John Purdue Club. Kirby took it upon himself to collect John Purdue Club members' dues, yet on a rare occasion he failed to take the next step. Jan Koehler said, "Kirby would collect a member's check for dues, stick it in his pocket, and forget about it. Then the John Purdue Club would get a phone call from the member saying, 'I gave Kirby my check six months ago!'"

JENKS REST

By 1960, JA needed a home. Again, Kirby turned to his friends in the Lafayette business world. Jan Koehler explained, "They found money in the Jenks trust, which was designated for building a rest area for seniors. That's why it became the senior center. It was named for [George E.] Jenks. The park needed another building. They liked the idea of the seniors sharing the building with Junior Achievement."

In 1921, George E. "Pop" Jenks of Lafayette died after a career as manufacturer of heavy paper boxes and editor of a paper industry newspaper called *The Shears*. Jenks sold *The Shears* around 1916 to Marshall Haywood of Haywood Printing Company, a printing firm that still operates in downtown Lafayette. In his will, Jenks left money to the city of Lafayette, "for the erection, on a suitable spot in Columbian Park . . . a pavilion for public uses and pleasures, said pavilion to be known as the Jenks Rest." The stipulation was that after the death of Jenks's grandniece, Georgia Jenks Mann, her trusteeship would end and all remaining money would be turned over to the city of Lafayette for the building of the pavilion to bear his surname. It was nearly forty years after Jenks's death that Kirby Risk would come along to facilitate the construction of Jenks Rest.

A photograph in the October 31, 1960, Lafayette *Journal and Courier* shows the Jenks Rest building under construction. The caption reads in part, "Installation of metal roofs, floorings and interior fixtures remains before completion in November. The $77,800 structure is 130 feet long and 76 feet wide, and is north of the Memorial Island stage at the shore of the park lagoon."

Joe Rush of Rush Metal donated the metal needed. Kirby handled all of the electrical needs. National Homes gave material, labor, and cost of labor to construct the flat-roofed building. From the front windows, visitors can see Memorial Island where Epsilon Theta conducted their Easter sunrise services. The unassuming cement block structure sits next to the train track where on summer days a child-sized locomotive moves families throughout the park.

A *Journal and Courier* story from October 23, 1965, entitled "Jenks' Kin Enthusiastic in Rest Building Praise," tells of George Jenks's great-great-great-niece, Mrs. Jess Jenks Parker of New Mexico, visiting Jenks Rest for the first time. She pronounced the building "quite nicely done," but the article also states:

> Mrs. Parker . . . found the building quite different from what she was sure George Jenks had in mind. She said he had seemed to be thinking about a place for rural folk to rest when they came to town by horse and buggy or slow car, "but you know how fast things changed" so that the original intent was outdated by the time the will was implemented. She added that she thought the donor's original intent had been developed well under the changing circumstance.

Today, Junior Achievement of Greater Lafayette still operates from offices at Jenks Rest, along with The Center @ Jenks Rest, which is operated by the Tippecanoe County Council on Aging. Seniors gather for coffee and bingo. High school students assemble to learn about commerce.

NATIONAL CONFERENCE

Each year, Kirby escorted Lafayette students to the National Junior Achievers Conference (NAJAC) held in August at Indiana University in Bloomington, a few hours south from Lafayette by car. Students attended from across the country and around the world. In the 1967 "Dateline Junior Achievement" twenty-fourth annual conference booklet, a black and white photo adorns the cover. The photo shows Kirby, balding, wearing his signature bowtie and checked sport coat with a silk handkerchief peeking from his breast pocket. He's handing out "Company of the Year" awards to three fresh-faced "achievers."

Kirby Risk presents "achievers" with "Company of the Year" awards at the twenty-fourth annual National Junior Achievers Conference in 1967.

An article in the conference booklet is entitled "The Best Week of My Life." The story states that more than 2,000 teenagers attended, and delegates were chosen for outstanding accomplishments in their local JA areas from among the more than 130,000 high school students who were members of JA the previous year. Delegates discussed such topics as organizing a company, personal salesmanship, annual reports, and public relations. The students competed for cash scholarships and awards, including $1,500 for "President of the Year." Top echelon business and industrial leaders from major corporations across the country spoke at the conference. Photos accompanying the article show happy teenagers gathering for refreshments, filling wax paper cups at a dispenser that reads, "Things go better with Coke."

Awards were given for President of the Year, Company of the Year, Marketing Executive, Treasurer, Personnel Director, Public Speaking, Annual Report, and more. A Miss Junior Achievement was crowned. In a black and white photo, Donna Stone from Atlanta smiles, wearing her tiara, sash, and corsage of daisies, as she holds her trophy and bouquet of roses.

Kirby's daughter, Julie, said, "I had the opportunity to go down to NAJAC. One year, I was in charge of our annual report, and it took third in the country. It was quite nice."

Jan Koehler remembered:

> Every year when we had NAJAC, the delegation went down on the Kirby Risk motor home. At the time, we would send twelve to seventeen kids. We'd have vans following with their luggage. They always stopped at a pie shop [Kelly's] on highway 67 in Martinsville. Kirby would order a bunch of different pies. The kids would say, "We had the best pie." He would pass the pieces around so everybody could try everything. Whenever you ate with Kirby, he always ordered desserts and encouraged you to eat them, even if you didn't want to. Everyone had a fun time.

In 1964, Kirby received the George Award given by the Lafayette *Journal and Courier.* The honor is given to "self-starters, individuals who see the need to accomplish something for their communities and then do it without thought of personal publicity or remuneration." The year prior, the newspaper had established the annual award for any person living in the area served by the *Journal and Courier.* Nominations are taken from the community. Kirby received the George Award for his "resettling refugees from Hungary, Cuba and The Netherlands," his work in organizing the Lafayette United Way Fund, and "fathering" Lafayette Junior Achievement.

NAED

In 1965 and 1966, Kirby served two terms as president of the National Association of Electrical Distributors (NAED), which annually sponsored the National JA Company of the Year contest. Kirby's professional, volunteer, and philanthropic lives always melded.

It was unusual for the same person to reign twice as president of NAED, founded in Chicago in 1908, as the Electrical Supply Jobbers Association. At the time of his election, there were 1,110 wholesale electrical distributors in the United States. A June 1966 article in *Electrical Wholesaling*, titled, "Kirby Risk: He's Very Persuasive," reads:

> Kirby Risk, one of three NAED presidents to be elected to a second term, is in the self-made category. Kirby's warmth and lack of pretension are apparent from the moment of first meeting him. He is one of the most gracious men in the industry. Even in a tense situation, his friendliness is unfailing. . . . He is attuned to the many subtle nuances of the electrical business. Yet he is a businessman who has managed to retain his ideals, which is not easy to do in a cynical world. Most of all, he's a doer who recognizes that persuasion is the straightest and surest road to a goal. And goals? They are apparent in the glint of determination that accompanies his smile.

Kirby Risk was president of the National Association of Electrical Distributors (NAED) in 1965 and 1966. NAED annually sponsored the National Junior Achievement Company of the Year contest.

Kirby's good friend John M. Newton, Jr., whom everyone called "Mr. Newton," preceded Kirby as president of NAED. Newton was thought of as one of the best speakers and speechwriters in NAED's history. In the 1940s, Newton, then owner of Oakes Electrical Supply Company, created a small electrical museum in Holyoke, Massachusetts. Kirby and Newton spent much time together, with Kirby visiting out east and Newton coming to Indiana where the Risks served him fresh sweet corn and tomatoes, a Hoosier summertime treat. Later, one of Newton's sons became chairman of NAED. Jim Risk said of his father and Newton, "They wrote back and forth and had a really warm relationship. Now the grandson, Jim Newton, is a business associate of mine."

Kirby surprised Newton and his wife when they celebrated their sixtieth wedding anniversary in a private room of a restaurant. Kirby flew to Massachusetts and borrowed a waiter's uniform and a tray holding a glass of water. Then, posing as the waiter, Kirby approached the table where his friend sat with family and friends and spilled the water on the lap of the unsuspecting Mr. Newton. Newton was indignant until he realized his dear friend was the prankster.

Other lifelong friends made through NAED were Art and Mary Hooper, who lived in Connecticut. Hooper was the executive director of NAED. At that time, NAED was headquartered in New York; now the headquarters are in St. Louis. The Hoopers and Risks visited each other's homes numerous times over the years. When Kirby, Caroline, Jim, and Mary Jo visited New York, the Hoopers were always invited to come into the city by train and join them for dinner and the theater. At NAED meetings, the Hoopers and Risks commonly shared a hotel suite. Jim remembered, "Art liked to talk about Dad 'setting up light housekeeping' and hanging his stockings over the lampshades to dry. It's fun to hear him. Dad liked to bring all types of food into the refrigerator in the suite. Art and Mary loved food, too."

The best friends traveled together, including extra days for vacations after industry meetings in places like California and Hawaii. Back then, NAED offered educational tour opportunities. For instance, members could go to England to visit distributors. Jim said, "The Hoopers were some of the dearest friends my parents had."

In April 1967, during the second year of Kirby's two-year term as NAED president, Caroline's perspective appeared in *The Electrical Distributor's* "The President Comments" column, which customarily Kirby would have written. The headline next to Caroline's photo reads, "The President's Wife Comments." She begins:

> It may come as a surprise to have this page "occupied" by an NAED wife instead of the President, but for the past two years Kirby has been doing the commenting to you people—and anyone who knows us well, knows that I am the talker in the family! . . . For nearly 34 years my life has been closely associated with the electrical business; and for many of those years, especially the past two years, NAED has been an important part of my life.

She comments further from the perspective of a wife in the late 1960s and, unbeknownst to the trade journal reader, the wife who holds down the fort, while Kirby keeps "vampire" hours:

> For those wives who come to the NAED conventions, I am sure that they, like me, find it a grand opportunity for a break from house-keeping and family responsibility. What a glorious feeling to leave the alarm clock at home; to see interesting and beautiful sights for which the planning has already been done; to eat delicious meals; and for me, to be able to sit in on some of the Association's fine programs. Through the years, the great satisfaction I have gained from being able to discuss business problems and new projects with Kirby cannot be stated in a few words.

DAUGHTER DREAMS

Julie Risk had different experiences than her siblings because she was so much younger than they. She and Kirby connected through sports, which ultimately helped her in business. She explained, "My time with my Dad was through Purdue and Jefferson High School football and basketball. Every Friday night for Jeff games, he'd say, 'Hey, call your friends. We'll pick them up.' I went with Dad to all the games. I loved it. Without question, that was our connection."

More than likely, Kirby didn't realize how profoundly his affinity with JA would affect the lives of his own children. When she was in high school, Julie thought she wanted to be an elementary education teacher, but after she experienced cadet teaching where students worked in a classroom for part of a school day, she knew teaching was not for her. To help Julie switch gears, Kirby set up a lunch at the Lafayette Country Club with Purdue's Dean of the Krannert School of Management John Day and the Director of Advising and Guidance Counseling for Krannert Dick Walbaum.

Julie said, "I had always been very involved in Junior Achievement, and so I had that business background. They talked to me about the Krannert School, and I decided to switch majors. Krannert was awesome. There were not very many women at that time. It was 1970 to 1974. I was the only woman in many of my classes. If there were two women in a class, that was a lot."

Julie became involved in the Krannert School and the Industrial Management Council (IMC). During her senior year, she worked as an advisor for Walbaum, helping to schedule pupils for classes by offering the student's perspective.

Julie said, "After I graduated, I went to work for General Motors, and I had such a leg up on so many other new graduates because I talked football with everybody. And I never realized what a bonus that was for entering the business world at that time as a woman. The general manager of the plant would come down on Monday mornings to talk to me about the game. So it was quite nice."

Did Kirby purposely expose Julie to sports to help her future in the workforce?

Julie said, "I wouldn't be surprised. He never said, 'Julie, you need to know this so when you go out into the world, you can talk football.' But it was within the first month of work that it was apparent that I had an in. There were guys who didn't talk football like I could. It was one of the best gifts my Dad gave me as far as entering the workforce, the business world. Working for General Motors, it was huge."

Julie was with General Motors in Indianapolis for fifteen years. After her second son was born, she tried to leave because juggling it all became too much, but the company begged her to stay. Julie said, "I went in and said I had to resign, and they said, 'You can't. You can work whatever number of hours you want. We will increase your staff, and you can keep your same job.' I called them 'Generous Motors.' They were a wonderful company to work for."

Julie ended up resigning after a nerve-racking turn of events with her son. Julie remembered:

> We got a call from the preschool, and one of our kids was sick. I was busy in the general manager's office and my husband, Mark, who is a lawyer, was involved with a case. Neither one of us could go. So, eventually, Mark was the one who went, and he got stopped for speeding. Mark said, "I'm going to pick up my child." And the police officer said, "Well, follow me." She gave him a police escort there. He didn't get a ticket, but we looked at each other and said, "Something's got to give."

Julie retired from the career she loved at General Motors, even though she said she could have worked there forever. She explained, "It gave me an opportunity to be a full-time mom, which is a real privilege. I was scared to death to leave because when you're an employee you get a lot of strokes. You get a lot of affirmation. That was after Dad died. Dad died in February of 1989, and I left General Motors in July of 1989."

COLGATE MEMORIAL AWARD

In the late 1970s, Kirby was on the National Board of Directors of JA. He also served on the National Long-Range Planning Committee. On February 2, 1978, Kirby was awarded the Colgate Memorial Award at the fourth annual Junior Achievement National Business Leadership Conference in Detroit, Michigan. Established in 1966, the award is

JA's highest honor, established to recognize outstanding volunteer contributions. The award is named after S. Bayard Colgate, who was chairman of the Colgate-Palmolive Company. Colgate was on the national board for twenty years and traveled extensively, speaking to business groups and promoting JA in scores of cities.

Kirby followed in Colgate's footsteps. A February 2, 1978, Lafayette *Journal and Courier* story about Kirby's honor states, "Risk has given numerous speeches to business groups across the country and informed dozens of other cities and thousands of other people about JA programs."

Previous recipients of the Colgate award included W. F. Rockwell, Jr., chairman of Rockwell International; Richard L. Terrell, vice chairman of General Motors; John deButts, chairman of AT&T; DeWitt Wallace, founder and head of *Reader's Digest*; and Richard A Jay, vice chairman of Goodyear Tire and Rubber Company.

Julie remembered the synchronicity of that day. "My father won the National Junior Achievement Award, and we got to go to Detroit for the ceremony," she said. "The chairman of the Junior Achievement board was Tom Murphy, who was chairman of General Motors, so I got to meet him. I was an employee there at the time. That was quite something. And Dick Terrell, who was the vice chairman of the GM board, was there as well. It was like, 'Wow.'"

Jan Koehler had been director of the Lafayette JA program for just a year when Kirby received the Colgate honor. She flew to Detroit with Jim and Mary Jo Risk and Julie Risk Pope, but their plane was delayed. Kirby and Caroline had arrived there prior. Jan recalled:

> We got in at 10:30. Kirby had already checked us into our rooms and had our room keys. He had food waiting for us in his suite, because he knew we would be tired. He was very thoughtful, thinking ahead about what people needed. Some people would find that controlling. But he really did it because he liked people for the right reasons. I thought that was very telling of the type of person that he was. And he was very humble about receiving the award.

Kirby received a silver Revere bowl during a luncheon in the Detroit Plaza Hotel. Henry Ford II, chairman of the Ford Motor Company and first grandchild of industrial pioneer Henry Ford, was the conference chairman and keynote speaker. Mark Scully, a student from Simsbury, Connecticut, presented Kirby with his award. Representing his high school company, Scully had won the National JA Annual Report Contest out of some 7,900 JA Companies the previous year. According to the master script for the event, Skully said, in part:

> One individual stands out as a "super volunteer" for all of Junior Achievement. Mr. Kirby Risk. . . . The man we are honoring today is himself so concerned that other JA volunteers should receive proper recognition that he chaired the Regional Council Committee, which developed a new system of National Leadership Awards for the Midwest Region. The experiment worked so well, it was adopted by the National Board for use nationwide.

> It was once said that a man never stands taller than when he stoops to help a young person. It is a great honor for me to represent over 200,000 achievers of America to say: Thank you, Mr. Risk. You are, to us, a very tall man.

That evening after Kirby received the Colgate Award, he hosted a party in his suite. Jan Koehler said, "He knew an amazing number of people, partly because of his JA national board experience. He would introduce you to people. Michael Eisner from Disney was one of the people in the suite that night. It was fun to do things with Kirby. He would lead you about anywhere." Michael Eisner was chief executive officer of the Walt Disney Company from 1984 to 2005.

The following April, JA in Lafayette established a college scholarship honoring Kirby and Caroline. It was presented to a student at the Future Unlimited Banquet. After the event, Caroline penned an encouraging thank-you note to inaugural director Jan Koehler. It reads in part:

Dearest Jan,

What a splendid banquet you had Monday night. Hundreds of Center Directors across the land would have been *proud* to have had such a large, smooth running, entertaining, delicious F. U. B. dinner for theirs!! The scholarship was such a surprise, and Kirby just could not have been more pleased. He couldn't really believe it!!

Throughout their marriage, work, church, and civic endeavors, Caroline's genteel notes and kind words softly bolstered Kirby's charge-ahead footwork.

In 1982, Kirby and Caroline traveled with Jack McDowell, manager of Lafayette's Green Giant plant, to Pittsburgh for the eighth annual Junior Achievement National Business Leadership Conference. The keynote speaker was then United States Vice President George H. W. Bush.

Jan Koehler said, "Kirby developed our gold, bronze, and silver 'Leadership Awards.' He felt the local board needed recognition from the national office. But he would never accept one. I tried to nominate him, and he said, 'No, no. I'm none of those. I can't have one.' He did not like recognition. It was very hard, but he wanted other people to be recognized."

Despite his aversion to receiving awards, in 1984, Kirby was recognized at the forty-first National Junior Achievers Conference with the Pioneer Award, which is given annually to the individual who has done the most to establish JA in a community and foster its growth to maturity. Kirby said, "I'm only accepting this award on behalf of all the sponsors of Junior Achievement in the Lafayette area. They're the ones entitled to recognition. I've just been lucky enough to get in with good groups of people."

The Bloomington *Sunday Herald Times* ran a story about NAJAC that year and mentioned Kirby's Pioneer Award. The article also stated that President Ronald Reagan had been invited, but he probably would be unable to attend, as he was in California. Nevertheless, the big news was that the US Post Office was issuing a commemorative twenty-cent postage stamp honoring Horace Moses, JA founder. A special stamp ceremony was held during the conference.

Kirby came to be known as the "father of Junior Achievement" in Tippecanoe County. As he aged, it became difficult for him to continue the pace of his volunteer endeavors. To ensure that the JA work was done on time, the two "Jans" in Kirby's life began gently relieving him of his many tasks, such as the Future Unlimited Banquet. Jan Koehler recalled:

> He got so mad at me. He'd say to Jan Lehnen, his secretary, "That whippersnapper doesn't know what needs to be done." Then Jan Lehnen would help him. She was truly his right arm. She could pretty much keep him in line. Jan Lehnen would say, "Well, now look. You go ahead and do this part, and let Jan do this other part, and it will take this off of the plate so you don't have to do it." And then Kirby would be all right. And I have to say, when we stopped doing some of the things Kirby's way, we didn't raise some of the money that we raised before. Because people give to people. Kirby was able to put that special spark into everything.

CHAPTER 16

TAKING RISKS

When he was in high school and college, Kirby's only son, Jim, worked for his father's two businesses, Kirby Risk Supply and Kirby Risk Electric Motors. He repaired motors at the "motor shop" and worked in the warehouse at the red brick building at Third and Ferry Streets in downtown Lafayette where customers walked in and purchased anything from lightbulbs to Sunbeam appliances to motor control. The supply business sold a full array of electrical and industrial goods. Jim also worked at the sales counter. He said, "We wore multiple hats in a small company. The focus was taking care of the customer."

Roger Swindle began working for Kirby Risk in 1954 and led the assembly of the National Homes fixture packages. He remembered Jim's teenage years in the business. Swindle recalled:

> One time Jim apparently left a bit early from an evening meeting that included customers. Kirby expected the sales people, and especially Jim, to stay until the last customer left. Kirby didn't tolerate not showing proper respect to customers. Kirby heard about Jim's behavior. Well, our upstairs had no air-conditioning. In the sum-

mer it could be miserable, and in the winter it was cold with no heat. We always had somebody work up there in the storeroom to pull inventory for the counter and warehouse personnel. We had a big chute that we would slide merchandise down from the third floor to the counter level. It was a pit to work up there. So, in response to Jim leaving early, Kirby came in and said, "Get yourself upstairs until you learn how to respect customers!"

Jim started with the family business as a counter sales person. Within several years, he moved to outside sales, calling on all types of Lafayette customers from industrial plants, like Fairfield Manufacturing, to small, locally-owned businesses, like Lawrence Bowers Electric located on Main Street.

Swindle described another Kirby creed taught to his son in his own Kirby style. He said:

> Jim was working outside as a salesman. One day, he returned to the office shortly before closing and parked his car in the customer lot. Only customers were allowed to park in the parking lot during business hours. Even Kirby parked across the street in the city parking lot. I went over to the main office shortly after five, and Jim was searching for his car. He went outside to the parking lot and came back in, and he said, "I can't find my car! Somebody took my car!" Kirby said, "You know you're not supposed to park in the back lot! Now, go find the damn thing!" Kirby had seen the car sitting in the customer lot, got in, drove it down Fourth Street, and hid it.

When Jim was in high school and asked his father if he could work for the business during the summer, Kirby told him to interview with Ralph Brassie, the controller who also served as the personnel manager. Swindle said, "Kirby never cut Jim any slack. Where Jim is today, he earned. Kirby did not hand it to him. He's earned everything by working for it."

At times, Kirby may have been harder on Jim than he was his other staff members.

Kirby had a subtle way of addressing many problems with his employees. Swindle recalled, "If Kirby saw that something wasn't like he thought it should be, he'd say, 'Now, why in the world would we do something like that?' That was his way of letting you know he didn't think it was the way it should be done."

One day around five o'clock in the evening, Kirby asked his staff of about sixteen to stay for a meeting. Swindle remembered, "Someone from Fairfield [Manufacturing] had called and asked one of our inside sales people a question. And our sales rep said, 'Well, that's not my department. You'll have to speak with somebody else.' Kirby heard about it and called this meeting, and he said, 'I didn't know we got so damn big that we were departmentalized.' That's all he said."

By the mid-1960s, Jim decided to leave Kirby Risk Supply to explore other career opportunities, including those in the life insurance industry. Jim said, "I sought advice from several sources and counseled with successful businessmen I admired. I did aptitude testing at Purdue that indicated my interests and capacities in common with people

Jim Risk called on Eldon Bowers of Ralph Bowers Electric in 1972, the year he became president of what was then called Kirby Risk Supply Company.

in sales, leadership, and service. I completed courses in sales and sales management."

Then Glenn Safford, Kirby's trusted, pipe-smoking, aide-de-camp, invited Jim for a visit in his home in nearby Brookston, Indiana. The sales manager had recently left Kirby Risk, and Safford asked Jim to consider staying on to assume the sales manager's position. The two men visited for several hours discussing the company and Jim's future. Jim said, "An unexpected opportunity suddenly was presented, and I accepted the challenge of managing the sales team and charting a growth strategy."

SAGAMORE OF THE WABASH

Kirby received the Sagamore of the Wabash Award in 1968 from his friend, Seventh Street neighbor, and wedding prank buddy, Roger D. Branigin. The Sagamore of the Wabash is given by the governor of Indiana to those who have made a significant contribution to the Hoosier state. The designation was created in the late 1940s during the administration of Governor Ralph Gates. "Sagamore" was a term used by Native American tribes of Indiana to describe a lesser chief or a great man whom the chief consulted for wisdom and advice.

The award has been bestowed upon ordinary people who have shown outstanding service as volunteers, veterans, or educators, along with presidents, astronauts, entertainers, and entrepreneurs. Recipients have ranged from Indiana University President and Chancellor Herman B. Wells to Garfield the Cat, the creation of Muncie native Jim Davis. The receiver need not even be from Indiana—singer Willie Nelson was honored for his work on behalf of American farmers.

MINUSCULE OFFICE

Beginning in 1969, Jan Lehnen served as Kirby's secretary. Later, she would continue as Jim's secretary, working for the company for a total of thirty-nine years. Kirby had difficulty keeping secretaries. Jan recalled the day of her interview with Kirby, who was sixty-eight by then.

"There was an ad in the paper," she said. "I went over and sat down in the teeny office, and we started talking, and all of the sudden, he said, 'Would you mind typing something for me?' He had some forms because he was going to the National Association of Electrical Distributors Convention. So he said, "Here's the typewriter," and I finished that, and he said, "Well, would you mind typing this?' I was there for several hours. Finally, it was getting late, so I had to leave, so he hired me on the spot."

Kirby was good friends with Jack Scott, the publisher of the Lafayette *Journal and Courier* at the time. Jan said, "After I was there for about a year, Jack Scott called one day, and I answered the phone. He said, 'You're still there?' Because Kirby was a great guy, but he was kind of a perfectionist, and he would criticize. But I was thirty-four, and I had worked many places and had a lot of experience, so it didn't bother me. I knew it wasn't me he was upset with if something wasn't perfect."

For several years after, each time Jack Scott called, he asked Jan, "Are you still there?"

When Jan started in 1969, the two businesses were officially called Kirby Risk Supply Company, a wholesale distributor of electrical products at Third and Ferry Streets, and Kirby Risk Distribution and Service, which sold plumbing, air-conditioning, and heating equipment and was an electric motor repair shop at First and Smith Streets. Kirby was chairman of the board of the supply business with Glenn Safford as president and Jim Risk as vice president and sales manager. Caroline was secretary-treasurer. For Kirby Risk Distribution and Service, Kirby was president, Stan Newhard was vice president and general manager, and Glenn Buschman was vice president of the motor shop. The two companies employed sixty-five people. The distribution and service business, which today is Kirby Risk Mechanical Solutions and Service, is still referenced by family and longtime staff members as "the motor shop."

Kirby's office at Third and Ferry Streets was very small, about ten by ten feet. When Jim became president in 1972, he shared this office with his father and Jan. Of course, Kirby was never there from eight to five. That wasn't his style. For the most part, he worked at night and slept late in the morning. He liked to work in the office when it was quiet and no one else was around so he could get things done. Jan said, "Jim would be there in the daytime, and Kirby would be there at night. And I would be there all the time!"

Kirby's desk was a sight. Just ask Jan. "Oh my God, you couldn't even see the bottom of it," she said. "He just had piles and piles. One day he was having someone come in and visit, and he wanted things cleaned up. So I just moved everything on his desk into the vault and put it back later. But stuff had been sitting there for so long that it was actually stuck to the desk, and I had to scrape it off."

After Jim became president, Kirby concentrated most of his efforts on his charity work, including Junior Achievement and United Way. Jan helped type many letters for all of his volunteer efforts and aided with John Purdue Club football and basketball ticket ordering. Jan said, "Years and years ago, Kirby had started handling the ordering for the John Purdue members. They'd pay us, and we'd pay Purdue."

Jim Risk had recently been elected president of Kirby Risk Supply when he stood for a picture in the early 1970s taken outside of the Kirby Risk building, formerly the Lafayette Milling Company, at Third and Ferry Streets in Lafayette, Indiana. Kirby purchased the building at auction in 1940, the year his daughter Sherry was born. The next year, Jim was born, and Kirby Risk Electric moved to this location.

Jan typed all of Kirby's letters on a Selectric typewriter using correcting tape. Jan recalled:

> I might have to type twenty-five letters in a night, especially if he waited until the last minute. After they'd have a meeting for United Way, he'd come back, and we'd want to get these letters out to report on what happened at the meeting. I'd get a long letter all typed up, and he'd decide he wanted to change one word. So I'd either have to retype the whole thing or go back and try to correct it with correcting tape. It would be just one measly word. Something that nobody ever would have noticed.

Fortunately, Jan was a fast typist. She said, "It's a wonder I have any fingers left. But Kirby had so many good qualities that if he did something that honked me off, I just let it slide. Everybody has moments like that, you know."

Besides typing her fingers to the nubs in cramped quarters late into the night, sitting next to Kirby's desk piled high with fermenting papers, Jan "smoked like a chimney," which added to the ambiance of the old, drafty building that once served as a flour mill. Jan said, "I'd be puffing away and there sat Jim and Kirby, but they never said anything."

In the background was Peggy Bennett, the switchboard operator, whose work filled the office with sporadic buzzing sounds. Jan remembered, "Kirby had a buzzer under his desk during my first few years. We were in our room and the switchboard was around the corner. When he would ask Peggy to place a conference call, he would buzz her, and when she was ready, she would buzz him. So we had these buzzers going off all the time. It was really cozy."

Jan loved Kirby and Caroline for their generosity, kindness, and fun. She said, "Caroline would come to the office to pick up Kirby, and he would say, 'We'll be done in a minute.' She would wind up waiting for two hours. She never complained. Every time we were working late she would bring food down for us to eat."

The "Late Mr. Risk" was known far and wide. The Purdue National Bank tellers were subject to Kirby's whims when it came to his last-minute daily deposits, yet they were fond of the charismatic man who enjoyed visiting the bank. Jan said, "The bank closed at five. Kirby would go to the bank every day at five. Sometimes he would call me at ten minutes before five and say, "'I can't make it today. Can you take it over?' I'd run over there and just get in the door before they closed."

After Jan worked at Kirby Risk Supply for three years, Jim became president. She said, "Jim is such an entrepreneur. He almost has a photographic memory. Jim had this firm foundation from Kirby. He had a good start. He did everything. Not all heads of companies start in the warehouse or shipping. He knew every aspect of the company. And he knew the products. Kirby did, too."

"The Late Mr. Risk" enjoyed visiting with the tellers at the bank when he made his daily deposits. He often rushed in just as the clock would strike five and the bank was about to close for the day.

COLUMBUS OPENS

In 1972, the same year Jim became president, the company opened its first location outside of Lafayette in Columbus, Indiana, 110 miles south. The sales staff had saturated the marketplace of Tippecanoe and surrounding counties, and it was time to stretch the boundaries to other parts of Indiana. Jim recalled:

> We were wanting to grow and expand the business. You stop and
> think about how you want things to look in five years from a fam-

ily, financial, business, spiritual, and social perspective and create a vision. It seemed obvious to create opportunities for people. We couldn't sit still. It was important to expand. The fact that we had seven outside sales people representing our Lafayette location, plus the sales supervisor who spent his day in the field, it was a challenge to develop more market share. So we needed to look for other opportunities.

Actually, Kirby and Glenn Safford first had kicked around the idea of opening a second operation about ten years before. They had surveyed the markets and had their eye on Columbus, even though most of the potential customers there had never heard of Kirby Risk Supply. Safford is quoted in a 1973 *Electrical Wholesaling* magazine article entitled "Making a Branch Succeed in Unknown Territory." He said, ". . . after a flurry of activity, one event led to another and the branch idea went fallow." The idea came to life again once Jim became president a decade later, and the three men made it happen in a time when the company had financial strength. By then, Safford was chairman of the board and Kirby was chairman of the finance committee.

The new location was called a "Distribution Center," because the term "branch" "sounded like it wasn't so important." Jim said, "From the beginning, our thought was to make it feel like it was a local business. So we gave them a lot of autonomy at the time. It's a different model today."

The men felt that Columbus was an attractive place to set up an electrical supply distributorship for three reasons. First, a large number of industrial plants were there, including the world headquarters of Cummins Engine Company. Second, businesses in and around Columbus were traveling out of the city to purchase much of their electrical supplies. And third, Columbus was a growing and thriving city known as the "Athens of the Prairie," a title derived from the fact that famous architects designed many of the buildings there.

Kirby Risk Supply was cautious not to criticize the competition in Columbus, so the staff canvassed contractors and industrial plants to clarify intentions and sound out reactions. In the *Electrical Wholesaling* article, Jim said, "In Lafayette, our company has done business for more than 40 years, and we would hope that if another distributor moved in down the street, our customers would continue doing business with us. This is the point we tried to get across to the companies in Columbus. We respect any existing customers-distributor relationship and do not try to tear it down."

The staff made it known to the Columbus companies that Kirby Risk wanted the chance to receive the business they were giving to out of town distributorships. Yet Jim also said—and this is where the Risk philosophy is like cream rising—"Just because a company doesn't intend to give us any business right away does not mean we aren't going to continue calling on them. They may someday need help in an emergency, and that's the chance we're hoping for."

Since 1926, Kirby had thrived on emergencies. A customer's emergency need gave Kirby and his staff the opportunity to out-luster the competition. Any time, day or night, at home or at the office, Kirby was ready to move into action to come to the aid of a manufacturer or business with a broken motor, a need for a generator, a part for an assembly line. He lived naturally what Jim came to call "sacrificial service," and his workers understood what was expected by watching Kirby's example. The Risk family lived "sacrificial service" at home and in business. The two aspects braided into uncommon strength and success. This caring culture of the company was evident in the people Kirby hired, and later, those Jim brought on board. Jim and staff carried forth the port-in-a-storm level of service that Kirby captained.

Once the Columbus distribution center launched, a two-day open house was held with five hundred invitations sent to area businesses. Suppliers were asked to participate. Jim's quotation in the *Electrical Wholesaling* article continues, "Some people thought we were crazy because we had no regular customers, and there was a chance that no one would come to see the place. I suppose we were taking a chance, but the whole open house was a huge success and a lot of good came from it." For a time, Jim traveled from Lafayette to Columbus three days a week to assist in the establishment of the new Kirby Risk distribution center.

The manager for the Columbus distribution center was the first husband of Kirby's daughter Sherry, Jim Stark. The prior year, Jim Stark had come to work for Kirby Risk. Sherry explained about her then husband: "Jim was in the Navy, then he sold insurance. We lived in Maine. Then my brother talked to him and encouraged him to come work for Kirby Risk. And my father wisely said, 'We need to be really sure that it is going to work.' So we met with an industrial psychologist in Chicago. Jim [Stark] spent quite a bit of time talking to them, and then I met with them, too."

Sherry liked living in Maine, where she was raising her two boys and had established friendships. But the couple scrimped to get by monetarily there, so the offer to move to Lafayette for a good-paying job was attractive. Sherry returned to her old life of "being a Risk." She recalled, "There was a company car. Mary Jo was my buddy from grade school. I was in bridge club. It was just way too easy. It didn't feel like I had earned any of it. And it felt like I was Sherry Risk. I wasn't Sherry Stark."

Jim Stark started at Kirby Risk Supply in Lafayette working the counter and graduated to working in outside sales. Then one night, Kirby and Jim took the Starks to the Lafayette Country Club. Sherry recalled, "They said over dinner, 'We are looking for a place to open a second facility, and we have decided Columbus, Indiana, is the right place to do that. We know you [Jim Stark] have been with the company for a very short time, but we feel you are the right one to manage it. Would you consider going to Columbus?'"

Sherry reported they immediately said, "Yes!" She recalled that her brother looked rather shocked, "because he had always lived in Lafayette, and I think to him the idea of asking someone to move away would be so difficult. Whereas in the Navy, my husband and I had moved thirteen times in the first ten years of marriage. So, to me, to have a fresh start in a place where we were the Starks, not Sherry Risk, would be wonderful."

Jim Stark began as the Columbus division manager and he became the district manager and a corporate vice president as the business expanded in southern Indiana.

MORE ACQUISITIONS

In Columbus, Kirby Risk served many markets: industrial, commercial, and institutional, along with residential, commercial, and industrial construction. They had a stronger emphasis on serving the industrial market than the typical electrical distributor because they offered automation and industrial products. A turning point for even more growth came when the Columbus site became a distributor of the Allen-Bradley line, which was founded in 1903 by Lynde Bradley and Dr. Stanton Allen as the Compression Rheostat Company. Jim Risk said, "That set the course for our continued expansion. With each new location our objective was to maintain the same major lines. There's only one authorized Allen-Bradley distributor per APR, area of primary responsibility, which made expanding our number of locations challenging."

In 1985, Rockwell International purchased Allen-Bradley. They made one of the first commercially manufactured Allen-Bradley brand of crane controllers for the St. Louis World's Fair. Today they offer a broad array of factory automation equipment.

The next distribution center Kirby Risk opened was in Crawfordsville, Indiana. Montgomery County, where Wabash College is located, has always been a strong market for the company, but at the time of their opening, Kirby Risk was losing some market share to a competing distributor that had recently opened. Jim recalled:

> We tried to buy the local distributor, but they were not interested in selling. Our core competency from the very beginning was relationships. So we would naturally create good, solid, trusting relationships with our employees and their families. And we'd do that with our customers, our vendors, and the communities that we served, and our fellow distributors around the state. We'd develop

trusting relationships with competitors, which put us in somewhat of a unique position to discuss the possibility of purchasing their business.

In essence, Jim and his staff understood many of their competitors, at the time, were family-owned electrical distributors just like Kirby Risk. Jim's quiet demeanor and sensitive nature helped him to understand the poignant side of letting go of a family-owned business, and his heartfelt understanding helped him obtain acquisitions in a respectful manner. Jim said, "It's definitely easier to start or open a new business location than it is to sell a family business. When you deal with these people, it's important to be sensitive to the emotional aspect of selling their business."

The locally owned electrical distributors that Jim befriended often did not have the next generation willing to take over the business, or the leadership did not have the necessary skills to take the company into the future, to embrace change and new technologies. Jim remembered:

> If you don't keep pace with the changing market dynamics, at some point you start drifting, and then you get out of the growth mode. Some of these local distributors were harvesting their business and lacked a vision for the future. At some point in there, I would find a nonthreatening way to meet with the owners and let them know we might have an interest, and be able to do it in such a manner that it would be good for them and their employees. We were reasonably successful at quietly acquiring fellow distributors.

The Kirby Risk team was more than reasonably successful with acquisitions. After Kirby Risk opened in Crawfordsville, they opened in Danville, Illinois, and then "marched around the state." Kirby Risk purchased other Indiana Allen-Bradley distributors, including a distributor headquartered in Muncie, Universal Electric, which had seven Allen-Bradley locations. During the 1980s and 1990s, Kirby Risk Supply expanded throughout Indiana, Ohio, and Illinois, purchasing the assets of other electrical distributors that bore family

names like Kulwin Electric and Kiefer Electric, and feel-good monikers like Hoosier Electric. Today, Kirby Risk Corporation operates
from forty-three locations.

In 1996, Jason Bricker was swayed by Jim Risk to leave his promising career path as senior manager with Olive Accounting (now BKD).
It was a job he loved and thought he had no intention of vacating;
however, Jason accepted the position of CFO for Kirby Risk Corporation after being "worn down" by Jim's quiet resolve. Jason said, "Jim
is a very sincere individual. It's just his complete style, charismatic
charm, and conscientious manner. He's very intuitive. He's very per-
ceptive. He understands people and relationships better than anyone
I've ever met. He values relationships, absolutely. They are paramount
to him. That combination is the most persuasive I have ever come into
contact with. Jim has the ability to do the uncommon."

The staff of the small electrical distributor companies acquired
were often surprised by the welcome they would receive as they were
assimilated into the Kirby Risk fold. Jim said, "Valuing people has
always been a part of the company. You really live that, and the new
employees that came on board with these purchases would typically be
wowed by the reception they'd get and end up recognizing they were
better off being part of the Kirby Risk team. We developed a can-do
spirit and had a lot of fun celebrating our successes."

CHAPTER 17

NEW DIRECTIONS

Through the 1970s and 1980s, the Risks and Prices continued to nurture their family bonds. Best friends Jim Risk and David Price led the companies their fathers had founded. David joined National Homes in 1965 and was named president in 1977. Jim and David had been buddies since grade school, playing basketball and football together and sharing family vacations. David's sister, Anne Price, said of the two, "They had such a competitive spirit. They were like brothers."

As adults, the two were always up for a good time, and not above the outlandish, like trick-or-treating (for drinks, not candy) costumed as "husband and wife" and ending one Halloween evening dancing as a "couple" at a local bar.

They started a gin tournament for their buddies. They deemed it the "Gin Classic," held on a weekend in February. David's wife, Jane, remembered, "Jim had creative ideas, and David was creative, too. They had favors. One time it was a paperweight that had a card on it like a jack or king—you know how the picture is in the corner? Well, it would be the faces of David and Jim instead of the jack or king. They also had a traveling trophy."

Jim and Mary Jo Risk, David and Jane Hovde Price, and Bob and Patti Peyton Truitt were part of what they called "PTR Gourmet Club," preparing elaborate meals at home for the group. Patti, who had been a member with Jim in the church youth group Epsilon Theta, recalled, "Jim inherited his love of food from his dad. So six of us had a gourmet group, and it was a lot of fun. We'd say, 'What do think this meal would have cost us if we bought it in a restaurant?'"

Patti's husband, Bob, was president of Rostone Corporation in Lafayette. Rostone made switchgear components for electrical equipment and was sold to Allen-Bradley. Allen-Bradley was Kirby Risk's largest vendor, so Bob was connected to the Risks through friendship and profession. Today, Bob serves on the board of Kirby Risk Corporation, and Patti is an attorney in Lafayette.

Like their fathers, Jim and David enjoyed staging practical jokes. David was renowned for pranking people with animals. He gave a friend a dog he didn't want, his sister a bird she promptly gave away, and he was responsible for the famous skunk at Jim and Mary Jo's rehearsal dinner on Owen Street. David's wife, Jane, said, "He brought an armadillo from Texas to my sister's wedding, just to be ornery. And then I had a fortieth birthday party for David. Everybody decided to bring animals to pay David back."

Jim Risk had already turned the animal tables on David during the Christmas of 1971. David and Jane's two-year-old son, Jimmy, wanted a "horsey." Jane and David were hosting the Price family Christmas at their two-story brick home in Vinton Woods. Jane remembered, "It was always a very fancy affair. We were still having cocktails, and somebody knocked on the door. This kind of straggly-looking man said, 'Is Jimmy here? I have a present for him.'" Little Jimmy scampered to the door and looked out into the falling snow. Tied to a tree was a pony.

"Jimmy just lost it, he was so excited," Jane said. "And then there's this snickering out in the yard, and Jim Risk and two other buddies, Tom Rush and Tim McGinley, unveiled themselves."

Upon seeing the gift to his grandson outside the front door, Jim Price led the pony to his son's back patio, through the sliding glass doors, and into the family room where the Price family was gathered in their best holiday attire. Jane remembered, "David's dad brings the pony inside my family room and makes Jimmy and I get on it. I was holding Jimmy. He slaps the pony on the rump, and the pony takes off. We had this long connected area from the great room to the laundry room. The pony takes off, and when he comes to the laundry room, there's no place to go, and he just screeches to a halt. Of course, Jimmy and I fall off."

The Prices kept Jim, Tom, and Tim's Christmas gift to little Jimmy in the backyard of their home, which looked out over the small Vinton Woods Lake. They had a lean-to built next to the swing set for the pony's shelter. In the summer, the Price children walked the pony down the streets of the quiet city neighborhood, and in the winter, the pony pulled their sled and toboggan. When the pony came to the back door, the kids fed him handfuls of sugar.

NATIONAL HOMES STRUGGLES

As the 1970s was a decade of growth for Kirby Risk, it was the beginning of a slow end for National Homes Corporation. A 1990 Lafayette *Journal and Courier* story states that the "decline was rooted in the company's move to expand and diversify just as the housing industry was entering a steep decline." In the 1970s, the prefab housing industry felt competition from conventional builders who were obtaining more prefabricated housing components, such as roof trusses. Another arrow to the heart of National Homes was the wage and price controls established by President Richard Nixon in 1972 to combat double-digit inflation. Home prices were frozen, while prices of lumber and other raw materials were not.

According to the *Journal and Courier* article, in 1972, Nixon also ordered an eighteen-month moratorium on federally subsidized housing, "locking the brakes" on the housing industry. Orders for new houses plummeted from 2.3 million in 1972 to 1.2 million by 1975.

National Homes had gone headfirst into three major new fields: mobile homes, modular homes, and land development. The result was a company that stretched itself thin financially and managerially. The *Journal and Courier* article states this about Jim Price, Kirby's good friend and professional ally: "In March 1972, Jim Price stepped down as chief executive officer, citing reasons of health. His wife later said the pressure of trying to solve the company's problems had stretched him to the breaking point." Jim's brother, George, was named successor.

Jim Risk said, "Jim Price was a passionate executive leader. He was a colorful and most unusual person. I have countless memories of my experiences with him, starting when I was six."

Another *Journal and Courier* piece from 1990 gives a glimpse into the personal toll brought about by the struggles of National Homes, what had been a family-owned business that became a Fortune 500 company: "The indomitable Price, who had overcome numerous adversities since the company was founded in 1940, was at the end of his rope emotionally."

After Jim Price left National Homes, he turned his entrepreneurial spirit to the Kentucky Fried Chicken restaurants he owned in Lafayette. He injected his franchise with personal touches out of the norm for the typical KFC. For instance, he offered a cucumber salad, made from a recipe that had belonged to Caroline Risk's mother.

On June 28, 1974, Jim Price died of a heart attack while at work. He was sixty-two.

Jim Risk remembered, "I was participating in a golf outing at Harrison Lake Country Club in Columbus, Indiana. We had recently opened our first location outside of Lafayette in Columbus. Someone from the pro shop located me on the course to inform me that Jim Price had just died."

Soon after, Jim Price's daughter, Anne, began managing the KFC restaurants in Lafayette. Today, her son, yet another "Jim," is also in the business. Anne said, "When I was ready to go to college, my Dad said, 'I want you to take some business courses. You're going to need

to know them in your life.' And I'm so glad I did. I definitely used it. It is interesting. A lot of the things that influenced me in my life were from my Dad."

JULIE'S GIFT

While Anne Price recalled the influence of her father, Jim, Kirby also impacted the life of his own daughter, Julie. She gave Kirby an unexpected gift, days before his seventieth birthday. Julie signed the same "pledge of intent" to never drink alcohol as a beverage, written and signed in 1916 by William Jennings Bryan, James Kirby Risk Sr., and Kirby.

Julie said, "I was in college. I took it to a frame shop where they took it apart so I could sign it, and they put it back together. Then I wrapped it up and gave it to him as his birthday gift. I was pretty emotional. I cried because I was overwhelmed and happy to be able to do that for him. I thought it would be one of the best gifts I could give him. You know, money can't buy that."

For decades, the pledge hung in a hallway of the Risk home where Caroline displayed family photos and memorabilia. It later was moved to the sunroom, which was the television room just off the kitchen.

"Dad wanted to make sure that I did it for me and not for him, but I'm sure he was thrilled," Julie said. "I never was a big drinker anyway. I had seen what it had done to other people, and it wasn't too attractive. I never regretted it."

Today, Julie has the pledge hanging in her home office. Each year, she tucks palm branches she receives at church on Palm Sunday behind the frame. The following year, she removes the branches and returns them to church where they are burned to honor Ash Wednesday.

The pledge of intent is a slip of yellowed paper behind glass in a modest black frame. Below the signature of her grandfather, James Kirby Risk Sr., whom she never met, Julie penned: "Julia Patricia Risk, Sept. 17, 1971."

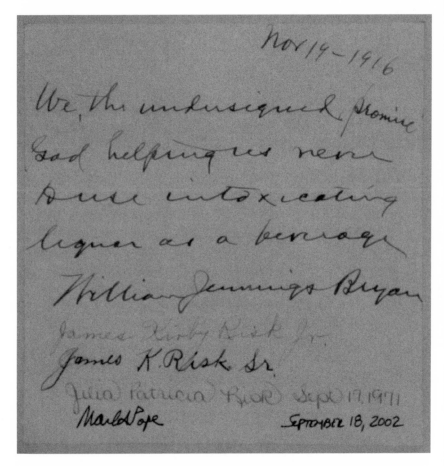

Nov 19—1916

We, the undersigned, promise, God helping us never to use intoxicating liquor as a beverage

William Jennings Bryan

James Kirby Risk Jr.

James K. Risk Sr.

Julia Patricia Risk) Sept 17, 1971

Mark Pope _____ *September 18, 2002*

Along with William Jennings Bryan and James Kirby Risk Sr., Kirby, at the age of fifteen, signed this letter of intent to never use intoxicating liquor as a beverage. He was true to the pledge for his entire life. In 1971, Kirby's youngest daughter, Julie, signed the letter as a gift to her father. Julie's husband, Mark Pope, signed in 2002.

TREATMENT CENTER

Swirling in the background of Julie's gift to her father was Kirby's quiet help with a new alcohol treatment center near Lafayette. After Jim and Mary Jo Risk married, young Julie cried because her big brother, her "rescuer" from Kirby's proverbial Sunday drives, would no longer be around. At that time, many of Kirby's country drives were to look over a spot for New Directions, a rehabilitation program that opened at the former Monitor School, which had been built in 1911 in the now "extinct" tiny burg of Monitor, Indiana, east of Lafayette.

Dale Cummings, who was a native of Caroline Risk's hometown of Boswell, was the director of the facility that was originally called "New Covenant Center." It served men from an eight-county area. In a 1975 Lafayette *Journal and Courier* story, Cummings, a recovered alcoholic himself, explained that the name meant, "A man can come to the center and make a New Covenant with God."

Cummings also said, "We try to help the alcoholic untangle the financial, legal and family nightmares. . . . He's got to have help working out the nightmares that he's created by his drinking or the drinking will remain a problem."

Cummings was supervisor, counselor, secretary, and cook for the nonprofit agency. Jim Risk described the accommodations for the men: "Shower curtains were hung from pipe to make separate rooms. Then we got the money to build the workshop, which allowed the men to earn some money. My father and I spent a lot of time at what we called 'the school,' because that's where they were living, in the old Monitor School."

Adjacent to the center was a "sheltered workshop" where the men rebuilt wooden pallets used by area manufacturers such as Alcoa, Ross Gear, Fairfield, Eli Lilly, and more. Clients of New Directions worked at the pallet rebuilding shop, earning money that helped pay for their treatment. A New Directions Industries (NDI) brochure states, "We build more than wood products. We start to rebuild lives."

Jim recalled, "Dale was really effective at working with people. When more expensive and elaborate facilities and institutions were having limited success, Dale was recording impressive results."

New Directions operated with money obtained through fund-raising, including collection boxes in area businesses, from United Way, and from state and federal grant money. The program grew to also treat clients with drug addictions. Outpatient treatment centers were opened in Crawfordsville, Indiana, and downtown Lafayette. In 2007,

New Directions closed due to lack of funding. Jim worked with Cummings to try to save the facility, but to no avail. In 2010, the old brick building—where schoolchildren once wrote on a slate chalkboard and later, where alcoholics vanquished nightmares—was set fire by an arsonist.

Several *Journal and Courier* articles were written about New Directions between 1975 and 2003, highlighting the need for funds to expand the offerings and improve facilities, but none of the stories mention Kirby's involvement. Kirby was in the background, moving mountains in his understated way. He was known to walk in, pick up a stack of bills, and pay them. He knew whom to take to lunch, whom to call, and whom to write to obtain the money needed to move his pet project forward. A pet project sanctioned by Kirby was golden.

Cummings told of the day he met Gene Kramer, president and CEO of Fairfield Manufacturing. "There's a story that I like to tell that epitomizes the community's trust and regard for Kirby Risk," Cummings said. "One day Kirby brought out this factory president to visit our facility. Afterward we went to lunch at the country club. Kirby got up to go somewhere, and this other man leaned over and told me, 'I don't need to know anything about you or your organization. All I need to know is that Kirby is in your corner. I'll pledge $10,000.'"

PERKS

When Kirby's youngest, Julie, was at Purdue University in the early 1970s, she was a member of the women's singing group the Purduettes. Her boyfriend was in the Purdue Men's Varsity Glee Club. Kirby was referred to as "the chief promoter of the Glee Club" for his efforts in fund-raising for the choral group's first tour of Europe. A large, framed photograph of the Glee Club posing next to the airplane that took them from the Purdue Airport to Europe hung on the wall at the Kirby Risk offices.

Julie said, "I wanted to be in the Purduettes so badly. I finally got up enough courage to try out and got in. I got to go on four trips my four years in school—Hawaii the first year. And my parents went on all of them. I always felt like I got benefits through life and especially through Purdue because I was Kirby's daughter. And I loved it."

Some of the Risk family held a different view of what it felt like to be known as one of Kirby's progeny. "I would hear grandchildren or others say it was really difficult to be Kirby's grandchildren," Julie said. "And I thought, 'What a different view.' I guess they felt that people had high expectations. I just thought, 'That's crazy. Take advantage of it.' I always, always said who my parents were with pride."

OLD OAKEN BUCKET GAME

On November 24, 1973, Purdue played archrival Indiana University (IU), which was coached by Lee Corso. The winner of the annual Purdue versus Indiana game receives the coveted "Old Oaken Bucket."

The tradition of the Old Oaken Bucket began in 1925, the same year Kirby quit school to start his battery company. A committee of four Purdue men and four IU men proposed that a football trophy be awarded annually. The small, wooden bucket was decided upon because it typified the Hoosier spirit. It was decided that the bucket should come from an Indiana well. There are several stories as to the origins of the bucket. Some say it came from an Indiana farm between Kent and Hanover. Another account claims that story is untrue, and still another tale claims the bucket actually came from Illinois.

Whatever its origin, the bucket is decorated with a bronze plaque that states, "Football Trophy, Presented by Indiana & Purdue Alumni of Chicago 1925." A chain is attached to the bucket with bronze to hold a block "I" or "P" letter representing the two universities and each game won, with the winning university adding a new letter to the chain each year. The winning team retains the trophy until the following year. The bucket is the second oldest trophy tradition in collegiate football, superseded only by the Little Brown Jug awarded to the winner of the game between Minnesota and Michigan since 1902.

Often Kirby, Caroline, Jim, and Mary Jo would sit around the kitchen table on Owen Street as Caroline crafted a poem that would become an invitation to their football day excursion. For the 1973 November away game, the Risks invited their guests to join them with this rhyme:

> Kirb's Old Home Place is the place to get braced
> On Saturday 'round about nine.
> The bus will depart for I.U.–(*Do* take heart!!)
> So we'll be at the game in good time.
>
> Boxed lunch served en route to the whole gosh derned group
> To prepare for the fray against Corso.
> But whatever the score–there still will be more:
> Fried chicken and pie, maybe more-so!!
>
> After we dine we'll be home before nine.
> We'll rehash, replay, and rejoice (?)
> The Bucket, "Old Oaken," we hope is our token
> For winning the game of our choice.

Guests who joined the Risks that day were from Purdue University, National Homes Corporation, Anheuser-Busch, Ross Gear, General Foods, Arnett Clinic, Rush Metal, the Shook Agency, and Kirby Risk Supply Company. Then Purdue President Fred Hovde and his wife, Priscilla, George and Marge Price, Jim and Roberta Price, and others who were a virtual "who's-who" of Lafayette, climbed into the bus and headed south to Bloomington. More than business associates, each Purdue or Indiana fan inside was a longtime, dear friend of Kirby and Caroline.

The bus always made a stop at one of Kirby's favorite shopping haunts–Sargent's 5 & 10 variety store in Cloverdale, Indiana. Kirby wrote in a 1975 letter to his friend Maury Knoy, the president of Rostone Corporation who was from Cloverdale, "Sargent's has also been an every-other-year Christmas toy shopping bus stop on our return

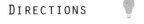

from the Old Oaken Bucket Classic. In fact, I'm writing this letter in a pair of blue flowered 49-cent BVD's purchased at Sargent's in 1959!"

DOUG MANSFIELD

Doug Mansfield came to Kirby Risk "motor shop" by way of Sam Lyboult, who was superintendent of the Lafayette Parks and Recreation Department. He was Jim Risk's basketball coach at Lafayette Jefferson High School. Today, Lyboult Sports Park in Lafayette is named in his honor.

In the 1960s, Mansfield worked at Columbian Park in Lafayette, Indiana, from age ten to twenty-one. He started on July 4, which was the biggest day of the year for the park. Busloads of people traveled from around the state to the park, which had a pool, amusement rides, a zoo, picnic areas, a scenic "lagoon," baseball stadium, and Independence Day fireworks. Mansfield was placed in the ticket window. "I sold nickel tickets, and all the rides and all the food took tickets," Doug remembered. "I sold eight thousand dollars' worth of nickel tickets that day. I started at 10 a.m., and we finished at midnight. We went to the bank three times."

The park, named after the Columbian Exhibition, also known as the 1893 Chicago World's Fair, was the center of activity back then, especially on a holiday. Thousands of people flocked to enjoy the summer day. Mansfield's work ethic and capable attributes were evident at a very young age. He worked at the park until he was twenty-one and graduated from Purdue University with an electrical engineering degree in 1971. Lyboult told Kirby about this hardworking young man. "Kirby got a hold of me," Mansfield recalled, "and he said, 'Why don't you interview with us?' I had no clue what Kirby Risk was."

Jan Lehnen, Kirby and Jim Risk's secretary for thirty-nine years, said that many people thought Kirby Risk sold Kirby vacuum cleaners, or they thought Kirby and Risk were two different people, like a law firm. Jan would tell these people, "Mr. Kirby Risk. Mr. J. Kirby Risk!"

Doug interviewed with Stan Newhard, president of the "motor shop." "In my interview, they took out a phone book, they opened it, and said, 'Now, print this page,'" Mansfield remembered. "I'm thinking, 'What's this have to do with double E? I'm an electrical engineer. I majored in thick film and thin film microelectronics and silicon wafers when I'm printing the Yellow Pages.' I had taken mechanical drafting, so it was a piece of cake. Lo and behold, it was because we had to write out our invoices. The customers had to read the invoices, and that was part of the job. They wanted to make sure I could legibly write an invoice for motor repair."

Kirby and Newhard hired Mansfield to work for $800 a month reporting to Bud Bushman, the service manager in the motor shop. The plan was that Doug would train for five years and then perhaps take over Bushman's position of running the shop where they repaired electric motors. Mansfield said, "Three months after I was there, Bud Bushman, who never smoked but chewed on cigars, died of throat cancer."

Soon after Bushman passed away, Kirby walked into the motor shop around 5 o'clock in the evening and said to Mansfield, "Young man, see what you can do with the place."

Mansfield thought, "Okay. I guess that means I'm taking Bud's spot."

Just as Mansfield showed his mettle as a boy of ten selling thousands of park tickets, he revealed his willingness to rise to a challenge as the Kirby Risk service manager at the age of twenty-two. He was one of the early hires who held a college degree. He would supervise men who had worked for Kirby Risk for years—and who were twice his age. Newhard was Mansfield's supervisor. He and his wife, Lillian, became like family. The Newhards took Mansfield and his wife under their wing. Mansfield said, "Stan wore the company name on his chest."

Mansfield continued, "I learned real quickly that I knew theory why motors worked, but I knew diddlysquat about how to repair them. But the guys on the floor knew how to repair them, so I learned to be humble. The approach was to ask questions. I'd keep asking, and asking, and asking, and then I'd interject once in a while the 'why' it worked, because I knew the theory. It worked out okay, and we developed mutual respect."

At that time, the motor shop serviced Lafayette industrial customers like Eli Lilly, Fairfield, Ross Gear, Rostone, and Anheuser-Busch. When an electric motor failed on their assembly lines, they needed a repair pronto to continue production. Mansfield said, "There was a huge amount of pressure in motor repair because, number one, the customer has a problem, and number two, they always need a motor repaired yesterday. Because if they can't run their equipment, they can't produce their product."

Sometimes there was a customer who required an "emergency service job." This was the kind of motor repair that received the highest priority at every level of the company—from sales, purchasing, management, and the actual mechanic. The customer was placed first in line. At 3 o'clock in the morning one hot summer day, the men in the motor shop were working on an emergency service repair for Eli Lilly. The large door to the shop was open to the early morning's air. Mansfield was in his tiny office where he could see the shop with two men working, dismantling the motor.

Mansfield said, "All of a sudden, two headlights came right up to the building, almost into the building. Howard Bell, the mechanic, yelled for me. I ran out of the office to figure out what was going on. Usually at that time of the morning, the only people out were police. The car drove right up to where we unloaded trucks, but we couldn't tell who it was. And lo and behold, who got out of the car? Kirby Risk."

Kirby asked the men what they were doing. Mansfield explained the emergency repair for Lilly, and then Kirby left. About a half an hour later, headlights appeared once more. Mansfield said, "I ran out of the office again, and out of the car pops Kirby with a gallon of Frozen Custard Fruit Drink and two cartons of frozen custard. We all sat down with Kirby, had a fruit drink and ice cream, and talked. Then he took off, and we got back to work."

Emergency service was available twenty-four hours a day. Mansfield and his team were prepared to serve 365 days a year, including Thanksgiving and Christmas. "The creed that we went by was to exceed our customer's expectations." Mansfield said. "We would promise on Friday and deliver on Thursday, or promise on Monday and deliver on Sunday. I brought a crew in one New Year's Day at four in the morning to work on a motor. We accomplished the near impossible, but we earned a great reputation and we grew the business."

Once again, the culture was "sacrificial service" before it was written in ink on the Kirby Risk mission statement many years later. Mansfield said, "We lived it in the motor repair, because that's the nature of that business." Kirby had lived sacrificial service since he opened up shop in 1926. He was "living it" the day he heeded an emergency to repair a grain elevator motor in Boswell, Indiana, and met a young girl named Caroline Robinson.

WILD GOOSE CHASE

In 1980, Mansfield became ill, and doctors could not determine what was wrong. He couldn't eat, so he lost weight and was unable to work. Mansfield said, "I felt like warmed over death, and they couldn't figure it out." One Sunday, Kirby visited Mansfield at his home. He was in bed. Kirby, then seventy-eight, said, "You know, I need a physical. I think you and I ought to go to Mayo."

Kirby was referring to Mayo Clinic in Rochester, Minnesota. For more than a century, people have found answers to medical problems at Mayo Clinic. Mansfield recalled, "So, we got on a plane and we flew to Mayo. They checked me out, and Kirby got a physical. We spent a week up there. On that Sunday, we sat in the hotel room and watched the American hockey team beat the Russians in the 'Miracle on Ice.'"

The "Miracle on Ice" is the name that was given to the men's ice hockey victory that occurred during the 1980 Winter Olympics at Lake Placid, New York. Team USA, made up of amateur and collegiate players, shocked the Soviet Union, beating them 4-3, then went on to beat Finland for the gold medal. In 1999, *Sports Illustrated* named the "Miracle on Ice" the "Top Sports Moment" of the twentieth century. As part of its one hundredth anniversary celebrations in 2008, the International Ice Hockey Federation (IIHF) chose the "Miracle on Ice" as the century's number-one international ice hockey story. The winning account was made into a movie in 1981.

Mansfield said, "We watched that on Sunday, and I'm lying on the bed cheering. We'd been in the hotel for three days in the middle of winter. Kirby said, 'You don't have any tests this afternoon. Get your clothes on. We're going out.'"

Mansfield dressed, Kirby slipped on his black cashmere topcoat, and the two stepped out into the Minnesota February cold. Kirby hailed a taxi. Mansfield remembered, "I had no idea what we were doing. We're in the back of the taxi, and Kirby says, 'Hey, hey, stop over there!'" The taxi stopped in front of a market. Kirby ran in and returned carrying four loaves of bread. Kirby gave the taxi driver an address and they zoomed off.

Mansfield said, "We stop and I see a big pond, and it's all snow and ice. It's cold. Kirby said, 'Let's get out.' We go trudging over, and I look out and there are ten thousand geese." The geese were gathered where the Mayo Clinic cooling towers discharged warm water. Kirby said, "We've got to feed the geese. Here's a loaf of bread."

"So we're throwing bread, and here come ten thousand geese, and they're just coming. And they're everywhere," Mansfield said. "They start biting the bottom of Kirby's cashmere coat. They're jumping up trying to get the bread, and Kirby says, 'Get out of here, you son of a . . .' Finally, he throws the bread down and says, 'Get back in the cab.' We got back in the cab and headed to Mayo."

It was true to Kirby's nature to escort Mansfield to Mayo Clinic and try to cheer him with an outing. Mansfield recalled, "Oh, it was hilarious. I didn't feel great, so it's a lot funnier now than it was then. But that was Kirby. He was trying to help."

It was the Kirby version of a "miracle on ice."

HARNESSED

In later years, Mansfield's tenacity and work ethic, and that of his team, paid off with what would become significant business opportunities for Kirby Risk Corporation. In 1982, the United States economy was suffering from double-digit inflation and manufacturing was slow. Sluggish production lines meant less need for motor repair. To repair a motor, the copper wire is rewound by craftspeople. Mansfield said, "Motor repair winders, who put the copper in the motor, are craftsmen, really artists. It takes about a year of practice for them to be extremely productive, with lots of training and lots of experience. Every motor is different, so it's really a skilled position."

At this time, motors weren't failing in the manufacturing world, because factories weren't working to capacity, and there was "nothing to wind." The fear was that Kirby Risk would have to lay off its four men who rewound motors. Mansfield said, "The buyer at Alcoa had asked us for many years to build control panels for their equipment. He had to send his engineers to Pittsburgh to have the panels built there, and then ship them back to Lafayette. He said, 'Why don't you guys build the panels, because you sell the product? You can build them, and then we'd have a local source.'"

The company decided to accept the opportunity to build Alcoa's panels, garnering the company more business, thus, avoiding the need to layoff the motor repair winders. Eventually, Kirby Risk also built panels for other customers as well.

Also in 1980, Caterpillar Manufacturing decided to build an engine plant in Lafayette. They set up a temporary office in Lafayette Shopping Center on Teal Road in a storefront where Big Lots, a discount retailer, exists today. At the time, A. J. Rassi had been named the plant manager of Caterpillar in Lafayette. He and his wife, Sonja, would become lifelong friends of Jim and Mary Jo Risk.

Mansfield made a sales call to the office, and Glenn Safford tagged along. "He was afraid I might promise more than I should," Mansfield said. "So we did a presentation on our capabilities—motor repair and building control panels. We got the order to build a lot of the control panels for Cat's facility, distribution panels and their test cell panels."

The test cell panels were the control panels used for a trial run of an engine in a testing environment at Caterpillar. They were as large as a conference table and painted "waterfall blue." Mansfield recalled, "I'll never forget the color, because they had the color [specified]. Everything had to be a certain color. Waterfall blue was ordered from Porter Paints. The panel had many push buttons and lights on top. Graphics and Mylar weren't available back then, so an artist was hired, and he came in and painted all the graphics."

Mansfield's staff was young and energetic, and they were willing to stretch and try new ideas. "It's not why you can't," Mansfield explained. "It's how *can* you? That's the philosophy we've always used. We aim for ten. We hit a seven or eight, it's better than aiming for a five and hitting it."

Soon after Kirby Risk began making the control panels, Mansfield was at Caterpillar visiting one of their buyers, and he saw the electrical wiring harnesses that attach to the engines Caterpillar produces. He had read about "just-in-time" delivery, a method that Roger Swindle had mastered at Kirby Risk downtown at Third and Ferry when he assembled the National Homes fixture packages decades before. "I had no idea what it was, but I'd read about it," Mansfield remembered. So he said to the buyers, "Why don't you let us build your wiring harness and bring them to you?"

The harness is a bevy of several insulated conducting wires that are bound together in one sheath or tubing that attaches to the engine and controls the electrical aspects and functioning of that engine. Mansfield used this analogy: "The engine is just like in an automobile. You have an engine with all these wires around it, and they go to the radio and to the ignition, and everywhere."

The buyer at Caterpillar liked the proposal to make the harnesses and deliver it "just-in-time" for their need, saving them money and inventory space. "He was young, about the same age as I was," Mansfield said. "He had four kids; I had four kids, and we both wanted to eat. We figured it would be a good thing."

A representative from Caterpillar called Kirby Risk asking if the company could braid their wire harnesses. Mansfield told the representative, "Sure." Then he hung up and said, "What's a braid?" Mansfield had no clue what a braid was, but he learned it is the nylon mesh sheath that encases the numerous wires that make up the harness. Most of the braiding at Kirby Risk is a strong, yellow nylon fiber. Some of the more expensive harness coverings that look more "polished" are like a black tube. That covering comes from a European company. Connectors are placed at the ends of the braids, and the final harness resembles an octopus.

Mansfield said, "A harness can be up to a couple hundred pounds in weight. When the harness gets to the Cat engine, they will lay it out around the engine and then just start plugging it in. So it's kind of like a computer plug and play." The harnesses go on Caterpillar engines for off-road mining trucks, cruise ships and other marine applications, and locomotive and industrial uses.

Kirby Risk builds wire harnesses for Caterpillar using fixed and "variable configuration." Each harness is specially configured to the specifications of the type of engine it is to power. In the beginning, Kirby Risk produced fifteen thousand different configurations. This was before the days of computers and Microsoft Excel.

Mansfield said:

> So we made a spreadsheet, basically. Here are the kits and then here are the parts in the kit. We'd know how to build each harness, and from that, we'd multiply everything out and make an inventory of the parts. All it was, was a math problem. So we became Caterpillar's very first just-in-time supplier in the world in 1982, in Lafayette, Indiana. Caterpillar came here and filmed our process and made a documentary. They took that videotape out to the world to say, "We want to do this, and this is how you do it."

*Doug Mansfield, president and chief operating officer at Kirby Risk
Manufacturing Group, and Curt Jenkins, service center plant manager,
stand next to one of the whiteboards where workers assemble made-to-order
wire harnesses for Caterpillar Manufacturing.*

The Kirby Risk crew built one harness per day at the motor shop on
First Street, and they delivered to Caterpillar on State Road 26 East.
During that time, Mansfield would see Caterpillar's plant manager,
A. J. Rassi, at functions with Jim and Mary Jo Risk, and Rassi would
say, "We're going to double your business next year."

By 1996 the harness business had grown monumentally, and a new
facility was built on McCarty Lane in Lafayette. The motor repair business at First and Smith Streets became Kirby Risk Electric Motor Repair and later Mechanical Solutions and Service. Kirby Risk purchased
twenty-five acres of land from Caterpillar and built a one-hundred-
thousand-square-foot facility. A second building of equal size was built

next door in 2008. Doug Mansfield is now president and chief operating officer of Kirby Risk Manufacturing Group. Curt Jenkins is the service center plant manager.

PLANT TOUR

Walking from the upstairs offices into the harness manufacturing plant of Kirby Risk is like walking from sepia tones into "Technicolor." A door opens from the ambient-lit office area onto a platform overlooking a vast, bright, white-walled warehouse. There are thirteen wire-cutting lines where a rainbow of wires are coiled and hung at the assembly cells where employees work. It's a clean environment where associates create harnesses to power colossal diesel engines.

First, wire is cut, stripped, and labeled with ink letters for the circuit ID. Much of this work is automated. About forty thousand circuits are produced per day. The length of the wire varies; some are one-foot long and some are sixty-feet long. After they are cut to configuration, the wires go to assembly where they are grouped together and tested.

Each group of wires goes to a giant whiteboard tilted perpendicular to the floor where workers stand to assemble the snake-like harness. Some harnesses have one or two wires, and some have as many as 750 wires. There are 240,000 possible wire terminal combinations, depending upon the configuration necessary for the engine that the harness will "plug into."

A "braider" puts the nylon covering over the cluster of wires, making one thick harness. The harness is made to order with nine thousand different part numbers from which to choose, and each group of wires is electrically tested. If one wire is in the wrong order, the entire harness is rejected. Nothing is made in advance, because Caterpillar orders the configuration they need when they need it for the engine they are producing. Kirby Risk delivers it "just in time."

Today, Kirby Risk produces fifteen hundred to two thousand harnesses each day. The harnesses are shipped to Caterpillar plants all over the country and the world. Wire harnesses go to the Lafayette plant just out the backdoor of Kirby Risk, plus they are shipped to such places as the Marine Center of Excellence in North Carolina; Griffin, Georgia; and cities in Illinois. Kirby Risk even makes harnesses that travel the globe to Caterpillar plants in Singapore, India, Japan, Brazil, and Ireland.

What would Kirby think of the wire harness operation? "He would be overwhelmed," Mansfield speculated. "If he could see the Service Center campus, including the two large manufacturing plants, he would be dazzled. Kirby would be more amazed if he could tour the plant floor and witness the efficient assembly processes developed by our capable Service Center team. This is something I dreamed about. My job is to look out and provide the vision."

A fitting statement from the young man to whom Kirby once said, "See what you can do with the place."

CHAPTER 18

BUILDING

Jim Risk took what his father began in an former blacksmith's shop and, with the help of an excellent team of dedicated people, harnessed it for growth. Jim had a vision for the business that he didn't necessarily announce, but it was his personal dream for the future of Kirby Risk. He envisioned a much larger enterprise. Jim explained:

After successfully establishing a few new locations, I had in mind a stretch target of five million dollars of gross margin, which would translate into recording twenty-five million or more in sales. We would typically use gross margin dollars as our objective; gross margin dollars are what you pay salaries and all expenses with. That was an initial vision. Then it was ten million gross margin dollars, meaning sales of approximately fifty million. Then an objective of twenty million; that would represent sales of one hundred million plus. Our capable team continued to reach these gross margin plateaus representing dramatic growth. In reflecting back on our growth journey, it was not as simple as it sounds. Our vision was to represent key vendors in each location, and this presented significant challenges. Much of our success was built on relationships and trust.

Carol said about her brother, "Our father was very inventive and creative. I think Jimmy is, too. But not the same. I often think they came in the right order, because I don't know if Jimmy could have started the business the same way Dad did. I don't think Dad could have grown it, because I don't think he could have let go of control the way Jimmy has been able to."

Throughout his career and especially in his later years, Kirby immersed himself in serving others and helping nonprofit organizations like Junior Achievement, United Way, and New Directions because he wanted to give back, but also to keep himself busy and out of the office to allow his son breathing room to take over the control of the company. Jim's style is that of the quiet, careful CEO who takes his time building relationships and making decisions.

By the late 1970s, the Kirby Risk building at Third and Ferry was bursting at the mortar joints with shortcomings. Jim said, "It was inadequate in every respect—the warehouse, the multiple docks, the offices, the showroom, the parking lot. But our success clearly demonstrates that it isn't the facilities that make for a successful business, it's the people. Some of our most profitable locations were not our most impressive facilities. Those top-performing locations had capable teams of people committed to responsive customer service."

The antiquated building restricted the growth and development of the company. It was very inefficient and required handling material multiple times. Jim said, "I remember when Caterpillar announced their new Lafayette engine plant, and the plant manager, who today is a very dear friend, A. J. Rassi, and his wife, Sonja, came to our modest showroom to select light fixtures for the home they were building. I crossed my fingers that they wouldn't ask to use our restrooms. They were a bit primitive."

After considering a move to an existing structure around Lafayette, the decision was to build a new facility on land owned by Caroline Risk. The property was on Sagamore Parkway North and was bookended between Vinton Woods and the Vinton Neighborhood, both built by National Homes Corporation. Today, the Kirby Risk

Electrical Supply and Corporate headquarters sits at Sagamore Parkway North and Beech Drive, the street that leads into the Vinton Woods Neighborhood. The Risk family deeded the property needed to create Beech Drive in the 1950s.

Jim and Curt Jenkins, warehouse manager at the time—today the plant manager of Kirby Risk Service Center—spent considerable time with Bob Footlik, a warehouse logistic consultant with Footlik and Associates from Evanston, Illinois. He is the son of Irving Footlik, founder of the manufacturing facilities design firm. Irving Footlik was best known for his palletless warehouse designs and the development of the first fully automated warehouse in the world at the Kitchens of Sara Lee. The two men, both sons of their respective company's founders, worked together to create a new building like few others.

Another son of a company owner was involved, Jason Bricker, who is CFO of Kirby Risk Corporation, having succeeded Gaspar Bejarano, the Cuban immigrant who had once lived in the Risk home. Bricker was just thirteen when his father, Jim Bricker, owner of Bricker Construction in Frankfort, Indiana, built the new 56,000-square-foot Kirby Risk headquarters using an innovative process.

Bricker said, "I was actually there when they broke ground. I still remember watching my Dad set the steel girders and walk along the steel like it was a balance beam. He is a very brave individual. It scared me to death. I was thinking, 'You are going to fall. It's thirty feet high!'"

Jason Bricker worked in the summer helping his father on the construction site. Little did he know then, he would one day be CFO of Kirby Risk Corporation after working as an accountant for Olive Accounting, which became BKD in Indianapolis. BKD was the accounting firm used by Kirby Risk Corporation. Jason and his father attended several of the Risk Purdue football pregame parties. By then, Jim and Mary Jo were hosting, but of course, Kirby and Caroline were there. Jason Bricker was folded into the Kirby Risk family and business at a young age. "As a matter of fact," Bricker said. "I was helping my Dad when he was putting together the contract to build the building.

I typed it. I recall sitting at our dining room table typing a contract. I took typing in high school. I think we were doing it on a weekend."

As Kirby and Caroline had conducted business at their kitchen table on Owen Street for years, the Brickers followed suit at their own family table.

The Kirby Risk building was constructed using the Solarcrete methodology, which was an innovative insulation process, offered at a time when oil prices were high and there was concern about energy conservation. "My Dad has always loved the latest and greatest thing," Bricker said. "It's six inches of polystyrene, which is basically what Styrofoam coolers are made from. And then you have wire mesh, steel rebar, and concrete sprayed on both sides, somewhere around two-and-a-half to three-inches thick. So the walls are about a foot thick. It's like a bomb shelter."

A tan and brown brochure from 1981 describes the building's framework as covered by "high density, pneumatically applied concrete, both inside and out. The roof system also incorporates 10 inches of rigid foam which completes the insulation envelope." At the time, the facility was touted as one of the most energy-efficient buildings in the country. The new building provided an expanded counter area where customers could walk in and order, as they did in the old brick building at Third and Ferry, but with improved efficiency, new displays, and added elbow room.

At the time of the grand opening celebration, Kirby Risk Supply represented more than 300 manufacturers and offered 22,000 products, including industrial controls, motors, heating and air-conditioning, refrigeration supplies, wire, cable, conduit, fuses, transformers, ballasts lamps, plumbing needs, and residential fixtures. One hundred and twenty-five employees worked at the new location, which had classroom facilities for continuing education.

Still today, the public may equate the Kirby Risk headquarters with the highly visible retail lighting showroom, first christened "Creative Accents" and today called the "Lighting Gallery." It offers a multitude of residential lighting. Hundreds of glowing chandeliers

The Kirby Risk Corporation headquarters in Lafayette, Indiana, was constructed using the Solarcrete methodology, an innovative insulation process. Completed in 1981, the building's framework is covered, inside and out, by high-density, pneumatically applied concrete. The roof system incorporates ten inches of rigid foam to complete the insulation envelope.

drip from the ceiling, sconces line the walls, table lamps perch at every level. In the beginning, plumbing fixtures were offered, including hot tubs. People who drive along Sagamore Parkway may have little knowledge of the breadth of electrical and motor offerings that are behind the name Kirby Risk—a name that belonged to a man who once said he was just a small town boy from the banks of the Wabash.

Jim said of the building, "It was definitely a major step for us at the time, size-wise and expense. But it positioned us for growth and allowed for much greater efficiency. The expanded brick and mortar provided our capable team an opportunity to expand our services."

The building opened before many of the Kirby Risk acquisitions took place. The distinctive facility helped position Kirby Risk Supply as a major player in the world of electrical distribution.

Jim said, "The building was a new technology and a new style that really had never been done—really energy efficient. So, it was bally-hooed in our industry and became somewhat a sense of pride."

Soon after the Lafayette building became a reality, a similar facility was built for Kirby Risk Supply in Columbus, Indiana. Cummins Engine was building a new world headquarters there, and they needed the spot where Kirby Risk was originally located. Cummins was a major Kirby Risk customer.

PLUMB WRONG

At the time that the new Lafayette headquarters opened, the motor shop, also known as the "Servicecenter" at First and Smith Streets, operated a wholesale distribution, plumbing, heating, and air-conditioning business in addition to the motor repair. Jim recalled, "My father was the Kirby Risk Service Center CEO, but he never was the typical eight-to-five executive, plus he was getting on in age. A capable team surrounded him; however, he continually asked me to become involved with the activities of the motor repair, plumbing, heating, and air-conditioning business. Yet my focus was growing the electrical supply business."

Kirby turned eighty the year the new supply headquarters opened, and there was no clear plan for the ownership and executive management succession of the Kirby Risk Servicecenter. The big question for the Risks was, "What was going to happen with the Servicecenter business?" Jim said, "Following considerable discussion, we then agreed to merge the Kirby Risk Servicecenter into the Kirby Risk Supply Company. It was a sudden change. We had just completed the new supply headquarters and warehouse, and now plans were to move the plumbing, heating, and air-conditioning business into our new building. The motor repair remained at First and Smith Streets."

It turned out to be a significant challenge for Jim and his team, who preferred taking adequate time to evaluate an idea prior to making a decision to implement. Perhaps, too, it was a lesson in how to handle a business with family involved. "It was a reactive situation," he continued, "rather than a well-studied, thought-out strategic move."

Shower stalls, bathtubs, toilets, plumbing pipes, and pumps moved into the new, sleek Solarcrete building to meld with electrical cable, panel boxes, lamps, motor control, fittings, and conduit. "It was a significant challenge for our people," Jim remembered.

About a year later, Jim thought about the next move. A planning meeting was convened of senior management, including executives from both the plumbing and electrical supply businesses. The thought presented at the meeting was, "Let's all put on the hat of the CEO and imagine we have a half a million dollars in cash. Where are we going to invest the money?" All in attendance, even the plumbing, heating, and air-conditioning executives, recommended investing in the electrical side of the business.

Jim said, "The team agreed we needed to exit the plumbing, heating, and air-conditioning business and focus all of our energy in the electrical segment. This exercise helped get a buy-in and brought clarity to our future direction. The process allowed the senior management to be involved in the decision."

To "exit" actually meant helping the current plumbing, heating, and air-conditioning employees start their own business. Jim said, "We were committed to assisting Don Leming and Dave Zimmerman establish their new business called L & Z Supply (today called Leming Supply). We helped at the bank and assisted with the start-up. They took over the plumbing, heating, and air-conditioning customers and inventory, and Kirby Risk Supply was back to being an all-electrical business. My father, who was a member of our Board of Directors, was not enthused about exiting the plumbing business. He abstained while all other board members voted in favor of selling the plumbing, heating, and air-conditioning business."

Why did Kirby abstain from "voting off" the plumbing, heating, and air-conditioning? Jim remembered:

> Some people, including myself and certainly my father, find it difficult to relinquish most anything. I am confident he saw the wisdom of the decision but found it difficult to give up a business he had helped create. However, the vision going forward was to focus on electrical. And boy, once we did that, we grew at a double-digit growth rate for many years. We were focused with a clear vision understood by the whole team.

The dedicated and capable team did, indeed, focus. In 2012, Kirby Risk Corporation has expanded to forty-three business locations in thirty-seven communities in Indiana, Illinois, and Ohio and has approximately one thousand employees. Perhaps Kirby's loyalty to his employees kept him from wanting to lose the plumbing, heating, and air-conditioning part of his business. Jim said, "It was most satisfying to witness our former employees nurture a very successful business. So it was a win-win."

There were few times when Kirby openly questioned Jim's business choices. By this time, Kirby was not involved in the company's major decisions such as taking on a new vendor, hiring a new executive, or making an acquisition. As Jim and his team acquired more small distributors and the company propagated, Kirby stood back, perhaps a bit in awe, but pleased to hear reports of the company's continued success. Jim recalled:

> I had no experience in buying a company back in 1972, but learned over the years by seeking counsel from advisors and industry friends and also by trial and error. Dad would ask, "What did we pay for that company?" It was a bit of a challenge to explain the complexities of the methodology we used. We had a wonderful relationship, but like many fathers and sons, we were not the best at communicating. But we had an extremely respectful and trusting bond. He truly was an outstanding mentor, devoted father, and excellent example on how to live one's life."

ROADRUNNER

Kirby was protective of his daughters, even when they were grown and he was in his eighties. His youngest, Julie, said, "Every time I drove to Lafayette for a visit and then returned home to Indianapolis without my husband, I'd get in the car and I'd see headlights behind me. Dad would follow me all the way home, see that I got in the house, never get out of the car, and then drive back to Lafayette. Every time. I think he thought that if something happened, he wanted to be there to protect me."

Kirby shadowed Julie for the 120-mile round trip when she was pregnant and happened to visit the night before each of her boys was born. Julie's babies were both born the day after a Lafayette visit, weeks before their due dates. It was as if Kirby knew something might happen and that his grandsons would make an early appearance. Julie said, "He followed me whenever I was driving alone. I don't know other people who do that. But you don't realize it when you are growing up with it. You just think that's the way the world works."

Did Caroline worry about Kirby, then in his eighties, driving to and from Indianapolis for a two-hour trip at night? Or by then was she accustomed to him zooming off to another city or the donut shop when night fell? She couldn't change the man who forever followed the rhythm of a different drummer. Kirby had been a fast driver in early years; he was a bit of a daredevil. Many people tell stories of him driving down sidewalks, cutting through parking lots and fields (sometimes to startle his passengers into a reaction). As he aged, his driving became much slower and more unpredictable.

Kirby's former secretary Jan Lehnen said, "People were always honking at him. He would drive up to the building at Third and Ferry and come up onto the sidewalk, right up to the door to pick me up. One day, when he was older, he drove through a stop sign, realized it when he was half way through, and then stopped in the middle of the intersection. Of course, everybody was honking at us."

Jim's wife, Mary Jo, said of her father-in-law, "He was an awful driver. I would scream, because the cars are coming this way and that way. His mind was going two-feet ahead. He drove the wrong way on one-way streets. Near the end, I didn't let my kids ride with him. Kirby would say, 'Mary Jo won't let the kids ride with me.' I'd say he was an awful driver, and Jim would say, 'Oh he was fine.'"

Daughter Carol spoke good-naturedly of Kirby's daredevil ways to get a rise out of people. She said, "He would take his children and their friends out for rides for Halloween and drive up over the sidewalk into people's yards. In that day and age, it wasn't so bad. He also bumped the car ahead of him at the stop sign, just to give a little nudge. That was when cars didn't dent so easily."

TRIBUTE

On May 25, 1984, a committee of Greater Lafayette comrades hosted a giant, community-wide surprise for Kirby and Caroline. Good friend Dick Liell respected Kirby as a mentor. He approached Jim Risk with an idea for the community to pay tribute to Kirby and Caroline. Those on the tribute committee included Liell, Bob Truitt, President of Lafayette Life Insurance Company Robert M. Whitsel, former Acting President of Purdue University John W. Hicks, and publisher of the Lafayette *Journal and Courier* Malcolm W. Applegate, among others.

This colossal thank-you was in spite of Kirby's lifelong rebuke of recognition for service. It was a chance for friends to expound accolades, one-liners, and roast-like jabs upon the man who quietly "worked the back alleys" to round up money and grease the wheels of benevolence. The homage also lifted up Caroline's role as a monumental component of Kirby's success. She had been there at any hour of the day or night to serve a meal and entertain. She was a wonderful conversationalist and thoughtful note writer who had covered for her husband for fifty-one years.

Kirby and Caroline were out of town prior to the hush-hush tribute. The Lafayette *Journal and Courier* published a story written by John Norberg that ran five days before the event and invited the community. A formal photo of Kirby and Caroline accompanied the article.

They stand holding hands in front of a bookcase, smiling to the left of the camera's eye. The headline reads, "Community to say 'Thanks, Kirby.'"

An editorial ran across the top of the "Opinions" page three days before titled "Thanks to Risks for lives full of good deeds." It states this about Kirby and Caroline, "They characteristically wouldn't stand still for gratitude and praise unless they were ambushed—which is how it's planned by their friends when they come back Friday and are shanghaied." The editorial written by George W. Lamb, editorial page editor, goes on to describe the Risks as having "a lifelong love affair with this community and its people."

Realtor James Shook, who was on the Tribute Committee, said, "Kirby likes to surprise people with nice things. We're just trying to turn the tables on Kirby and his wife, Caroline. There aren't many ways you can say thank-you to them. If he knew this was in the works, he would be in Timbuktu by the night of the ceremony."

Norberg quoted several Lafayette movers and shakers in his story. E. Joseph Bannon, chairman of Purdue National Bank, said, "I have never seen a better human being so dedicated to the well being of his fellowman. He is one of nature's noblemen. The only person sweeter than Kirby is Caroline."

Many commented on Kirby's quirky ways to command money for charity. Al Stewart, director of the Purdue's Varsity Glee Club, said, "We were at Rotary Club meeting one time. Jim Reifers (owner of Reifers Furniture) came in, Kirby said, 'Jim, give me $100.' Jim said, 'OK, but dare I ask why?' Kirby said, 'Yeah, but if you ask why it'll cost you $200.'"

James Shook put it this way, "He can get his hand in and out of your pocket (for charity) faster than anything you've ever seen."

Joe Bannon commented on Kirby's inventiveness, "He's unpredictable and fun to be around. You never know what he's going to come up with next. He does more things for people accidently than most people do on purpose in a lifetime."

Robert Whitsel said, "Kirby is very opinionated. I've always said there are three ways to do things—the right way, the wrong way, and Kirby's way. When you deal with Kirby Risk, you do it his way. And he's usually right."

More than five hundred people braved pouring rain and filled a tent set up on the lawn north of Kirby Risk Supply headquarters on Sagamore Parkway for "A Tribute to Kirby and Carolyn Risk." Jack Scott, chairman of the Gannett Foundation, was master of ceremonies. He said of Kirby, "He does a lot of secret things for people. He's got tremendous clout in so many different areas. But he doesn't use it for himself. He uses it for others."

Kirby and Scott, formerly the publisher of the *Journal and Courier*, had always good-naturedly harangued each other. Kirby had once surprised Scott when he was in Hawaii at an editorial gathering by crashing the meeting dressed as a native "warlord"—bare-chested, wearing nothing but a floral print, shin-length sarong, and a headband atop his bald head. At the tribute, Scott said, "I stay with Kirby and Caroline whenever I come to Lafayette. He charges me, but it's lower than the hotels."

Kirby, a dog lover, had worked to obtain Lafayette's first police dog. Scott recalled:

> One time he told me to meet him at Coney Island [Diner]. When I got there, I said just one hot dog and an orange pop. He said he was raising money for a police dog and only a limited number of people were going to be allowed to participate. He wanted $100. I said, "I haven't got $100 on me!" He said, "Only the most prominent people in town are being asked to give." By the time I left, I had given him $200.

Kirby and Caroline sat at the head table, while friends spoke from all walks of their life. Reverend Ken McCullen of Central Presbyterian Church gave the invocation. Kirby had been a quiet leader at Central and instrumental in creating the church's foundation. Those who spoke included Chairman of Allen-Bradley Company I. Andrew "Tiny" Rader, and Art Hooper, Kirby and Caroline's good friend from

Connecticut who was executive director for the National Association of Electrical Distributors.

An eight-page, tan and brown program skimmed the high points of the Risks' life together. Photos spanned eight decades, from a baby Kirby in the buff to Kirby in a tuxedo, collar open, bow tie dangling, taking a nap on a couch in the Waldorf Towers suite. The inside cover was inscribed with the words, "Mankind is my business." The back cover left the reader with Kirby's favorite Bible passage, Matthew 6:3, "But when you do a kindness to someone, do it secretly—do not tell your left hand what your right hand is doing."

Maury Knoy, who had been president of Rostone Corporation and was president emeritus of Purdue University's Board of Trustees, said, "The Risks like to do things no one knows about. We'll never know how much they've done for everyone."

Ralph Crockett, manager of distributor sales for General Electric Lighting, said, "A man no one dislikes must be blessed from above."

Lafayette Mayor James Riehle created a new award to honor community service—the Order of the Marquis de Lafayette. He made Kirby and Caroline the first recipients. The city of Lafayette was named for the French general, the Marquis de Lafayette, who aided the American armies during the Revolutionary War. The new award was a miniature replica of the Marquis de Lafayette limestone statue that stands above what was an artesian well, now a fountain, at the northeast corner of the Tippecanoe County Courthouse on the downtown square.

Purdue Athletic Director George King made Kirby the seventeenth honorary member of the Purdue Letterman's "P" Club. King said, "There are hundreds of young men and women who got through college through the generosity of Kirby and Caroline." The Risks had established several ongoing scholarships. Bob Truitt, then president of Lafayette Junior Achievement, gave Kirby its 1984 Pioneer Award, and said, "We have seen them touch so many people's lives, so many children's lives."

Kirby and Caroline's daughter, Sherry, spoke, and Jim Risk ended the ceremony by saying that his parents were "painfully shy about recognition," and that Kirby "relishes the opportunity to perform the impossible."

The Purdue Varsity Glee Club sang Kirby's favorite song, "Mankind Should Be My Business." The fabulous team of Kirby and Caroline were showered with love and gratitude. Caroline wore a floral corsage; Kirby was in his famous striped bow tie. His white mustache spread across his face as he wore a constant smile.

A *Journal and Courier* article that ran the day after the surprise quoted Kirby's and Caroline's reactions. Kirby said, "You folks almost had me believing we're fairly nice people. Caroline deserved it all! It was a beautiful evening. I knew nothing about this. It was a complete surprise—probably the greatest surprise we've ever had in our lives. We are extremely proud of our family and dear friends."

Caroline said, "I was overwhelmed. It was unbelievable. Everything was exaggerated, I can tell you that. It was a beautiful thing. And we loved it. Words just fail me."

The grand finale to the weekend was a gift from the Kirby Risk Supply Company to Kirby and Caroline—a trip to England on the *Queen Elizabeth II* (QE2) with their good friends Art and Mary Hooper. The QE2 crossed the Atlantic between New York and Southampton for nearly forty years between 1969 and 2008. It was one of the fastest and grandest passenger vessels ever built.

The gift also included a rented flat located at 49 Hill Street, City of Westminster, London. The Hoopers would stay in a flat next door. Kirby and Caroline sailed to England on the QE2 on August 30, 1984, and they returned to America on October 8 via British Airways Concorde. A Concorde's flight time between London's Heathrow Airport and New York's John F. Kennedy International Airport was a little over three hours. A Boeing 747 averages more than seven hours for the same journey. Commercial Concorde flights ended in 2003, and the seven Concordes in the British Airways fleet have gone to their final resting places at museums around the world.

While in London, Kirby and Caroline visited Pedro and Barbara Granadillo who were residing there at the time. Pedro, the fourteen-

In 1984, Kirby Risk Supply Company gave Kirby and Caroline a trip to England aboard the Queen Elizabeth II *as part of a community-wide thank-you and tribute paid to the couple.*

year-old Cuban refugee who had lived in the Risk family's basement apartment was now working in London for Eli Lilly. Pedro said, "Kirby and Caroline had lunch at our house, and we took them to high tea with scones, cream, and jam."

Kirby and Caroline sailed in opulence, holidayed in London where Kirby celebrated his eighty-third birthday, and saw Pedro, whom he had advised to take the job with Eli Lilly decades earlier, and then zipped back home to 719 Owen.

LONDON LETTER

On September 12, while his parents were in London, Jim Risk wrote a three-page letter asking about their voyage and updating them on personal and business happenings. Much of what Jim wrote about were shades of his parent's lives, now his life. He mentioned the annual Junior Achievement cookout that was held the night before. He talked of upcoming Purdue football games and who would attend. Additionally, he told of his three children who had much homework, and that the Jefferson High School football team was undefeated.

He updated his parents on Caroline's mother, "Gram," who was in poor health. He reassured them that Caroline's brother, Russell, has been visiting Gram three times a week where she lived in Westminster Village Retirement Home in West Lafayette.

Jim wrote, "Business continues to be reasonably good. In fact, August ended ahead of budget and *both* Bloomington and Bedford were *profitable*. I am still trying to develop a way to purchase Walker Electric."

During this time, National Homes Corporation was in dire straits financially. David Price, president and chief executive officer, said in a *Journal and Courier* article that in August of 1984, the company had considered selling part of the Lafayette plant to keep it open. But it was determined that the sale would not be enough to keep the company afloat. Management had no recourse but to inform union employees that the plant would stay open only if the workers accepted a 25 percent wage cut, along with other cuts in pension and insurance benefits.

Jim wrote in his letter to his parents, "The National Homes employees voted *not* to accept the wage concessions, therefore it appears they will be moving the manufacturing operation to Effingham, Illinois. I have been attempting to influence the situation with discussions with Dave, the union and the mayor; but it doesn't look good. I have a meeting scheduled with Dave and Mayor Riehle in my office this evening as a final effort."

David Price said of the union vote that was 137-72 against, "I don't understand it. We begged them to please vote yes."

In January of 1985, the National Homes Sagamore Parkway plant closed its cavernous, money-consuming building in Lafayette and moved its Midwest operation to a more compact, lower-overhead structure in Effingham. In Lafayette, nearly 250 people lost their jobs. Two of the key managers of the Effingham plant were Lloyd W. "Duff"

McKenzie, president of manufacturing, who was married to David Price's sister, Anne, and Ed Safford, vice president of sales and marketing, who was the son of Kirby Risk Corporation's Glenn Safford. In the newspaper article, David Price said, "This is not the end. This company is going to be more viable in the next ten years than it ever has."

The company kept its headquarters on Earl Avenue and continued to employee sixty-eight people. In another *Journal and Courier* article from that time, black and white photos appear of George, Jim, and David Price. The separate headshots, printed side by side, show the three family members, their resemblances extending beyond their suits and ties. Founding brothers, George and Jim, smile slightly in their pictures taken decades before. In the then current photo of David, he looks off into the distance, his eyes dark with a stunned veneer. David, the prankster, golfer, and gin tournament host, said, "This has been a very painful time. This is the last thing I wanted to happen. I hate it. I don't want to leave Lafayette. This is our home."

CHAPTER 19

DISTANCE RUN

In his later years, Kirby began having heart-related medical problems. His youngest, Julie, said, "I can remember he was in the hospital, and he had to miss a basketball game. I think it was IU/Purdue, and he wanted to go so badly. Doctors wouldn't let him go, and he was making a fuss." Indiana University is Purdue's archrival. To miss the IU game was added sacrilege for the diehard fan. And for Julie, who connected with her father by attending games with him, Kirby's inability to be in the Purdue stands filled her with foreboding.

Julie continued, "A few years later, when he had a second heart attack, that did it. He didn't care to ever go to a game again. That fight to go was gone."

The following fall, Kirby, the man who attended every home and away Purdue football game since the 1930s, stopped attending the fall gridiron matches of his alma mater. Julie said, "He could have gone. I'd come home after every game, and we'd go through the whole game, together. I had to talk to somebody about every play. Mark, my husband, thinks that Dad chose not to go to the games at the end, when maybe he still could have, in order to prepare me for being at games

271

without him. Dad was preparing the family for when he was not around."

Even from a hospital bed, Kirby influenced his adult children. Julie said, "I went to see him in the hospital, and I was telling him about one of my husband's cases; he's an attorney. I said one of the judge's names. Oh, did Dad lecture me on confidentiality! I learned my lesson to never mention a name ever again. I was just visiting my father in the hospital trying to make small talk, you know? So, even when he was at the end, he was teaching and parenting with total integrity."

On February 1, 1989, Jim Risk helped his father into the car to take a drive by the various Kirby Risk locations in Lafayette. The two drove past the cement-encased, modern headquarters on Sagamore Parkway and the old, ruddy brick building at Third and Ferry where Kirby had spent countless hours building his business one lightbulb and relationship at a time. Then the father and son, bearing the same name, tooled down to the motor shop at First and Smith Streets.

Doug Mansfield, then the division manager, remembered, "Jim had Kirby in his car. Kirby was in the passenger seat, and they pulled right into the motor shop because he couldn't get out. The door was open, and shoo, into the bay drives Jim's car, which was highly unusual. Jim said, 'Come here.' And I went around and talked to Kirby for a few minutes about all the things that were happening in the motor repair business."

Three days later, on Saturday, February 4, 1989, J. Kirby Risk Jr. passed away.

"I know now, it was like a last hurrah. I didn't know then," Mansfield said. "It was touching, particularly later, when I thought about it."

EULOGY

Kirby's obituary and a story appeared in the Lafayette *Journal and Courier* with this headline: "On a 1-to-10 scale, he was 11." It was a quote from Gordon Kingma, president of the Greater Lafayette Chamber of

Commerce. On February 7, the day of Kirby's memorial service at Central Presbyterian Church where Reverend Dr. Donald R. Ewing officiated, an editorial ran. (The service was purposely delayed be a few minutes as a nod to "The Late Mr. Risk," making Kirby tardy for his own funeral.) The newspaper piece said that Kirby "radiated benevolence like sunshine, yet hid in its very shadow, shying away from those who would say their thanks." *Electrical Wholesaling* trade journal was quoted: "He was a tireless worker, an indefatigable telephoner, and inexhaustible traveler, a persistent nudger. Nothing second-class about this gentleman."

Reverend Ken McCullen, former minister at Central Presbyterian Church, who by then lived in California, wrote a "Witness to the Resurrection" for Kirby and mailed it with a letter to Caroline. When McCullen had first arrived to serve Central Presbyterian years before, Kirby met with him and said, "I'll be one of your greatest supporters but one of your damnedest critics." To which McCullen replied, "Kirby, if you can take it as much as you can give it, we'll get along fine." Kirby had installed a clock in the pulpit so the minister wouldn't go long on his sermon. He was faithful to his statement, praising McCullen when he did something "right" and telling him pointedly when he "messed up."

McCullen wrote:

> Kirby worked at his faith. Whenever he was in town, he was on the east side of the sanctuary. He listened to the sermons with a critical but attentive ear. One time, when I preached on disarmament and provided an opportunity for people to sign a petition at the close of the service, Kirby admitted he had never signed such a petition in his life, but he was moved by the sermon to "sign the damn thing." He could be moved by his faith to a new position.

In McCullen's letter to Caroline, he wrote of her contributions in the shadows:

> You, indeed were very much a part of the "Risk ministry" throughout the greater Lafayette community. It is true that Kirby was the

one who was always "out front," but it was your constant and consistent support that gave him an opportunity to do what he did so well. To us, Kirby and Caroline were a team. You complemented each other, gave strength to one another, and shared both good and bad together. No doubt, that team was started in heaven and was shared with us on earth.

McCullen ended his "Witness to the Resurrection" with an excerpt from the poem "If" by Rudyard Kipling, published in 1910 in *Rewards and Fairies* when Kirby was nine.

> If all men count with you, but none too much;
> If you can fill the unforgiving minute
> With sixty seconds' worth of distance run,
> Yours is the Earth and everything that's in it,
> And—which is more—you'll be a Man, my son!

McCullen plucked one phrase from the poem as a summation of Kirby's life: "Kirby filled every minute with sixty seconds' worth of distance run."

CHAPTER 20

Without the Gentleman

After Kirby passed away, Caroline adapted and found her way. It was the first time in her life that she lived alone. Her oldest daughter, Carol, who lives in Florida, said, "She is stronger than I knew, growing up. Because when Dad died, she started spending her winters in Florida, which was wonderful for me, because I'd never lived in the same town with her as an adult. She really reinvented herself."

Kirby died in February 1984, and Caroline's mother passed away eight months later on October 19. To lose two significant others in one's life within such a short timespan could take its toll, but Caroline's robust faith and family buoyed her. Jim is especially attentive to his mother, to whom he has always been close.

His wife, Mary Jo, said:

> After Kirby died, Jim was the substitute. Caroline doesn't move without him as far as any kind of decisions, whether it's her checkbook, a contribution, a new car, moving, or anything. He's her security blanket. I've said to him, "Your sisters are going to think you're a real pain in the patoot because you can do no wrong as far as your

mother is concerned." He's more than any son ever was. He is totally there for her. It's been wonderful, because he is fabulous with her.

Because Julie is Caroline's baby, combined with Julie's calm demeanor, mother and daughter have a close relationship. Mary Jo said, "And Carol and Sherry are close, too."

Jane Hovde Price, wife of Jim's best friend, David, said, "Jim is a son like no other son I've ever known. He probably talks to Caroline every day. And sees her, if he's in town, five times a week."

By the next October, Caroline moved from 719 Owen Street to a "patio home," a duplex-type house, on Almond Court in the Vinton Woods Neighborhood behind the Kirby Risk headquarters. Jim said, "The Owen Street property had three heating systems. It needed paint, a new roof, and maintenance. It seemed appropriate to move Mom into a more manageable space. She went along with it."

Caroline had moved into her mother-in-law's home as a twenty-year-old bride. Nearly sixty years later, she moved out at the age of seventy-eight. Caroline, with her family's assistance, moved to Almond Court. The furnishings and pictures in her new patio home were arranged to replicate how they graced her 719 Owen home.

Caroline ended up living in the Vinton Woods Neighborhood, built by her good friends the Prices. She and Kirby had owned land next to where the Price brothers, Jim and George, built homes on Cypress Lane, a cul-de-sac, but Kirby never built a new home there. The land remained vacant for years. Jim Price's former house sits next door on land that dips below street level. It is 1960s "contemporary," with several patios fanning from the foundation. His son and daughter-in-law, David and Jane, lived there for a while after Jim passed away. George's former house is next door to his brother's, a white French Provincial-style with a semi-circular driveway.

Jim Risk said of his parents' Vinton Woods lot, "Dad had blueprints done and then just never pulled the trigger. You know, Dad was born in the house on Owen and never left."

Before the Owen Street house sold in 1992, Caroline opened the doors for all to see as part of the Tippecanoe County Historical Association home tour celebrating the centennial anniversary of the Highland Park Neighborhood. Much history had graced the rooms, from William Jennings Bryan dining on Dora Risk's fresh corn on the cob, to Pedro Granadillo, a Cuban refugee and later a top executive for Eli Lilly, living in the basement and eating bowls of ice cream dipped by Kirby. Pregame football parties and summer cookouts had been hosted, friends had supped, and hospitality had been offered while babies were raised and company board meetings were held around the kitchen table.

A story about the neighborhood and its sense of sanctuary ran in the Lafayette *Journal and Courier* with a quote from Caroline, "When we went to Hawaii for our twenty-fifth wedding anniversary [in 1958], we didn't even take the key to the house with us, and we were gone three weeks. We just knew everybody. It was a warm, friendly place." Actually, in all the years that they had lived at 719 Owen, the Risks never locked their door. They didn't even *own* a key.

Stretch to Grow

In 1991, Kirby Risk Corporation opened in Indianapolis, Indiana. It was the nineteenth electrical distribution center. Jim said:

> People cautioned that our business style would not work in Indianapolis. A year and a half after opening in Indianapolis, we had grown to become one of the largest Indianapolis distributors. They thought our small town model wouldn't work in the big city. But it works in all markets—valuing others and exceeding expectations, wowing the customer. Noticing people. Having a passion. We were consistently willing to do more than expected.

Jim became involved in a project for Batesville Casket Company in Batesville, Indiana, and he exceeded expectations with a very "Kirby-like" move. Jim remembered:

> Our team in Columbus asked me to assist with a lighting project for the casket company. When we finished that evening, I drove back to Lafayette and happened to remember that in our warehouse we

had the perfect commercial fixtures for the project. We normally would not stock this particular fixture. They were leftover from a job. I laid out the lighting project, loaded up the van, and at seven o'clock the next morning delivered the fixtures to Batesville Casket. We had just left them at six the night before.

Hustle is part of the game, and wherever Kirby Risk Corporation landed, the dedicated team of people put a lot of energy together. Jim made certain to demonstrate appreciation. During the heavy growth years of the late 1980s and 1990s, he distributed a handwritten "thank-you card," summing up the year, good or bad, to every employee and included a "thank-you" check. Every note began with, "Dear Fellow Employee."

Jim was candid in his yearly thank-you notes. In 1999, he mentioned a paralyzing snowstorm that slowed business activity and how the implementation of a new software system demanded a major investment of time and resources, disrupting normal sales and service initiatives. In each note, he rallied the troops with sincere appreciation of their concern for others, and when necessary, cheered them on to "rekindle growth." Jim said of the thank-you card to fellow employees, "It had a warm, sincere feeling. Employees posted them on their bulletin boards or at their cubicles."

Each month, Jim sent out one-page notices on the "state of the company." In 1994 and 1995, the headline shouted in bold print "A RECORD MONTH." He compared the percentage growth for the month with that of the prior year. He congratulated and listed the locations that achieved a new monthly record. Every staff member knew which location had been successful, perhaps instilling a sense of competition among sites, in a subtle "Jim" way. He welcomed suggestions on how to integrate a newly acquired electrical supply company into "our corporate family." In March 1995, the business name was changed from Kirby Risk Supply Company, Incorporated, to Kirby Risk Corporation.

Jim ended one monthly "state of the company" notice with, "I have truly been overwhelmed by the outpouring of support in response to our announced acquisition." It appears as the company gathered more independently owned distributors under its wing, the team embraced the assimilation of each newly adopted business.

As sales continued to rocket, one particular month established a most impressive record, so Jim, CFO Gaspar Bejarano and Vice President of Development Charlie Stroop visited each Kirby Risk location. Jim said, "We each went in a different direction making certain each location was visited and commended on the same day. We delivered a fruit basket to each location to celebrate the record month and expressed personal thanks and congratulations. We also took one to Allen-Bradley's district office in Indianapolis to let them share in our success. We created a winning culture and a team spirit."

As his father before him, Jim is active in the National Association of Electrical Distributors. He said, "For being as small as we were in the earlier years, the company had developed a reputation of being an industry leader. My father and Glenn Safford and others had established our industry reputation on a national basis. I started going to NAED meetings when I was twenty-one. I've probably been to more of their meetings than anyone living today. I'm still going."

Today, John Burke, a proven professional, is president of Kirby Risk Electrical Supply and chief operating officer of the corporation. Burke continues the Kirby Risk tradition of active involvement in NAED. He currently has taken the lead on several initiatives that will make a positive impact on the future of the electrical distributor industry.

Part of Jim's training came through community involvement. He was elected president of the Greater Lafayette Chamber of Commerce at age twenty-nine and president of the United Way at age thirty. In his mid-thirties, he was chairman of the Greater Lafayette United Way Campaign.

Another organization that Jim is still involved in is the National Association of Wholesaler-Distributors (NAW). NAW encompasses more than one hundred national line-of-trade associations. Jim was NAW chairman of the board in 1996. He said, "It was an educational experience and an opportunity for personal growth where it gets you out of your comfort zone."

Jim's willingness to go where he has not been before, literally for the company (as in a new city) and spiritually for himself (as in personal growth), speaks volumes about his method of attainment for Kirby Risk Corporation.

While in his thirties, Jim became involved in the Young Presidents' Organization (YPO), which also prevented him from settling for "cruise control." YPO is known for its excellent educational and unique idea exchange opportunities.

Jim said:

> We attended universities and colleges sponsored by the Young Presidents' Organization where we experienced classes led by recognized business consultants, best-selling authors, world leaders, and other noted experts. I was surrounded by leaders who were success-oriented and interested in personal development. These educational experiences stretched your imagination and fostered a desire to excel ... stretching your boundaries, so you think, "Maybe I can do this."

Jim continues to participate in his original YPO forum with other past and current CEOs with whom he has developed a trusting relationship. He said, "We serve as a board of advisors for each other. Our meetings provide a unique opportunity for members to seek counsel on business issues, health challenges, estate planning, and so forth, with all discussions in strict confidence. You can't put a value on the benefits of the forum experience. Some of the members are from private companies, some public, providing important guidance and encouragement."

The takeaway may be that any CEO, president of a corporation, or even owner of a local bakery should not go it alone. A network of like-minded colleagues eases the burdens and opens the doors to possibilities. The adage, "It's lonely at the top," is only true if the one at the pinnacle fails to reach out to other people at the apex of their work worlds. Jim continued:

When counseling others, I encourage them to seek advice from success-oriented folks whom they admire. I caution the tendency to share frustrations and unhappiness with those who are experiencing similar troubles. Those people will typically say what you want to hear, agree that you are not understood, and reinforce the negative. Meanwhile, success-oriented folks will offer positive coaching and constructive criticism, encouraging you to stop blaming others and take control of your life.

CHOICES

Three life facets that Jim Risk values—family, relationships, and business—collided in 1991. Two years after Kirby Passed away, Jim Stark, vice president and district manager of the Kirby Risk southern district, and husband of Kirby and Caroline's daughter, Sherry, came to Jim with a heart-breaking confession. Stark was seeing another woman who was an employee of Kirby Risk in Columbus, and he wanted a divorce from Sherry.

By this time, Sherry had made her mark in Columbus. She had been hired by the mayor to manage community development for the city deemed "an architectural mecca" by the *Chicago Tribune*. Sherry said, "Being deputy mayor really put me in the limelight. I was in the newspaper and all that. I think that was really hard for my husband."

Even though Sherry and her husband divorced, Stark remained with the company until his retirement in 2000. Sherry said:

> That was very, very difficult for all of us. Very hurtful for me because of the circumstance of his relationship with somebody in the business. I still feel he should not have stayed with the company, but he did. I think my brother had a real challenging situation to deal with, with my personal pain. I truly believe marriage is for life, no matter what. So the betrayals and then him still having a position in the company, and his new wife accompanying him to the events that I once attended with him, that was brutally painful for me. And I thought incredibly unfair.

Yet Sherry can see her brother's point of view. She said, "The flip side is, from a businessman's standpoint, my husband's knowledge of the industry and business relationships could have been a detriment. Could he have taken company information to other industries? I don't know what all went through my brother's head, but my ex-husband stayed with the company until he retired, and he and his wife still come to Lafayette for the annual Christmas party."

After years of being alone and questioning her personality as being "too strong" for a man to handle, Sherry is now in a long-term relationship with a gentleman she describes as gentle, brilliant, and supportive. Over the years, Sherry maintained a close relationship with her former in-laws. Sherry said, "When she died, I was the only one with my former mother-in-law, whom I still called "Mom." Her family asked me to speak at the funeral. And I invited all the family to my house afterward, including Jim Stark and his wife. So for the kids, you do what you have to do."

Sherry became president and CEO of the Heritage Fund, the Community Foundation of Bartholomew County in Columbus. Upon her retirement in 2011 after twelve years in the position, *The Republic* ran a story that read: "Her retirement not only caps off an era of tremendous growth and enhanced responsibilities in the institution's thirty-five-year history, but serves as a capstone to a remarkable career in public service."

LOSS AND FRIENDSHIP

As Jim Risk mourned the loss of his father, his good friend David Price was experiencing his own industry turmoil. National Homes Corporation, which had started in Lafayette in 1940, was sold by a controlling interest to a Canadian company, marking the end of an era in Lafayette history. The company headquarters moved to Richmond, Virginia. In December of 1991, National Homes filed for bankruptcy. The following May, several investors including "Duff" McKenzie, Anne Price's husband, bought what was the last operating factory in Effingham, Illinois, with plans to continue making prefabricated homes.

Throughout the National Homes waning years, Jim Risk wrote formal letters of encouragement to David Price. In a letter on Kirby Risk Supply letterhead dated June 10, 1985, Jim wrote, "Just wanted to put in writing my congratulations and compliments to you on bringing National Homes through many, many difficult years. . . . Hopefully good times are ahead. You certainly deserve it."

In August, the Lafayette *Journal and Courier* ran a five-part series of stories titled "The Rise and Fall of National Homes," with the National Homes logo on a graphic of a house breaking apart at the foundation. The series of articles highlights the wonder years of National Homes and includes photos of the Benton County brothers who were close, Jim and George Price. It tells their stories of rising from Midwest roots to become the leaders of the housing industry. Their personalities and home lives are analyzed and painted in type. Homeowners were interviewed. Some were post-World War II couples who bought a National Home, moved in, and lived there for decades into their retirement years.

The rough years are splashed across the pages, as well. A headline reads, "Workers rejected 25% National Homes pay cut." This story interviewed some of the "blue-collar workers" who still carried a bitter memory of the labor disagreement that led to the plant closing in 1984.

The words "doom," "decline," and "Home-building king loses its crown" appear on the pages. And there is David Price's photo—his ebony eyes look away, not meeting the camera. He's a deer in the headlights of economic downturns, government regulations, overzealous diversification, and changes in customer buying habits.

David started working at National Homes when he was twelve. He said in a rare 1987 interview with the *Chicago Tribune*, "One summer I was an apprentice for the electricians, the next summer an apprentice plumber, then carpenter. Mainly, my work was in the field, but I began selling houses at 18." For a while, David nurtured his own National

Homes dealership in Kokomo, Indiana. In 1965, he returned to Lafayette, and in 1990, the walls came tumbling down on his watch.

In another story in the Lafayette *Journal and Courier on August 15, 1990,* David said, "This experience has not been fun because to survive you were involved with many, many distasteful decisions. Eliminating profit centers or cutting back on people or a combination of those things. You lose a lot of sleep." Accompanying this article is a 1960s photo of David's father, Jim, his mother, Roberta, his sister, Anne, and himself, a fresh-faced teenager, sitting on their patio on Cypress Lane. The caption reads in part, "Jim Price cared deeply about two things: National Homes Corp. and his family."

On the patio, at the dinner table, out in the community and the world, National Homes was always a part of the Price family—nearly a living and breathing member of the household.

Nearly two decades later in 2008, David Price died of esophageal cancer. His sister, Anne, said, "Two days before he passed, we were sitting on the bed with him eating candy and watching a ball game. It was so amazing. He wanted to do his taxes. I said, 'David, I'll go get them for you but . . .'"

David died on January 1. Good friend Patti Truitt commented that he died happy "with the tax break." David's wife, Jane Hovde Price, said, "He planned his funeral. He had friends speak from each part of his life." Jim Risk was one of four men to speak. He summoned memories of his lifelong friendship with David, including their families' shared vacations, David's notorious pranks, and their crazy Halloween costumes as man and wife. The last song to play at the service was "Hail Purdue."

In 2012, David and Jane's grandson, Scotty, is a high school football player in Michigan. Jane said, "When Scotty was at quarterback camp at Purdue, he and his dad took some of David's ashes and put them on the fifty-yard line in Ross-Ade Stadium. Hopefully, Scotty will be walking on that turf someday. He just broke a school record for touchdowns and yards. He wants to go to Purdue in the worst way."

Jane and Anne agree that Jane's father, former Purdue President Fred Hovde, would have loved to see his great-grandson grace the playing field of Purdue University.

RETROSPECTIVE

After Kirby passed away, he continued to receive awards, which Caroline accepted on his behalf. In 1989, Kirby was posthumously presented with St. Elizabeth Hospital's "Elizabethan Award" for his nine years of involvement during the formative years of the St. Elizabeth Hospital Lay Advisory Council. In 1991, Kirby was one of the first inductees into the Junior Achievement Business Hall of Fame. In 1992, Kirby received the first Arthur W. Hooper Award from the National Association of Electrical Distributors, named after the man with whom he had shared a steadfast friendship. The award would "pay tribute to individuals whose horizons extended far beyond a business enterprise to encompass a deep concern for abiding dedication to the welfare of the industry represented by the National Association of Electrical Distributors." Kirby had guided the growth of NAED during some of its most crucial years of development, serving an unprecedented two terms on the NAED Board of Governors.

WESTMINSTER VILLAGE

In 2000, Caroline agreed to move from Almond Court to Westminster Village Retirement Community. She was in Florida when Jim moved her belongings in and placed all the furnishings and decorative pieces as close to the same arrangement as that at Almond Court, and prior to that, at the house on Owen. Jim said: "When Mom and Julie arrived from Florida, they both cried tears of happiness and appreciation because they were so pleased with what they saw. It was an emotional move, and it turned out to be so positive."

He continued, "She understood the move was the proper decision but was a bit apprehensive. She was relieved and truly overwhelmed when she entered her new residence. It was exactly like home. It looked like Owen Street. That's all part of the family culture—we were raised to exceed expectations in all we do."

Caroline was now living where her mother had lived in her later years. Also living at Westminster was Caroline's longtime friend, Roberta Price, and another Benton County crony, Martha Graham, widow of Dr. Thomas Graham, who died in the National Homes airplane accident in 1951.

In 2012, Caroline lives at Westminster Village as she turns one hundred years old.

SACRIFICIAL SERVICE

Today, the Kirby Risk Corporation written mantra rings of "Kirby fuel": "Going above and beyond what it takes to provide the right parts at the right time, to the right place, and at the right cost is not a sacrifice . . . it's a minimum requirement. Staying committed to this concept of 'sacrificial service' the customer has fueled Kirby Risk since 1926." Kirby Risk Corporation consists of four operating business units:

Kirby Risk Electrical Supply is a full-service electrical distributor providing high-quality, state-of-the-art electrical, automation, lighting, and power distribution solutions.

Kirby Risk Service Center designs and builds custom-engineered systems, wiring harnesses, and subassemblies for JIT manufacturing requirements, providing line sequencing and inventory services.

Kirby Risk Mechanical Solutions and Service offers ISO 9002-quality electrical apparatus repair as well as motor, power transmission, and generator sales. Off-site services include predictive maintenance programs, motor cleaning, and analysis.

Kirby Risk Precision Machining provides quality precision-machined components using the latest CNC technology. KANBAN and other manufacturing logistics capabilities extend the level of service to customers in a wide range of industries.

Arco Electric Products also resides under the Kirby Risk Corporation umbrella. Arco specializes in the manufacture of Roto-Phase converters and power factor correction systems. Kirby Risk represents more than 2,000 manufacturers and carries more than 90,000 products.

Kirby and Caroline had a love that transcended the everyday.

MEMORIES

Sometime after Kirby left this world, Caroline began jotting down notes about her life with her husband of more than a half a century. Some pages are simply lists of years and a sentence or two about happenings for each. Another sheet is titled "Kirby's Quirks," and her typed, almost cryptic one-liners march down the page: "Hitchhikers," "Maid at Waldorf Towers," and "Birthday party—Kirby under bed."

Other journal-like pages carry more of a storyline about how Kirby began his business and the intermingling of their family with the company. Caroline understood that her life with Kirby was extraordinary, and it needed to be recorded. On Kirby Risk Supply graph paper she wrote, "Countless memories dance across the screen of my memory and for some of the younger members of our family that didn't have the opportunity to share these times, I've thought it might be of interest to know some of the more memorable stories."

She begins what turned out to be just four paragraphs of memories with this wistful homage to the man she married amidst the glimmering backdrop of the 1933 Chicago World's Fair: "There's no need to tell anyone in this family that J. Kirby Risk, Jr. was a 'one-of-a-kind.' What a privilege to have shared 55 ½ years with that warm, loving sentimental, fastidiously clean, untiringly polite, unbelievably generous, extremely determined, soft-spoken gentleman."

CHAPTER 21

GHOST OF CHRISTMAS PAST, PRESENT, AND YET TO COME

Every December 25, Kirby wore his Christmas coat. Kirby bought the sport coat at a favorite store, Maus & Hoffman. In 1940, William Maus, Sr. and Frank Hoffman founded the business based on a simple idea—"always offer the best." It was a store after Kirby's own heart. Kirby loved fine apparel for himself and for Caroline. Even though he bought high-quality clothes, he often wore them in an unorthodox fashion, pairing plaid pants with a checked shirt and a striped bow tie. Patterns and colors need not match in Kirby's couture.

Jim said, "Dad loved to go to Maus & Hoffman because he appreciated being remembered and enjoyed receiving special service. They'd fall all over him, take care of him, and they became family friends."

In Kirby's day, Maus & Hoffman was located on Las Olas Boulevard in Fort Lauderdale, Florida, and in Petoskey, Michigan. The Fort Lauderdale shop remains open, and there are now locations in Palm Beach and Naples. Their website states, "For over 70 years at Maus & Hoffman, we've been offering men and women clothing with a Floridian flair—comfortable, colorful and always of the finest quality."

"Colorful" always called to Kirby, and his Christmas coat beckoned with a "come hither" hue. A dazzling kelly green and made of supple cashmere, the equally emerald silk lining bears the Maus & Hoffman label. Kirby had a yellow felt bell with a red bow stitched to the breast pocket. He wore the Christmas coat with a silk green and red polka-dot bow tie.

Kirby sported his green coat when he lavished his family with gifts. Sherry recalled, "Christmas was totally over the top. We'd go to church Christmas Eve. We'd come back, and we'd open all of our presents. They would fill the living room—gorgeous, wonderful things. There would be some kind of surprise for mother. One year it was delivery of a melodeon [pump organ]. One time it was a white mink coat."

Kirby and Caroline shared a laugh at a company Christmas party in 1981 with Jan Lehnen, Kirby's secretary. During the holiday season, Kirby wore his cashmere Christmas coat, which he purchased at Maus & Hoffman in Fort Lauderdale, Florida. He had the gold, sequined felt bell sewn onto the pocket.

Jack Halsema from Michigan Town, Indiana, played the Risk family Santa for thirty-nine years. Santa, the real deal who always had the same face, came to the house on Christmas Eve and said to Kirby's children, and later his grandchildren, "If you're good and you go to bed, I'll be back later tonight." Each year, without fail, pictures were snapped of Kirby, Caroline, and some of their family members taking a turn to sit on Santa's lap.

Kirby enjoyed purchasing clothes for Caroline. In the 1980s, he gave her a white mink coat as a Christmas gift. The unpretentious girl from Boswell wore the coat once.

"Then on Christmas morning, Santa came," Sherry said. "We could hear the bells. I remember being scared and hiding. There would be a gift for each of us from Santa. Christmases were everything a child could dream of."

Kirby sat back as his family opened presents in the living room of 719 Owen, the house where he had been born upstairs in the front bedroom, where he signed the William Jennings Bryan letter of intent, and where he and Caroline had fostered fun, support, and unconditional love to Junior Achievement teenagers, Epsilon Theta youth, international students, and Cuban refugees.

"Dad would wait to open his gifts," Sherry said. "He loved to watch us unwrap. He loved to experience it. So it was hard to get him to open his gifts. They would stack up around him."

Throughout his life, Kirby's gifts stacked up around him. The man whose days hummed to music inspired by the words of Charles Dickens "knew how to keep Christmas." Kirby was like his Maus & Hoffman Christmas coat—comfortable, colorful, and of the finest quality.

Giving was Kirby's gift, unwrapped his way.